A SHORT HISTORY OF WAR

Jeremy Black is Professor of History at the University of Exeter. Black has published widely in military history, including *War and the World* and *Air Power*. His other works include *Maps and History* and *Naval Warfare*.

T0024174

JEREMY BLACK

A SHORT
HISTORY
of
WAR

YALE UNIVERSITY PRESS
NEW HAVEN AND LONDON

Copyright © 2021 Jeremy Black

First published in paperback in 2022

For information about this and other Yale University Press publications, please contact:
U.S. Office: sales.press@yale.edu   yalebooks.com
Europe Office: sales@yaleup.co.uk   yalebooks.co.uk

Set in Minion Pro by IDSUK (DataConnection) Ltd
Printed and bound by CPI Group (UK) Ltd, Croydon, CR0 4YY

Library of Congress Control Number: 2021937081

ISBN 978-0-300-25651-2 (hbk)
ISBN 978-0-300-26707-5 (pbk)

A catalogue record for this book is available from the British Library.

10 9 8 7 6 5 4 3 2 1

For Virgilio Ilari

Contents

Acknowledgements

I would like to thank Heather McCallum for her backing for this project and, in doing so, mark three decades of working together. Caleb Karges, Heiko Henning and three anonymous readers provided very helpful comments on an earlier draft. They are not responsible for any errors that remain. Charlotte Chapman has proved an excellent copy-editor. This book is dedicated to Virgilio Ilari, a key figure in keeping the academic study of military history vibrant and intellectually rigorous, and a much-valued supporter of my work.

Acknowledgements

CHAPTER 1

The Origins of Conflict

> If we forbear to fight, it is likely that some great schism will
> rend and shake the courage of our people till they make
> friends of the Medes [Persians]; but if we join battle before
> some at Athens be infected by corruption, then let Heaven but
> deal fairly with us, and we may well win in this fight.

Herodotus' dramatic account of Miltiades the Younger outlining in 490 BCE what was at stake for Athens when threatened by a Persian invasion, the threatening great power of its day, captured the role of will and the place of divine support in understandings of success in warfare. This remark from the 'ancient world', however, is one that in terms of the species is really that of very recent history. Humans from the outset were involved in conflict, but not on any great scale, and certainly not that of the 490 BCE invasion that culminated with the total Athenian victory at the Battle of Marathon over the larger Persian force.

Instead, humans had to compete with other animals for food and to prevent themselves from being food for others. They also had to fight for shelter. Warfare did not therefore only emerge as some result of the corruption of humankind by society, in the shape of agriculture and related social organisation, as was enthusiastically argued in the 1960s by commentators who were unconsciously copying Judaeo-Christian ideas of the Fall of Man due to Adam's sin. Such an account would have warfare begin about 90 per cent of the way into our history as a species. Instead, fighting is integral to human society. Indeed, the pattern for modern hunter-gatherer societies, such as those in Amazonia and New Guinea, reflects a formerly more common practice, notably of conflict between human groups, whether hunter-gatherers or settled. Fighting with other human groups, whether to secure hunting areas, to seize slaves, not least for mates and/or to incorporate into the tribe, or to assert masculinity, was part of a continuum with fighting with animals. Indeed, the last bear in Germany was not killed until 1797.

The success of humans over animals in the conflict that has lasted across human history, and which continues today in new forms with creatures that cannot be seen with the naked eye, owed much to inherent physical and mental characteristics, but also to humans' ability to use these to improve their chances. Physically, a key factor was that of being able to perspire and move at the same time, rather than having, as with many animals, to stop in order to perspire. This capability provided a major advantage in both pursuit and flight.

The ability to communicate through language was vital in helping humans to hunt and fight as groups. A significant ability in resisting other predators, and in hunting megafauna, notably mastodons and mammoths, group activity could then be translated to conflict with other humans. Language was also important in helping ensure that innovations spread and were improved.

This was a key aspect of the learning process that has remained significant to the present day, and that helped differentiate humans from other fighting animals. This process was not some automatic response to circumstances or an unconscious process of evolution, but, instead, a matter of testing opportunities and evaluating responses, with humans acting as agents of change. This was a process in which social organisation and language played roles and in which humans differentiated from other species.

A major, but not sole, aspect of this was the development of tools as the properties offered by stone, wood, bone, hide, antler, fire and clay were used to create and strengthen both weapons and shelters. Flint stones proved particularly useful, notably for axe heads, and techniques of working on them improved. Composite tools, particularly points and blades mounted in wood or bone hafts, were especially important, and spears and arrows were stone-tipped, providing greater penetrative power for the weight.

Throwing weapons helped humans overcome animals with stronger combat characteristics, including innate weapons and protection, especially claws, antlers, tusks and hides. Humans needed weapons to keep outside the range of the animals. Moreover, tools, such as large stone points able to pierce mammoth hides, made it possible not only to kill but also to cut up bodies and thus eat them, gaining protein accordingly. Protein from meat and fish did not require the long processing needed to digest raw vegetables and fruits.

In Europe, large megafauna, including sabre-toothed tigers, giant deer and the woolly rhinoceros, all became extinct, as in Central America did mastodons and giant armadillos. Changing habitats were doubtless important, but so was the ability of humans to exploit the situation. Their skill in hunting helped ensure that humans were better able than other animals to adapt to the unpredictability and possibilities created by the retreat of the ice sheets at the end of the last Ice Age in around 10,000 BCE. Thus, the population of the woolly rhinoceros, which appears to have been essentially stable from about 27,000 BCE to about 16,500 BCE while humans were present, possibly because the rhinoceros was too dangerous to hunt, fell from 12,700 BCE, possibly due to the consequences of global warming, before the species became extinct.

Taima-Taima, a site in coastal Venezuela with human occupation back to 12,200–10,980 BCE, has yielded a mastodon bone pierced by spear point. A burial pit recently found in Alaska revealed the bones from humans who died about 9500 BCE, laid on a bed of antler points and weapons. Humans fighting animals were widely depicted in early rock paintings in caves, as later in Roman mosaics. In Spain, the rock paintings in Cueva de la Vieja show men with bows hunting stags, while rock art from the Tassili n'Ajjer plateau in the Sahara, dating from about 6000 BCE, present the hunting of giraffes, and in Kashmir, the Burzahama site from about 4300 BCE depicts hunters and a bull. Hunting is also a key element in Mayan art in Central America. So also with stories about humans and animals fighting, stories found in all mythologies.

The range of human capabilities assisted in the struggle with other carnivores, in the domestication of some animals that enhanced human capabilities, notably in agriculture and movement, and in creating a safe context for a new stage of human action upon the land in the shape of cultivation of crops and the related development of permanent settlements. The timetable varied by region, in part due to the spread of innovations, but also to the density of humans, to the routes between their groups, and to terrain, cover and the differing impact of the Ice Ages. Diversity owed a great amount to the physical environment, but humans could affect this, notably with the clearing of woodland for agriculture, which also reduced the cover for wild animals. The development of harpoons and bows and arrows helped in catching fish, as did the adaptation of boats to particular maritime environments, for example *fassonis*, flat-bottomed, reed-built boats used to catch fish in the marshes and lagoons off the Sinis Peninsula in Sardinia, with similar boats found elsewhere.

As the human population rose, and as rival carnivorous animals were driven to the margins, away from areas of settlement in the war that had to be won, so fighting with other humans became more important. The extent, timing and explanation of this fighting are all matters of controversy, and calling it war has proved controversial. To some, the use of weapons does not mean conflict, and skeletal remains showing violence as a cause of death may be due to murder or feud, rather than war. Thus, Ötzi, the 'iceman' from South Tyrol, who lived around roughly 3300 BCE, had a copper axe, a flint knife and flint-tipped arrows. He had probably attacked others, and was wounded, if not killed, by similar weapons.

So also with the different problems posed by what, after evidence of it was discovered in 1996 by an amateur archaeologist in the Tollense valley in north-east Germany, appeared to be one of Europe's oldest known battles, if not the oldest known evidence of war in Europe. In addition to human remains, notably a skull with blunt force trauma, possibly from a club, and an arm bone pierced by an arrowhead, weapons, including a bronze sword, flint and bronze arrowheads, cudgels, spearheads and daggers, have been discovered there. Initial investigations suggested that the battle, in about 1200 BCE, roughly when Troy was destroyed, involved as many as four thousand warriors, of whom possibly 1,400 died, and arose from an invasion of north from south Germany; but more recent genetic analysis has established few ties of kinship among the dead and thus made a migrating group improbable. Instead of a battle, an ambush of a trade convoy is now suggested. Similar contrasts in evaluation are possible for other sites, and should also be applied to tales, texts and images.

In part, the problem in establishing the terminology, and therefore assessing the history, of war can also be that of assuming that a state level of warfare was more significant than that of other organisations such as tribes. While convenient if war is to be seen as a 'social construction' and an aspect of state building, this approach does not make sense for much of the world, including for societies whose past bellicosity is very well affirmed in the continuing oral record, as with New Zealand Maori, Australian Aborigines, Pacific Polynesians and Melanesians, and Arctic Inuit. Bellicosity is also a theme in accounts of social order in which warriors play a major role, as with the account of the creation of the world in the *Purusha Sūkta*, the *Hymn of Primeval Man*, from tenth-century BCE India.

Rather than the nature of organisation, the will to fight is the key element, whatever the scale. This will, which can be seen as bellicosity or warfulness, overcomes the unhelpful distinction sometimes drawn between rationality and irrationality in leading to war. Bellicosity can be regarded as both, or as either, a rational and an irrational response to circumstances. In addition, hostility and conflicts are not clearly separate but, instead, on a continuum.

Bellicosity in the shape of the will and readiness to fight leads to war, rather than war arising because misunderstandings produce inaccurate calculations of interest and response. The resort to war is both a choice for unpredictability and the positive connotations of risk, and also a product of individual and social norms, notably of masculinity and competition.

Evolutionary factors aiding survival, as well as the companionship and excitement, indeed pleasure and release, that many feel in fighting, both by themselves and with others in the group, is an important aspect of this situation, and one present across a range of cultures. Modern re-enactments of battles testify to this factor, although it does not relate to those who are forced to fight. Belonging and status are important elements in warfare, but also culturally dependent and politically contingent.

The focus of human conflict certainly swung from animals to organised fighting between humans, although may, at some level, have been the case from the outset of human society, or at least from when foraging clans came into contact with one another. Moreover, the oft-repeated argument that early warfare was ritualistic and, partly as a result, limited, and that the true history of warfare is different, has to be handled with caution as evidence for the purpose and nature of early warfare is limited. Moreover, ritual did not mean that conflict was not deliberate, deadly and harsh; no more than do rituals that continue to the present, such as uniforms, or martial music, or structures and words of command. This is a dimension of conflict that should always be borne in mind. Thus, writing of the Caribbean in the seventeenth century, Colonel John Scott observed of native cannibalism:

They rather eat out of malice, chewing only one mouthful and spitting it out again, and animating one another thereby to be fierce and cruel to their enemies, as a thing pleasing to their Gods, and it hath been a great mistake in those that have reported the Southern Indians eat one another as food.

Such social conventions as an aspect of group dynamics were probably at issue from the outset of conflict.

CHAPTER 2

War and Early States

They display in battle the speed of horse, the firmness of
infantry; and by daily practice and exercise attain to such
expertness that they are accustomed, even on a declining and
steep place, to check their horses at full speed, and manage to
turn them in an instant.

Julius Caesar on the British chariots he encountered
when invading in 55 BCE

Shrouded in myth, the war over Troy in about 1194–1184 BCE
near the Dardanelles in Turkey in the Late Bronze Age captures the
extent to which the narratives by which humans made sense of
themselves related to conflict, both between gods and between
humans. Thus, the *Iliad*, the epic account of the Trojan War, is one
of the earliest war stories to survive. In this account, honour was
the key spur, honour in the shape of control over a woman, Helen,
wife of King Menelaus of Sparta, taken to Troy, but also, and more
consistently, in this and other war stories, of relations between

men. So also in India with the role of dynastic feuds and major battles in the great Sanskrit epics, the *Mahabharata* and the *Ramayana*, notably the battles of Kurukshetra and that of the Ten Kings.

Similarly, war played a central role in religious narratives, such as the Old Testament of the Bible, with the children of Israel capturing Jericho and other targets. War rituals, like those in the South West Pacific, nowadays re-enacted for tourists, have survived. These rituals frequently present struggles against other clans and against creatures that are semi-animal, and semi-gods. In narratives and rituals, gods were usually presented as warlike, with the rulers their representatives, a situation that pertained in Japan until the end of World War Two.

This situation was part of a process in which tribal success over other tribes involved conflict between gods, cosmic struggles, in an inherently competitive system, a process, moreover, that led to the spiritual union of conquerors with the land they had conquered. The polytheistic (many gods) nature of most religious systems encouraged narratives of struggles between gods, while for monotheistic religions, such as Judaism, there was struggle between the 'true God' and pagan cults, such as those of Baal. Thus, the Jews' struggle with the Philistines was presented as a religious conflict at all levels.

Separately, but related to this, religious rites and buildings were an aspect of the protection of communities, but also required security. Protected temple complexes were a key element in early cities, as with Nippur in Mesopotamia (Iraq), which from 2100 BCE had a series of temple walls.

The story of conflict related not only to the endless time spans of religion but was also as old as humanity, indeed is the story of humanity. It is not separable from the human experience. While hunter-gatherer societies with their bellicosity continued to be important, the standard narrative of human development focuses on those of agriculture, settlement, metalworking and trade. War and improved weaponry were part of the equation, with weaponry developed to be more useful for combat, both in lethality and from ease of use. The replacement, at different times, of the Stone Age by successive ages of metal saw Stone Age weapons, such as those fashioned from flint and obsidian, gradually superseded. Metal weapons were easier to use and more mobile. In turn, flint weapons, which themselves reflected multi-stage work and assembly, were much sharper than their metal counterparts, but, unlike metal, did not hold their edge with use. They were also heavier.

In 7000–5000 BCE, in both West Asia and South-East Europe, it was discovered that heating could be used to isolate metals from ore-bearing deposits. As a consequence, fire was an important part of the development of weaponry, and an instance of the dependence of war on technologies that were not specialised to its end. No metal weapon could have been fashioned without the technology to smelt and work metal. Soft metals, which melt at low temperatures, were the first to be used, so that more easily worked copper was the basis of metal technology before more difficult iron. Copper was succeeded by bronze, which was made by alloying copper with tin, and was stronger and more durable than pure copper. The oldest bronze swords were produced before 3000 BCE in what is now Turkey. This shift in weaponry had social consequences, as metals required trade, notably for tin, and manufacturing.

Sophisticated sword-fighting techniques developed, and combat style improved, and, by 1300 BCE, these swords were found across Europe. Such techniques were important in the case of all weapons and were part of the multi-faceted nature of the adaptation and application of human skills in warfare.

The sling was another long-lasting weapon, definitely known to Neolithic peoples, although possibly older, and generally underrated. Despite being relatively short range, and notably so compared to the bow, the sling was dangerous, especially in the hands of experts who knew how to pick stones that would fly true to the target. Slings have been found by archaeologists around the world, including in Peru, Nevada, Egypt, the Balearic Islands and Anatolia. Sling staffs, moreover, offered an improvement in projection. As such, they perform a role akin to spear throwers which, in effect, extended the throwing arm.

There were also developments in forts. Early fortifications relied chiefly on terrain features, such as slopes with the height they offered, as well as on concentric walls to protect successive walled precincts. Multi-storey towers were a later development, and probably one learned from areas where there were earlier examples, notably the Eastern Mediterranean. Alongside major Bronze Age fortresses, such as Mycenae in Greece, the ruins of which remain impressive, and Troy, most were smaller scale. Thus, the Argaric Bronze Age of south-eastern Spain, which flourished in about 2200–1550 BCE, had walled hilltop settlements. Archaeological research has provided evidence of sophisticated fortifications, for example at the site of La Bastida where, in 2012–13, masonry walls were discovered which in part flanked an entrance passage exposing attackers, as well as five solid square protruding towers resting on carefully prepared foundations to prevent sliding down the steep hill, a considerable feat. The close-backed towers provided an opportunity to throw objects. Fortifications located on hills or *tells* were widespread, as with the Hittites in Turkey, height providing both visibility and defence.

Horses were domesticated as early as 4000 BCE north of the Black Sea, and by 1700 BCE were being used in a new weapons system, the war chariot, which, as later with the tank and the internal combustion engine, reflected the employment of a new power source, in this case the horse, as well as the working of metals. Chariots were denied to societies lacking the horse, which underlines the significance of the natural environment for the development and utilisation of weaponry.

The use of wheeled vehicles, in existence in South-West Asia by about 3500 BCE, were a key element in the development of chariots, which eventually used spoked, rather than solid, wheels, reducing their weight, while reins linked to bits provided a means to control the horses. Chariots, which also served to differentiate between soldiers and to organise the battlespace, served as platforms for archers and other warriors, offering an effective challenge to cavalry and infantry alike. As an instance of the range of skills that had to come together, the composite bow, which can store compressive and tensile energy by virtue of its construction and shape, evidence of which dates from Mesopotamia in about 2200 BCE, was, like the chariot, a piece of engineering reflecting considerable skill, and a capacity to develop within an organic-goods environment.

Horses and chariots also had symbolic roles, as with the *aśvamedha* in Vedic India, in which the wanderings of a sacrificial horse followed by warriors, provided a claim to suzerainty and a cause of conflict. In Mycenaean Greece and Iron Age Britain, the powerful were buried with their chariots.

To be most effective, weapons such as bows had to be wielded by large numbers of trained men, and alongside the weaponry used, this was important to effectiveness. When the Romans invaded England in 55 BCE, 54 BCE and (successfully) from 43 CE, their Celtic opponents suffered from their lack of effective missile power and body armour, and their chariots, although a formidable challenge, were vulnerable to Roman archers, and their hill forts, such as Maiden Castle, to Roman siegecraft. Yet, alongside the short swords, javelins and body armour of the Romans, it was their well-honed discipline in combat that was a key element in their repeated success across a wide range of environments.

The requirement for large numbers of troops helped change the character of warfare in at least some areas, for the ability to field men brought with it the requirements to feed, water, house and equip them. These were major obligations, and ones generally addressed both by a mixture of burdening subjects and the conquered alike, and, on the other hand, the shifts and expedients that were apt to press hard on soldiers and sailors. For most of history, the latter are nameless, as individual service was not recorded. Even when it was, there was little the soldiery could do to ameliorate their conditions unless they could enforce their value by refusing military service or unless they were difficult to replace. The first, of which mutinies and coups are the bluntest expression, captured the conditionality of much military service, even in the most onerous of systems and most authoritarian of ideologies. The second was a product not simply of the particular skills of some troops, but also of the degree to which an often only limited size of population could make them difficult to replace.

These are instances of the implicit bargains, within armed forces, and between them and their human and physical environments, that have probably always underwritten military service and the use of these forces. For the bulk of history, and notably much of the ancient world, we have no evidence of the nature of these bargains, the difficulties they reflected or the tensions they caused, but that does not mean that we cannot consider the point. Indeed, repeatedly in military history, as in the other branches, we have to counterpoint the limited material we have with which to work, and the assumptions we bring from the anthropologies, sociologies, economies and environments of warfare. Using the plural for the latter is deliberate because we should not assume that there is only one of each, with the necessarily more limited choices, both for contemporaries and for later analysis, that might suggest.

For example, an element in the importance of symbolic factors in conflict was seen with the long-standing practice of fighting at particular places as in ancient Greece and, later, Anglo-Saxon England. There was a correspondence between places appropriate for assemblies, legal, political and/or religious, and for peace-making ceremonies, and places appropriate for conflict. These places were often associated with river crossings, passes, forests and heaths as well as specific waypoints, such as barrows or other monuments, places that had pragmatic benefits, including logistical ones, as in access to routes of communication, visibility and space for large numbers of people to gather. But they could also have sacral significance and explicit associations with kingship, as in places where gods or other figures had shown themselves, or barrows associated with a legendary ancestor. As these places were memorialised, and the battles that took place there were recorded, they could convey territorial control and collective identity.

In the ancient world, as more recently, leaders had to respond to a multifaceted background while pursuing advantage and what seemed their destiny, and there was no single direction of control or influence. Nor is there today. Humans are agents of change.

Thus, different human geographies meant, as they still mean, great variations in conflict as humans adapt to their local situations. This was especially so in the pre-modern age, as the difficulty of travel was linked to the slow diffusion of technological developments. Moreover, alongside unique geographical patterns that came into being, culture formed a sort of 'feedback loop' that could accentuate unique variations. There was no one world of war.

CHAPTER 3

Egypt, Assyria, Persia

Susa, the great holy city, abode of their Gods, seat of their
mysteries, I conquered. I entered its palaces, I opened their
treasuries where silver and gold, goods and wealth were
amassed . . . I destroyed the ziggurat of Susa. I smashed its
shining copper horns. I reduced the temples of Elam to
naught; their gods and goddesses I scattered to the winds.
The tombs of their ancient and recent kings I devastated,
I exposed to the Sun, and I carried away their bones towards
the land of Ashur. I devastated the provinces of Elam and
on their lands I sowed salt.

King Ashurbanipal of Assyria describing the capture of Susa,
the capital of Elam in south-west Persia, in 653 BCE

The Greek world that attacked Troy was for a long time on the
periphery of more powerful Middle Eastern empires and, together,
these were a key centre of the development of warfare between
states. This development owed much to the scale of activity made

possible by river-based irrigation agriculture of fertile alluvial soils and its capacity to support significant populations. This was especially the case in Mesopotamia (Iraq), with the valleys of the Tigris and Euphrates, and Egypt with the Nile. From early times, the Mesopotamian cities were at war with one another and massively fortified. Uruk, the possible background for the late second millennium BCE poem the *Epic of Gilgamesh*, is a case in point: its walls in the fourth millennium BCE were about 9.5 kilometres long. Earth ramps were vital as means for assaulting cities and were frequent in Mesopotamian warfare. A number of empires were based in Mesopotamia, notably that created in about 2300 BCE by Sargon the Great, king of Akkad; and their rise and fall reflected conflict, both within Mesopotamia and with neighbouring areas.

Warfare in part arose as empires were established, sought to expand and then were overthrown. Empires, a developing form of human organisation moving beyond tribal systems, were also seen in Egypt, China and northern India. These regions also saw walled cities, those in Egypt beginning with Nekhen (Hierakonpolis) and Naqada.

Egyptian history has left relatively plentiful records, including inscriptions and decorations. Its armies advanced north into the Near East and south into Nubia (northern Sudan), and frequent conflict was important in the development of the army, which was depicted in temple carvings. The Egyptians probably learned chariotry from the Palestinian Hyksos, who conquered Egypt at the end of the Middle Kingdom (*c.* 2040–1640 BCE). The combination of the compound bow with the light, two-wheeled, horse-drawn chariot, beginning probably in the seventeenth century BCE, was shown in temple reliefs of the New Kingdom (*c.* 1550–1077 BCE). Their employment by Thutmose III against a Syrian coalition at Megiddo in about 1460 BCE helped win the day: speed and hitting power enabled him to employ enveloping attacks successfully.

Subsequently, chariots were important both to Egypt and to its rival in the Near East, the Turkish-based Hittite kingdom which, with both employing large numbers of chariots, maybe five to six thousand in total, fought the Egyptians at Kadesh in 1274 BCE.

Depicted in the bas-relief monuments at Thebes as a chariot rider, Rameses II, the Egyptian ruler, claimed victory but, in practice, narrowly avoided defeat. The Hittites, who made major use of chariots, regarded themselves as benefiting in war from the support of the Sun God, while their capital of Hattushash had mighty walls supported by projecting towers and with twin-towered gateways.

The end of the Bronze Age in about 1200 BCE saw a widespread collapse, including of the Hittite empire and possibly of Troy, as well as the invasion of Egypt by the 'Sea Peoples'. The Hittites had made a precocious, but only very limited, use of iron weaponry, and the first empire to make a systematic military use of iron was Assyria. Based in Upper Mesopotamia, its empire was strongest from 911 to 609 BCE. The Assyrians had determined leadership, a militaristic culture, and a sense of providential support, notably from the god Ashur. Their conquests included Babylon (689 BCE) and Elam in south-west Persia in 653–640 BCE. Assyria had a large, well-organised army effective in both campaign and battle, and especially good with both cavalry and siegecraft. The latter robbed opponents of the safety of remaining behind walls. The dramatic stone reliefs from the palace of Nineveh, the Assyrian capital, depict the sieges of cities from the mid-seventh century BCE, with men fighting from the tops of the siege towers that protect battering rams.

Aside from devices that came into direct contact with the walls, notably battering rams and siege towers, there were siege engines including those that fired projectiles, especially catapults; although their range, accuracy and aiming required fire from close proximity. As with other weapons, catapults served a variety of purposes and could be fired from a number of platforms. Large catapults could throw heavy stones designed to inflict damage to the structure, while medium-sized catapults launched bolts, and lighter hand-held ones fired arrows and small stones designed to clear away defenders from their positions. Such anti-personnel weaponry provided an opportunity for gaining tactical dominance and, thereby, for the use of siege engines close up against the walls. Thus, they were an aspect of the degree to which sieges involved stages in order to suppress the defences, just as defences involved stages with which to resist attack. In turn, these stages required different facets for the defence. This included firepower mounted on the walls, and notably in the towers that were their strongest features. The Assyrians also used mining operations.

Assyrian cavalry rested in part on an ability to ensure the supply of plentiful and useful horses, a key consideration in all cavalry-based empires, and one that remained very important to success in the eighteenth century, as with that of the Afghans in India from the 1750s CE to the 1790s CE. The Assyrian preference was for heavy chariots, with four rather than two horses, and carrying four men rather than two, thus greatly increasing firepower.

Assyria's capture of Memphis in 671 BCE and Thebes in 663 BCE was an impressive demonstration of their capacity to take Egyptian cities, but the effort involved was weakening, and Assyria was overthrown in the late seventh century BCE as a result of Babylonian rebellion and the rise in Persia of the Medes.

The regional struggle resolved itself with the victory of the Persians under Cyrus the Great (r. 559–530 BCE), who conquered the empire of the Medes in 550 BCE, overthrew the Babylonian empire in 539 BCE and created what was up until then the largest empire of the world, his titles including King of the Four Corners of the World. As with the Assyrians, the Persians were particularly effective in cavalry and siegecraft.

After Cyrus defeated Croesus, king of the Lydians, in 547 BCE at Thymbra, allegedly because the Lydian horses were frightened of the smell from Cyrus' camels, his general, Harpagus, captured the wealthy Greek cities on the Ionian coast of Anatolia, a major part of the Greek world. Having surrounded their target with a rampart, the Persians weakened it before capturing it by storming. In response, in the fifth century BCE, the Greeks strengthened their defences, building higher towers and using carefully hewn masonry.

As with other empires, the Persians faced the situation that they were more effective in some contexts than others. Thus, Cyrus was killed by the nomadic Massagetae when he campaigned into

Central Asia, which was all too often a threatening area for forces from Persia, a pattern seen in campaigning into the eighteenth century. Sources, however, are often limited. Thus, the Battle of Opis, in which the Babylonians were defeated in 539 BCE, can be located, but the cause of the defeat is not known. So also with Cambyses II's victory over the Egyptians at Pelusium in 525 BCE, a Persian victory followed up by the successful siege of Memphis and by establishing not only control over Egypt but also suzerainty over eastern Libya. This was both an impressive instance of power projection and the first of a sequence of rapid conquests of Egypt that revealed both surprising vulnerability (one, in turn, that, with Alexander the Great, was to affect Persia) and the lack of any obvious land boundaries to conquest.

Frontier zones were a problem for all empires, notably due to a lack of clear borders, combined with a will to expand. The mighty Persian empire was no exception. Wide ranging, it was dependent in part on an impression of success, and this dependence encouraged the determination to crush opposition in the Greek world. Under Darius I, the Great (r. 522–486 BCE), as part of a more general process of expansion, Thrace was conquered in 513 BCE, and a rebellion in 499 BCE by the Greek cities in Ionia on the eastern shores of the Aegean, conquered in 546–545 BCE, was crushed in 494–493 BCE.

Darius then decided to punish Athens and Eretria (on the island of Euboea), which had provided support for the rebellion, this punishment being a way to deter further action. In 490 BCE, an expeditionary force conquered the Cyclades islands and then destroyed Eretria, before landing at Marathon on the Greek mainland. A rapid Athenian response, however, led to the defeat of this larger force which had not yet had a chance to deploy adequately beyond the beachhead, the battle becoming crucial to the Athenian sense of their special destiny. Not one to accept failure as anything bar a stage to revenge, Darius planned a return match, but postponed it due to a revolt in Egypt in 486 BCE.

In turn, his successor Xerxes constructed a bridge across the Hellespont (Dardanelles) in 480 BCE and, in the face of a massive invading Persian army, many Greek states remained neutral or, as with Thessaly and Boeotia, allied with Xerxes. An attempt to hold the pass at Thermopylae against the Persians advancing south was outflanked thanks to advice on a route supplied by a traitor, and the Greeks withdrew, leaving a small, largely Spartan, rearguard under King Leonidas, which fought on to the death. The Persians pressed on, capturing Athens.

A very different verdict was delivered at sea, where a far larger but swell-shaken Persian fleet was defeated in the narrows of Salamis, when its ships were too tightly packed and its formation in difficulties. Modern full-scale reconstruction and use of triremes, a galley employed for classical warfare, has helped greatly in appreciating the choices of the period. Galleys could have rams on their prows, but the usual tactic was to bombard by means of catapults, archers and javelin throwers, weakening resistance before trying to board, a technique still very much seen with the Christian victory over the Ottoman Turks at Lepanto in 1571 CE. The necessity for considerable manpower to propel these vessels by rowing them greatly limited the cruising range of such ships, as they had to stop to take on more water and food, which encouraged them to stay close to the coastline. Xerxes left Greece after Salamis and his son-in-law, Mardonius, although with a considerable army, was defeated on land at Plataea in 479 BCE, after which the Persians lost control of the areas they had conquered in 480 BCE.

The inscription on the pedestal of the ruined statue encountered by the traveller in Percy Bysshe Shelley's poem *Ozymandias* (1818), 'My name is Ozymandias, king of kings:/ Look on my works, ye Mighty, and despair!', might seem a comment on the rise and fall of empires. Indeed, a sense of futility is captured by Shelley: 'Nothing beside remains. Round the decay/ Of that colossal wreck, boundless and bare./ The lone and level sands stretch far away.' Possibly the specific inspiration for Shelley was the announcement by the British Museum that it had acquired a fragment of a statue of the powerful Rameses II of Egypt (r. 1279–1213 BCE), and the name Ozymandias is a Greek version of part of his throne name. That was a reasonable prelude to reflection on the recent fall of Napoleon

Bonaparte in 1815, and, indeed, captured a cyclical character to history, one in which war devoured its products and brought down pride. This indeed was a counter-cultural response to be expected of Romantic figures like Shelley when looking at the process and product of civilisation and, more specifically, at militarism.

In the context of the values of the ancient world, however, that approach is more problematic. The reliance on force reflected needs and values. There were economic drives to control land, resources and people, as well as the pressures of social roles, and the hierarchies and masculine images involved. In addition, conflict appeared natural, necessary and inevitable. It was part of the divine order, the scourge of divine wrath, and the counterpart of violence in the elements, as well as the correct, honourable and right way to settle matters.

CHAPTER 4

Early Chinese Warfare

Buried near the tomb in Xi'an of Zheng, the First Emperor (r. 221–210 BCE), the Terracotta Army provides in its thousands of life-size soldiers and horses a silent testimony to power. Such power was long-standing.

Large-scale agriculture had been the case in north China by about 7000 BCE, and, as with Mesopotamia and Egypt, with which it had some similarities, this provided the resources both for conflict and for state-building, the two being closely linked. In the north China plain in the third millennium BCE, walled settlements and metal weapons appeared, and walled towns were found in areas with an appreciable density of population, as with Chengziya in about 2500 BCE. The urban civilisation of the Shang dynasty developed in about 1800 BCE in the valley of the Yellow River, although this civilisation was only a fraction of the size of modern China, and its control beyond the core Shang territory was limited.

Nevertheless, built in about 1550 BCE, the walls of the Shang city Zhengzhou were 10 metres high and nearly 7 kilometres in circumference, and would have required millions of working days to construct. Such works indicate the level of political control, social cohesion and organisational ability prevalent at the time, as well as the presence of plentiful labour, for these walls were not machine-made. This widespread development of city walls, beginning at an early stage in Chinese history, was functional, but also revealed a cultural 'show' dimension, in that every self-respecting city had to have a wall. The scale of Chinese walled cities dwarfed those elsewhere, and their rammed earth walls were extremely thick and impervious to siege engines, which resulted in additional defensive features focusing on gates, as these were the main point of attack. The gates protruded from the walls and commonly had a number of additional internal gates and courtyards that served as 'killing zones' for fire from archers on the walls above.

These fortifications were aspects of a formidable military system. The Chinese use of chariots, composite bows and bronze-tipped halberds and spears developed in the second millennium BCE, chariots spreading from Central Asia in about 1200 BCE. Subsequently, chariot-borne nobles played a crucial part in battle in China, a form of warfare focused on a social élite requiring the costs of both horses and chariots, and also seen in the Near East and in Europe. Making particular use of chariots, the Zhou dynasty (c. 1050–256 BCE), originally a frontier power to the west, overthrew the Shang dynasty (c. 1600–c. 1050 BCE), but, in turn, was attacked by other chariot- and cavalry-using border people, especially the Di and the Xianyun from the bend in the Yellow River to the north-west.

In the lengthy Warring States period (403–221 BCE), competing regional lords ignored and overthrew the now weak Zhou; and improved weapons, such as the crossbow, as well as the use of mass, disciplined infantry formations, led to some of the largest military engagements yet recorded. Much of the infantry was armed with spears. However, on a more general pattern, the reliability of the literary sources that record very large armies and high casualties is problematic.

In 230–221 BCE, Zheng, the king of Qin, conquered China and took a new title, First Emperor. The most successful of the autonomous lords in the Warring States period, he brought it to an end, rather as Philip II of Macedon was to do in Greece in the 330s BCE, and as Jiang Jieshi in China was to curtail greatly the warlords of the period, with his Northern Expedition of 1926–8 CE. The scale of conflict in this period helped ensure that chariots became relatively less significant than infantry. Yet, the key element was not military technology, but rather politico-institutional development in the shape of the extension of state authority over the countryside, and the ability, as a result, to conscript large infantry armies, with their scale offsetting the advantages offered by chariots.

Organisation was also seen in the formidable walls of Wei, Zhao and Yan, built not only against Chinese rivals but also to protect north China from the nomadic steppe people to the north and their well-trained mounted archers. Zheng ordered the construction of a long wall to fortify the northern frontier.

The Qin dynasty (r. 221–206 BCE) also used its power to extend its control south of the Yangtze River in 209 BCE, which very much contrasted with the Shang and the Zhou, both of which had held loose hegemonies limited to north China. As with many military systems, however, in a pattern that has lasted to the present, the Qin empire was overly dependent on the character of the emperor, and Zheng's death was followed by conflict in the ruling family, military disaffection, popular uprisings, civil war and collapse.

The Terracotta Army of Zheng might be a resonant legacy of ancient China, but he did not create a lasting system, being followed, instead, by a civil war won by Liu Bang, who founded the Han dynasty (206 BCE–220 CE). This turned the Qin socio-military system built for conquest into a system for rule in which internal politics and social structure helped produce cohesion. As with Imperial Rome, the government sought to monopolise force and thereby to ensure a demilitarised interior that would not rebel; but frontiers posed a problem as the Han confronted hostile external challenges, notably the Xiongnu confederation of nomadic tribes. Unified in 209 BCE, it was the first empire to control all of Mongolia, in a pattern of challenge that lasted until the mid-eighteenth century. The Han responded with defensive walls, but also with large-scale offensives during the years 201–200 BCE (a disaster that ended with the army encircled and the emperor suing for peace) and 129–87 BCE, that of 97 BCE involving the use of about 210,000 troops.

To confront the Xiongnu, the Han had to build up their cavalry. Chariots, which were vulnerable to mounted archers, ceased to play a role. The earliest Chinese figurine with two stirrups probably dates from about 322 BCE. Stirrups provided stability in motion, helping in both shock action (heavy cavalry) and with firing or throwing projectiles from horseback (light cavalry). Neither depended on stirrups, but stirrups helped make them more effective: like many developments, they were an incremental improvement. More effective edged weapons were also significant.

Wu, the 'Martial Emperor' (r. 141–87 BCE), found it difficult to engage the Xiongnu when he advanced onto the steppe, and was obliged to retreat for logistical reasons. At the same time, the establishment of garrisons and colonists, including into Central Asia, both limited the Xiongnu and won allies (and horses) for use against them. The Han repaired the Qin wall against attack from the north, and built new walls to the north and south of it, partly in order to support territorial expansion. Moreover, garrisons were established in Ferghana (an important valley on the Silk Road), Korea and Champa (Vietnam). From 104 BCE a major effort was put into getting herds of Ferghana horses, which were superior to the existing Han ones. The Ferghana ones then formed the basis for an improved cavalry.

Providing another instance of the process of trial and error that drove human adaptation, Wu's successor, Zhao (r. 87–74 BCE), switched to a defensive strategy towards the Xiongnu, which was easier to maintain, albeit costly in the shape of the provision of ample gifts. In part, these were a matter of divide and rule, helping to turn some tribes against others. More significant for the long term was Wu's success in extending power southwards, where rivals had access to fewer horses and therefore lacked mobility and offensive shock power. The kingdom of Southern Yue was conquered after 137 BCE and the Dian of Yunnan defeated in 109 BCE, while subsequent rebellions were suppressed. The Qin presence in the south was expanded and consolidated by the Han, and this secured a southward migration of settlers that was of permanent importance in the reshaping of China, although also leading to periodic rebellions by indigenous people.

With the emperors increasingly weak, the government of Han China was to collapse in the face of rivalry between generals initially given command in order to suppress rebellions. One forced the Han emperor to abdicate in 220 CE, launching the age of the Three Kingdoms (220–280), which resulted in unity under the weak Jin dynasty (266–420), only for the revived Xiongnu to storm the Western Jin capital, Luoyang, in 311. Northern China splintered into the 'Sixteen Kingdoms' (304–439), while, south of the Yangtze, the successive Eastern Jin, Song, Qi, Liang and Chen dynasties (317–589) were each founded by generals. Force was crucial to power, and warlords vied for regional control. China was a concept, thanks in large part to the Qin, but not a political reality.

The strength of the cavalry of the north, however, enabled Yang Jian, a general who founded the Sui dynasty in the north in 581, to conquer the south in 588–9. To do so, it was necessary to adapt to (and adopt) the riverine-based maritime supply systems of the south. It was the greater ease of northerners moving onto the water, than of southerners moving onto horses, that largely created the north–south military gradient of China. The horsemen of the steppe lands were the source of instability there as elsewhere across much of Eurasia.

Chinese relations with nomadic and semi-nomadic peoples of the steppe combined military force with a variety of diplomatic procedures, including *jimi*, or 'loose rein', which permitted the incorporation of 'barbarian' groups into the Chinese realm. Their chiefs were given Chinese administrative titles, but continued to rule over their own people in traditional fashion. As a reminder of the role of ideology, an element of continuity in the location of Chinese border walls has been seen as reflecting both a practical understanding of the topography and its possibilities and, on the other hand, beliefs about the structure of the universe and concerning a border between China and the 'Barbarians'.

The success of particular Chinese dynasties varied greatly. Thus, the Tang dynasty (618–907) pursued expansion, with fortresses and military colonies from Xinjiang to Sichuan. A permanent army, in place of the earlier system of military households, was introduced from 737 and the frontier was organised into regional commands. Initially reliant on heavy cavalry, the Tang increasingly favoured light horse archers instead. The infantry, most of whom used spears but with crossbows also common, increasingly were equipped with armour. However, in 751, an Arab army under Ziyad ibn Salih, governor of Samarqand, defeated a Chinese counterpart under Gao Xianzhi at Ablakh near Lake Balkhash, a battle decided when an allied contingent of Qarlug Turks abandoned Gao for Ziyad: such changes of side in what were generally composite armies often including ancillary forces were common, and not only in Asia. Thus, at Bosworth in 1485, Richard III of England lost when some of his army defected to Henry Tudor, who became Henry VII.

The battle at Ablakh can be accounted truly decisive, for it halted Tang expansion into western Turkestan and helped to drive forward the Islamisation of Central Asia. However, this was the sole major battle between Chinese and Arab armies, as the Arabs made no effort to press east into the Tarim Basin and Xinjiang, prefiguring the Russian failure to seek to advance against China between 1690 and 1857. Choices, and thus will and perception, the geopolitics of conflict, were affected by geography, but not generally dictated by them. One such was limited Chinese interest in blue sea naval activity, although riverine navies were critical in campaigning within China.

Ablakh dented Tang prestige, but the An Lushan Rebellion in northern China (755–63) was more serious for the dynasty. A different Chinese military geography was at stake under the Northern Song (960–1127), with linear defences, including a network of hydraulic defences such as deep irrigation channels and marshes, to protect the vulnerable province of Hebei. Reliant on volunteers, not conscription, the dynasty had reportedly over 1.25 million troops by 1041. Crossbowmen were the main defence against nomadic cavalry. The Song had relatively few cavalry. The Northern Song developed new fertile lands, which helped to sustain the new garrisons and new towns, which was a classic instance of a strategic direction in which the local was subordinate to the imperial state. So also with other expansionist empires, notably in the nineteenth century.

In turn, bringing Song rule to a close, China was to be conquered in the thirteenth century by the Mongols, who proved more successful than the Xiongnu, and indicated the continued vulnerability of settled agrarian societies, which has been a major theme in much military history.

CHAPTER 5

Greece and Macedon

Victorious over Persia in 480–479 BCE, the major Greek city-states were to fall out, pursuing influence, indeed, control through rival alliance systems. The historian Thucydides described Athens as an economy, state and society transformed and empowered by maritime commercialism, and presented its growing strength as a destabilising force in Greece, not least as its agrarian rival, Sparta, felt threatened. This difference was seen by Thucydides as responsible both for a destabilising shift in relative power and for a degree of cultural animosity that made it difficult to adjust disputes.

Modern commentators have tended to emphasise a shift in relative power, although the cultural animosity between Athens and Sparta was also very important. A common 'Greekness' did not prevent important politico-cultural differences within the Greek world. A comparison can be made with the background to the outbreak of World War One in 1914, if the European empires are seen as latter-day Greek alliance systems. More profoundly, in classical Greece as today, ideas of self-interest aligned with those of ideology: there was a convenience of congruence between the two that eased the path to war.

As an instance of the role of written history in supposedly teaching timeless lessons, Thucydides' text is currently deployed in order to argue about the likelihood or probability of conflict between a declining United States and a rising China. The use of the text in this fashion raises specific issues to do with the understanding of it, including its translation, but also more general questions about the relevance of historical texts as providing supposedly timeless lessons, which is a deeply suspect idea. Argument by analogy is also question-able, with writers and their writings employed as both analysis of the past and prospectus for the future, which is problematic. There are also relevant points about the extent to which the understanding of the 'lessons' can itself change the very applicability of the example. This can be seen with the contentious use over the last century of 'lessons' from examples such as Munich, Suez and Vietnam, refer-ences to the episodes of 1938, 1956 and 1963–75.

As a key aspect of a mini-states system in Greece, the Peloponnesian War (431–404 BCE) saw Sparta finally victorious over Athens, an outcome that was far from inevitable and one that was handled in the literature with far less mention of divine intervention than the coverage of the far earlier siege of Troy. The cruelty of war was seen in the Athenian invasion in 416 BCE of the neutral island of Milos, which had been offered alliance or destruction. Athenian victory was followed by the slaughter of all the adult males and the enslavement of women and children.

Initially, the Spartans invaded Attica and ravaged the agricul-tural land near Athens, which was protected by its long walls and supplied by means of its maritime strength. The Athenians gener-ally avoided battle, while mounting amphibious attacks on the Peloponnese. In turn, the Athenians suffered a terrible blow when their siege of Syracuse, the major city in Sicily, in 415–413 BCE proved a total and very costly failure. Whereas the siege of Troy had a mythic character, and was essentially recalled much later from oral tradition, Thucydides left a lengthy account of Athens's attack on Sparta's Sicilian ally. As he made clear, the mismanagement of the campaign by the Athenians was a key element. This included a lack of security such that the Syracusans knew they were coming. Sparta sent help to Syracuse. The Athenians defeated at Syracuse were enslaved, a common fate. Athens fought on, but Persia came to the support of Sparta, which heavily defeated the Athenian fleet in 405 at the Battle of Aegospotami as the Athenians tried to protect their route for grain supplies from the Black Sea. The Athenians surrendered the following year.

In turn, Sparta's strength troubled former allies, leading to the inconclusive Corinthian War (395–387 BCE) in which Sparta was hit hard at sea, while Persia was able to intervene in Greek politics. The Theban–Spartan War (378–362 BCE) that followed saw Thebes defeat Sparta at Leuctra (371 BCE), in part by using the attack in oblique order, that by a strengthened flank. The war, in which there were repeated invasions of the Peloponnese and a major victory at Mantinea (362 BCE), left Thebes as the major power.

Macedon to its north, however, became the nemesis of Greek independence, with Philip II (r. 359–336 BCE) remodelling his army and progressively advancing southwards, defeating at Chaeronea in 338 BCE the forces of Thebes and Athens. As with many battles in antiquity (and not only then), the details of what occurred are few and the accounts capable of differing interpretations. The following year, as another instance of the coalitions that were important to Greek warfare, Philip created the League of Corinth, which was designed as the basis for the invasion of Persia, with himself as leader.

In the event, after Philip's assassination in 336 BCE, this was to be carried out by his son, Alexander the Great, who captured the potentially decisive role of individual leadership, as well as the expectation that leaders would be personally involved in the fighting. Calling himself Lord of Asia, Alexander conquered the Persian empire, and then tried, for prudential reasons as well as due to his quasi-mystical sense of his own mission, to transform the rivalry of Greeks and Persians into a new imperial unity.

Alexander invaded Asia Minor in 334, defeating larger Persian armies at the Granicus River (334 BCE) and Issus (333 BCE), before turning south, via the Near East, to conquer Persian-ruled Egypt in

332–331 BCE. In 332 BCE he had successfully besieged the well-fortified port city of Tyre in modern Lebanon. His catapults were able, alongside more rapid-firing archers, to provide covering fire for battering rams employed to breach the walls, and also for boarding bridges from which troops moved into breaches from ships. Cannon were later to provide the breaching force of the battering rams without needing their close contact, although, as a reminder of the need to be wary about assuming transformations in warfare, cannon displayed similar characteristics to catapults in requiring direct sight and close range. Alexander used ships, as at Tyre, but his was essentially a land power.

Alexander then returned to Syria and turned east to defeat Darius III, the Persian emperor, at Gaugamela (331 BCE) near Nineveh. This proved the decisive defeat of the Persians. Alexander's force was seven thousand strong, the Persian forty thousand, but many of the latter were weak and poorly trained infantry who lacked the spirit of the battle-hardened Macedonians. Despite being affected by the Macedonian javelin throwers, the Persian cavalry seriously pressed the Macedonians, but Alexander's cavalry itself hit the Persian left, and, with Darius apparently killed (in fact the charioteer behind him was the victim), many of the Persians fled, destroying the cohesion of their centre. In 330, Alexander burnt down the Persian capital, Persepolis, while Darius was over-thrown by conspirators, notably his cousin, Bessus, and killed.

Alexander campaigned to the east in an attempt to crush resist-ance, including by Bessus who had proclaimed himself king of kings only for Bessus to be betrayed by his followers. Alexander also sought to affirm the frontier of Persian rule, which meant defeating local satraps (governors) and tributary rulers. Alexander also sought the wealth of India and, possibly, to advance to the end of the known world. After difficult operations in Afghanistan, against determined opposition, Alexander fought in the Indus Valley, encountering opponents with plenty of elephants. Porus, king of the Pauravas, was defeated at Hydaspes on the banks of the Jhelum River in Punjab in 326 BCE and, having surrendered, became an ally, a frequent process. However, Alexander's troops had had enough of the apparently unending warfare and, in 326, demanded to leave India. He was accordingly obliged to return to Baghdad where he died in 323 BCE, leaving no heir.

Alexander's army had a multi-purpose effectiveness, not least with its disciplined phalanx formations of pikemen with their sarissas (long spears), its heavy cavalry, the two providing a combined-arms force, and its skill in siegecraft. Such an effectiveness is always significant as it increases the range of opponents that can be challenged, indeed overcome. The army also came to include local troops, first as auxiliaries, but, eventually, in the infantry. Persians were recruited, as were Scythian horsemen, and Alexander benefited from horses from Central Asia.

In another instance of over-extension, Alexander's generals could not sustain his position in north-west India. They also fell out over his succession, establishing a number of rival kingdoms, notably Egypt (ruled by the Ptolemies), Syria, Iraq, Persia and Southern Turkey (the Seleucids), and Macedon (Antigonids). These competing families remained in control until Roman conquest, although the Seleucids lost Persia in about 255 BCE. At Ipsus (301 BCE), the largest of the battles, the victorious Seleucus I made good use of elephants, which frightened the horses of the opposing cavalry. There was scant sense of subsequent geographical limits. In particular, Seleucus, having gained control of the Asian territories, invaded Thrace in 281 BCE, only to be assassinated.

Hellenistic armies drew on the different resource bases of the particular kingdoms, although their cores, reliant on the phalanx of pikemen, fought in a similar style, which was to be a pattern followed in Western warfare over the last millennium and a half. At the same time, infantry recruitment, formations, weaponry and tactics also varied in the Hellenistic world, with circumstances helping ensure these changes. Thus, the length of the sarissa became greater, which, however, helped limit flexibility. The Hellenistic period saw publications on warfare, including Philon's *Poliorcetica* on fortification, as well as the development of more formidable siege weapons such as battering rams sheathed with iron and mounted on rollers, early versions of armoured vehicles. At the siege of Rhodes in 305–304 BCE, a massive iron-plated mobile tower carrying catapults was used by Demetrius 'Poliorcetes', the 'Besieger'. Iron plates helped siege towers to resist the fire missiles and catapults launched from the positions they were attacking.

Alexander became a potent image of heroic rulership, one that was to resonate widely and for a long time, helping to provide a validation for the glory to be gained through war. Indeed, the totemic character of conflict was to be seen in the determination across all cultures to hold onto the legacy of the past, of its honour and power. This has been seen across the cultures, from antiquity to the present, with military units eager to list past battle honours on their standards. Giovanni Panini's painting *Alexander the Great at the Tomb of Achilles* (*c.* 1718–19) depicted the episode in which Alexander, who believed he was descended from Achilles, allegedly ordered that the tomb of Achilles in Troad be opened so that he could pay tribute to the great warrior of the past, and thus acquire his magic. There was a wider meaning in the popularity of images of Alexander's exploits as they came to validate Europeans' sense of their destiny in the world, as in Napoleon's approach to his conquest of Egypt in 1798 or Marzio di Colantonio's painting *Alexander the Great in His Conquest of Asia* (*c.* 1620). This was an aspect of the *traditio imperii*, the inheritance of classical imperial power, so important in Christendom.

This process was also very significant in other cultures, and notably in China when non-Chinese dynasties were established. However much it looked to the future in technology, war was often in the shadow of images of the past. That is a pattern that is still with us today, not least due to the role of past examples and weaponry in present thought, training and force structures, and to the impact of the present on the future.

CHAPTER 6

Indian Warfare

Ustād Ali Kuli discharged his guns many times in front of the
line to good purpose. Mustafa, the cannoneer on the left of
the centre, managed his artillery with great effect. The right
and left divisions, the centre and flankers having surrounded
the enemy and taken them in rear, were now engaged in hot
conflict, and busy pouring in discharges of arrows on them.
They made one or two very poor charges on our right and left
divisions. My troops making use of their bows, plied them
with arrows, and drove them in upon their centre.

> Babur, the Mughal victor over the Lodi Sultanate
> of Delhi, on Battle of Panipat, 1526 CE

The patterns of military development and activity seen elsewhere
in areas of advanced agriculture were also present in South Asia.
Thus, it saw the development, by the mid-third millennium BCE, of
agricultural settlements that were walled, such as Mundigak (near

Kandahar), which eventually had massive walls. Archaeological remains extend to fortifications on a formidable scale, and notably so for the Indus Valley-based Harappan culture of 2800–1600 BCE, as with the citadels at Harappa, Kalibangan and Mohenjo-daro. In addition, the lower towns were protected with thick walls, which were of baked mud bricks. The Sanskrit-spreading Vedic Aryan invaders, marauding nomads, possibly from Baluchistan, who spread across northern India in the early second millennium BCE identified themselves, in the *Rig Veda*, as the 'destroyers of forts', and may have caused the overthrow of the Harappan culture. This transition to the Iron Age was slower in southern India, underlining the extent to which, like sub-Saharan Africa and Western Europe, India was a subcontinent with much diversity.

In turn, in the early first millennium BCE, fortified settlements reappeared in the Punjab, both for local protection and as expressions of the power of developing regional states. Moreover, major cities across southern India were fortified in the context of intense competition, which was reminiscent of Mesopotamia and Greece. So also in the mid-Ganges Valley with the Magadhan capital, Rājagrha, and the city of Pātaliputra, which was fortified against the Vajji confederation in the sixth century BCE. The Magadhan empire had a large force of elephants, cavalry and chariots. On what was later the North-West Frontier of British India (and now of Pakistan), the tribes who unsuccessfully opposed the advancing Alexander the Great in 327 BCE relied on walled towns, such as Arigaion, and rock fortresses, such as Aornos.

The invasions of northern India by Central Asian peoples had more impact than what became in hindsight the short-lived expedition of Alexander. The northern Sakas, the Yuezhi, the Scythians and the Kushans, were each invading groups, but their precise identity and relations with one another are an ethnographical nightmare and the chronology of much early Indian history is uncertain. This is also true of that of most of the world, but there is a shortage of written sources for Indian history. Difficult to date, Kautilya's treatise *Arthaśāstra* claimed that 'Victory for a king depends primarily on elephants.'

Much of northern and central India was united in the fourth century CE by the Gupta dynasty, but it was put under great pressure by invaders from Central Asia. The White Huns launched a major attack in 480, following up with more wide-ranging advances in the 500s and 510s. These greatly weakened Gupta power, preparing the way for the division of India from about 500 among a large number of regional powers, a division that lasted until the thirteenth century. As in China, armies in the north, which were closer to areas where horses were bred and could be readily sustained, could deploy large numbers of cavalry. Those further south had limited access to horses, which were also harder to keep in health, and, therefore, lacked the mobility and offensive shock power of the northerners.

Subsequently, in the period of their rapid early expansion, Muslim forces, having overcome Persia, advanced, like Alexander the Great, to the River Indus in the late seventh century, with expansion into the valley itself in 711–13, and major raids beyond in 724–43. They were to be more effective in India than further north at the expense of China, which was a more formidable as well as distant opponent. Muslim powers established themselves in the region and raided widely, not least in order to gain slaves. Slave-raiding was a major cause and consequence of conflict in this period, and, indeed, for much of human history. Thus, based at Ghazni, south-west of Kabul, the Ghaznavids expanded into Persia, to the Aral Sea, and into the Indus Valley, in the early eleventh century, and also raided far into India. They retained their position until overthrown in the late eleventh century by the Ghurids, another Afghanistan-based empire. After victory at Chandwar near Agra in 1194, the Ghurids had also taken over the Ganges Valley. Although attacked by the Mongols in the 1290s, northern India was not brought under their control. Instead, the Delhi sultanate controlled, directly or indirectly, much of northern and central India, although it was conquered in 1398 by Timur, a closer threat than the Mongols and one for whom India was more important than China. However, the Timurids were not to sustain a presence in northern India.

Although the north of India was vulnerable to cavalry invasions, the south and the north-east contained environments, notably of thick semi-tropical forest and marshland respectively, that were resistant to such attacks, disease playing a role alongside terrain. In these regions, elephants continued to be particularly important, with the Indian elephant, although a heavyweight, more malleable than its African counterpart. Elephants could be more impressive than effective but, in the hands of an experienced general, could be much more than just a scare tactic. Indeed, elephants had some of the characteristics of later tanks. They had a crew, carried weapons that were used by the crew, were armoured, and were employed to smash opposing lines and pursue the enemy.

In the forest valley of the River Brahmaputra in the north-east, the Ahom developed fighting techniques well adapted to the terrain, using archers, flexible tactics including surprise night attacks, and rapidly created fortified positions based on bamboo stockades which made attacking them a costly and difficult task. They proved a formidable opponent to Mughal expansion in the seventeenth century. India could not support war China-style, in large part because of geographical limitations, with arable areas broken up by wilderness and, as a result, internal frontiers everywhere. As a result, in a similar 'states system' to Greece, small states tended to be able to resist or limit empire-building attempts.

India was divided into a number of states, in part reflecting the physical environment, but also a more general absence of cohesion in territories that essentially rested on the military prowess of the ruler and his ability to win over support through continued success. In turn, the large number of states that resulted made any conquest lengthy, and a process, rather than an event, as the Mughals discovered in the sixteenth century.

Prior to the spread of cannon, Indian fortification focused on cities, where it was a question of walls and citadels, or fortresses in the countryside, usually on hilltops. Particular effort was devoted to citadels at capitals. This was especially so at Delhi, the key centre of power in northern India. The citadel there was a residence, political centre, military stronghold and protector of both mosque and mausoleum. Rulers founded their own citadels or adapted those of their predecessors. Separately across India, the town dwellings and rural centres of prominent families were fortified, with walled and gated compounds being a significant feature in towns.

Many Indian rulers placed a major emphasis on cavalry, whether the rapid-firing mounted archers who were important in the north or heavy cavalry. In contrast, in Western Europe, there was no force of mounted archers capable of challenging the firepower of the infantry. Instead, whether armed with longbows or crossbows, archers fought dismounted.

Zahir ud-din Muhammad Babur, the energetic and able founder of Mughal power in northern India, inherited his father's principality of Ferghana in modern Uzbekistan in 1494, and in 1497 occupied the city of Samarqand, but was driven from both by the Uzbeks, being defeated at Sar-e-pul in 1501 in one of the cavalry battles that were so important in Eurasian history. He went on to invade northern India, overcoming the Lodi sultanate of Delhi at nearby Panipat in 1526.

Yet, the grounding of his conquest proved extremely difficult, and encountered serious resistance, including one period of major reversal. In part, eventual Mughal victory depended on triumphs in successive battles, but, to a considerable extent, it was a product of expedient alliances with local interests, notably many of the Rajputs. This was more generally the case with imperial conquests. It was not until the late seventeenth century that the Mughals came to dominate the Deccan, south-central India. They displayed an ability to adapt to a bewildering variety of environments, from the equatorial heat and humidity of the forested Brahmaputra valley, where they fought the Ahom, to the arid plains and snowy mountains of Central Asia. Their troops, military system, generalship and (on the whole) logistics proved equal to the challenge, even if success could not always be won. This range is an important measure of military capability, but range tends to be underrated, not least because many famous Western forces, such as those of Frederick the Great, Napoleon and Moltke the Elder, largely or only operated simply in one type of military environment.

Even so, the Marathas posed a challenge to Mughal control over western India that, despite major efforts, could not be overcome. Indeed, this challenge was not to be overcome until the 1810s, and then only by the British. It was they, in co-operation with many Indians, who brought territorial unity to South Asia, although that was to be fractured in turn in 1947.

CHAPTER 7

Rome and Hannibal

Like the Hittites and the Assyrians, the Romans were formidable warriors. They were particularly impressive for the training and discipline that enabled them to march at a formidable rate, as well as to deploy in a variety of planned formations, including the *testudo*, which was the means to conduct sieges, and also to perform complex and effective manoeuvres on the battlefield. The Romans were able to deploy and operate in a range of physical and military environments, and to produce an infrastructure of military power and persistence by fort- and road-building.

Indeed, Gnaeus Domitius Corbulo (d. 67 CE), a general who fought in Germany and conquered Armenia, observed that the pick was the weapon with which to beat the enemy. Trajan's Column in Rome shows Roman soldiers digging. Roman forces were trained and adept at building marching camps every time they stopped. These generally occurred at 25-kilometre intervals, the average daily rate of march expected of a legion. The camps followed a common pattern and, in what would today be referred to as a standard operational procedure, each element of the marching group understood its role in the construction process. The camps provided security and good communications on their line of advance. Many camps became the bases of settlements.

Originally a modest settlement in central Italy, the Romans gained strength and power by conflict, both local and distant. Having subjugated other peoples who were made to become allies, Rome unified Italy. This campaigning also entailed resistance to Celtic attacks from the north and to invasion, on behalf of the Greek settlements, in 280 BCE by Pyrrhus, king of Epirus in Greece, an effective general whose army included elephants. This paragraph so far covers several hundred years of history and presents, as a smooth process, what was in reality quite a difficult one. In practice, Rome encountered considerable resistance. Rome's major opponent in the interior, the Samnites of southern Italy, proved a formidable foe, with wars in 343–341, 328–304 and 298–290 BCE, and a key Roman victory at Sentinum in 295 BCE. As a consequence, the Samnites were forced to become allies. Rome cemented its position by establishing colonies (settlements) of Latin citizens at key places, and by building roads, notably the Via Appia from Rome across the Apennines to Capua in 312 BCE, and the Via Flaminia from Rome to Rimini on the Adriatic in 220 BCE. Such infrastructure was crucial.

Roman victory over the Samnites permitted pressure on the Greek cities of southern Italy, especially Tarentum (Taranto). Although victorious at Heraclea (280) and Asculum (279), Pyrrhus was defeated in 275 at Maleventum (which changed its name to Beneventum after this victory). He then returned to Epirus. This led to the Roman capture of Tarentum (272), to the other Greek cities coming to terms with Rome, to the establishment of more Latin colonies, and to the extension of the Via Appia, so that most of Italy was under Roman control by 250.

Incessant warfare helped ensure that Rome's culture, public memory, public spaces, religious cults, society and political system were militaristic, and citizenship was linked to military service.

Indeed, in many respects, Rome was Italy's Sparta. It praised martial values, and promoted and honoured politicians accordingly.

Roman success against the Greeks brought them into rivalry with Carthage, a Phoenician settlement founded near modern Tunis that had become, by the third century, the major maritime and imperial power in the western Mediterranean. The three Punic Wars between Rome and Carthage were wide-ranging struggles that involved conflict in mainland Italy, Sicily, Spain and North Africa. In the First Punic War (264–41 BCE), Rome's struggle with Carthage focused on the control of Sicily which then, and repeatedly, suffered from being a meeting place of civilisations. In this struggle, the Romans were hit hard initially by their lack of naval power and this led them rapidly to develop a navy that proved able to defeat Carthaginian fleets off Sicily. In battle, the Romans rammed their opponents and then used the plank-like *corvus*, which had a spike that attached it to the enemy ship, to form a bridge between ships, and thus enable rapid boarding of the enemy vessel, war at sea thereby transformed into land battle afloat to the benefit of Rome. However, the *corvus* appears to have been a one-war wonder, possibly because it had been linked to the loss of many Roman ships in storms.

Naval strength provided Rome with a crucial margin of advantage that allowed it to conquer Sicily and, more tangentially, to project power to North Africa, although the expeditionary force sent there was defeated, in part by the Carthaginian use of war elephants. Having lost that war and ceded Sicily, which became Rome's first province, Carthage faced a rebellion by its mercenaries. As an instance of the serendipitous way in which the Roman empire expanded as opportunities were exploited, this rebellion gave the Romans the opportunity to annex Corsica and Sardinia in 227 BCE. In his *Histories*, Polybius recorded, 'The Romans, from the moment they concerned themselves with the sea, began to entertain designs on Sardinia.' Their horizons literally expanded.

Subsequently Carthage and Rome came to compete over southern and eastern Spain in which both powers were vying for influence. This competition, which touched off the Second Punic

War (218–201 BCE), reflected the extent to which Rome's ambition increasingly extended over the Mediterranean. This extension indeed proved more significant to Rome than expansion north over the Alps. Hannibal (247–183 BCE), the key Carthaginian general, who had taken a vow to seek revenge for the defeat in the First Punic War, having done well in Spain, decided to attack the base of Roman power in Italy itself, and thus to secure the Carthaginian achievements. To do so, he marched across southern France, crossed the Alps, a formidable undertaking, in 218 BCE, and attacked the Romans in Italy. Hannibal bringing his elephants across the Alps helped posterity to see this as an epic struggle, although only one survived the crossing and it died soon after.

Hannibal's arrival created an acute crisis for Rome. His highly professional force was ably led and gained control of the dynamic of campaigning. Major Roman armies were defeated at the River Trebia (218), Lake Trasimene (217), Cannae (216) and Herdonia (210). Cannae proved one of the biggest defeats of antiquity and one that was to have a disproportionate influence in Western military thought: the Roman army had its flanks driven in, and then, the victims crushed together, was slowly and systematically slaughtered, with about fifty thousand Roman casualties. Defeat led some of Rome's allies to desert and also created acute political pressures within Rome. Different commanders and strategies were pushed to the fore in a desperate search for solutions. Deciding whether or not to engage in battle was a key choice. The commander, Quintus Fabius Maximus, known as Cunctator, 'the Delayer', urged avoidance to such effect that this evasion is known as Fabian tactics. Brought to the fore after Hannibal's victory at Lake Trasimene, Fabius avoided battle on the plains, preferring to rely on attritional conflict in the hills where Rome's infantry was particularly valuable as opposed to Carthaginian cavalry. Popular impatience led to the abandonment of his strategy and then to disaster at Cannae, after which Fabius was reappointed.

In the event, Hannibal failed not because of defeat in battle in Italy but as a result of his inability to translate victory in battle into his intended outcome: the collapse of Rome and its territorial system. Hannibal's army was small and lacked a siege train. The city of Rome proved too strong to attempt to storm and most of Rome's allies remained firm. Advancing from Spain to back him, Hasdrubal's army was defeated by the Romans at the Metaurus (207), while maritime supply to Hannibal's army in Italy was effectively blocked by the Roman navy. Moreover, the Romans quickly freed a great number of slaves so that they could join the Roman army.

Instead, the Carthaginian system was brought down, first by Roman successes in Spain, where Scipio won the decisive Battle of Ilipa (206), and then because of a transfer of the war to North Africa in 204. Hannibal had to return home in order to address the threat posed by Scipio who proved more successful than the Roman force that invaded North Africa during the First Punic War. In 202, Scipio, thereafter called Africanus, won a crucial victory over Hannibal at Zama in part because the Romans had learned how to thwart Carthaginian elephants. After Zama, Carthage accepted the harsh Roman peace terms, and Hannibal went into exile.

Rome's victory in the Second Punic War left Rome dominant in the western Mediterranean, including eastern and southern Spain. It was not thenceforth to face so wide-ranging an opponent, and was therefore better able to direct resources against opponents.

The large size of the army of republican Rome derived from the organisation of the peoples of Italy into various citizen and allied statuses, all of which were required to serve in the Roman army. Like the Han rulers of China, the Romans believed in a mass army based on the adult males of the farming population, which provided huge reserves of manpower for use against Carthage. Maybe up to a quarter of a million Italians were in the Roman army in 31 BCE, nearly a quarter of the men of military age.

Having defeated Hannibal, the Roman legionaries, with their short stabbing iron sword, heavy javelin and shield, fighting together shoulder to shoulder, were involved in conflict further afield. Benefiting from superior manpower, resources, willpower and organisation, they had taken control of the eastern Mediterranean, Egypt, Gaul (France) and Spain by 30 CE, following up with most of Britain and the Balkans by 100 CE. Julius Caesar was the key figure in the conquest of Gaul, most dramatically by overcoming Vercingetorix, his major opponent, in 52 BCE.

Caesar also launched expeditions against Britain in 55 and 54 BCE. In 55 BCE, Caesar did not move from his precarious beachhead in Kent. The Romans were victorious in hard fighting, but the damage done to their ships by equinoctial gales, and the scale of the resistance, led Caesar to come to terms with the local tribes. In 54 BCE, he invaded anew with a larger force, benefiting from his opponents' naval weakness, which meant that they could not contest the passage of the English Channel. Moving from the beachhead, Caesar defeated the local tribal leader and imposed a settlement.

Gaining success, as Caesar very much did in Gaul and sought to do in Britain, as Gnaeus Pompey (the Great) did in Spain and against Mediterranean piracy, and as M. Licinius Crassus unsuccessfully sought to do in Syria, commanders then used their resulting reputation to pursue their ambitions in Rome. Inherently, this was an unstable process. A political player in its own right, the military was factionalised, and the factionalisation very much focused on the ambitions of men who were not interested in compromise which, indeed, they understood as likely to cause a loss of face. Competition cascaded down the decades, as military factionalism sustained enmities. Pompey (106–48 BCE) had backed Sulla in the civil war in 83–81 BCE and was sent by him to overcome Marius' supporters in Sicily and Africa. Pompey and Marcus Licinius Crassus joined Julius Caesar in the First Triumvirate (55), an agreement to share power, notably over Rome's areas of military activity and in support of the Roman people, an agreement that pushed the Senate (oligarchs) aside.

This pact, however, did not last. Defeated at Carrhae by the Parthians in 53, Crassus was killed. In turn, Pompey, who presented himself as the champion of the Senate, and Caesar went to war with each other in 49, Caesar leading his troops across the River Rubicon (near Rimini) from Cisalpine Gaul into Italy. He won a key victory over Pompey at Pharsalus (48) in Greece. The civil war continued even after Pompey was killed, as his sons' supporters fought on, notably in Spain and North Africa, only to be defeated.

The new situation proved unstable. Caesar, the leading *popularis*, although himself a patrician, very much associated with the plebeians, while his opponents, most prominently Brutus and Cassius, the leading *optimates*, sought a republic directed by the aristocracy. This division led to Caesar's assassination in Rome on the Ides of March (15 March) in 44, and then to a civil war in which a triumvirate of Caesar's supporters totally defeated the conspirators at Philippi (42) in Greece.

In turn, the triumvirate fell out. Its weakest member, Lepidus, was pushed aside, while Mark Antony allied with Cleopatra, ruler of Egypt, only to be defeated in a great naval battle at Actium on the west coast of Greece in 31 BCE by the forces of the third triumvir, Caesar's heir, also called Caesar, who in 30 BCE pursued Mark Antony to Egypt where Mark Antony and Cleopatra both committed suicide. The Roman conquest of Egypt marked a major transition in the geopolitics of the ancient world.

CHAPTER 8

Imperial Rome and Its Fall

Agricola then encouraged three Batavian and two Tungrian
cohorts to fall in and come to close quarters; a method of
fighting familiar to these veteran soldiers, but embarrassing to
the enemy from the nature of their armour; for the enormous
British swords, blunt at the point, are unfit for close grappling,
and engaging in a confined space.

> Tacitus of the Roman victory at Mons Graupius,
> Scotland, over the Caledonians, *c.* 83 CE

A wonder of engineering some 3,724 foot (1,135 metres) in length,
the first bridge built across the lower Danube was constructed near
the Iron Gates in 103–5 CE by the Emperor Trajan (r. 98–117) in
pursuit of his conquest of Dacia (Romania), finally achieved in 106.
The bridge superstructure was later demolished, possibly in order
to thwart a 'barbarian' invasion from the north.

Augustus had neutralised the army politically, but only temporarily. The importance of gaining military reputation was seen with

Claudius' victorious invasion of Britain in 43 CE, and his successor Nero's neglect of the army led to a rebellion in 68 CE that precipitated his fall and a contest between army commanders, notably in 69, the Year of the Four Emperors, eventually won by Vespasian, who founded a new dynasty. Having done really well as a conquering republic with ambitious generals, Rome proved a still formidable conqueror in the first 120 years CE, with the gods repeatedly called forth in the cause of success. Conquests included the finishing of those of Armenia, Iberia and Israel.

Warrior values were to the fore. Trajan, an experienced general, was adopted as son and successor by the elderly Emperor Nerva (r. 96–8), whose lack of military credentials was a problem. Trajan arranged the dedication of his column in Rome in 113 for the anniversary of the dedication of the Temple of Mars Ultor in 2 BCE in order to invoke the help of that god in the new war against the Persian-based Parthian empire, a war in which he might have sought to emulate Alexander of Macedon or only to settle a more defensible frontier.

Roman rule also brought peace to the Mediterranean for the first time, with piracy crushed, notably as a result of victories off Sicily in 36 BCE. As a result, the Romans were able to use the Mediterranean as a crucial trade system and with singularly low protection costs. The unique circumstance of having all the Mediterranean under the same military and fiscal authority made large-scale overseas trade possible, not least providing Rome with food. Fleets based at Misenum near Naples and at Ravenna, supported by smaller squadrons around the empire, including at Alexandria in Egypt, Fréjus in France, and Seleucia in Syria, kept the peace.

At the same time, Rome, like other empires, relied not only on conquest but on co-operation, both with neighbours, including client states, and in ruling subject peoples. The conquered leadership was frequently given the chance to become Roman, which led the élites of many areas to become loyal allies and provide ancillary troops. This co-operation was economic and cultural, as well as political and military, and ensured that conquest could be a process as well as an event. For example, Mauretania in modern Morocco was conquered by the Romans in 46 BCE, turned into a province in 40 BCE, became a client kingdom in 30 BCE under Juba, and was annexed in 44 CE.

As well as co-operation with their own subjects, empire had to work with outsiders, 'barbarians' from beyond the frontier, where the careful politics of mutual advantage, and the ability to create a sense of identification, were both useful.

However, a major defeat in Germany in 9 CE, born of over-extension east of the River Rhine, was also followed in the late 110s CE by the lack of staying power east of the River Euphrates in modern Iraq at the hands of the Parthians, even though Trajan advanced to the Persian Gulf in 116.

The experience of over-extension, one repeatedly seen with empires, led instead, eventually, to a shift to a policy of stabilisation, consolidation and fixed, defensive frontiers. Formidable systems of walls and fortresses were designed to provide both sites for defence and bases for attack. The Romans were major fort-builders in Britain, not least with their substantial legionary bases, particularly Deva (Chester), Eburacum (York) and Isca (Caerleon), as well as with shorter-lived legionary bases, such as Exeter (Isca) and Wroxeter.

In addition, the Romans built supporting forts, such as Housesteads, as part of Hadrian's Wall, a 110-kilometre long forti-fied stone wall constructed from about 122 across Britain at its narrowest from the River Tyne to the Solway Firth (estuary). Wallsend on the Tyne remains as a place name at the eastern end of the one-time wall. This wall took advantage of features in the terrain, notably a sill of hard volcanic rock which gave added height. The Emperor Hadrian (r. 117–38) was a consolidator of empire who also built defensive works in Germany and fixed the border with the Parthians on the Euphrates, abandoning Trajan's intention to gain Mesopotamia. He also retreated from part of Dacia.

The Romans later built the Antonine Wall further north in Britain. A turf rampart set upon a stone base, defended by forts, this wall was not retained for as long. Also in the reign of Antoninus

Pius (r. 138–61), the frontier was advanced in Germany, with a palisade defended by stone watchtowers and forts.

Rather than being intended to resist attacks, the walls and their forts were bases for operations, as well as being a control on transit into the area of Roman rule. Vindolanda Fort on Hadrian's Wall is a good example of a large fort used as a legionary operating base. Roman defences made use of ditches to protect positions, both permanent and temporary. These were sloped or pointed V-sectioned ditches that were difficult for attackers to cross, not least because of their steep slopes and pointed bottoms.

Attacks from 'barbarians' outside the empire became pressing from the late second century, with the Marcomanni and Quadi invading northern Italy in 167–70, and Berber tribesmen raiding Spain from the 170s. The Roman world was an attractive target and suffered a particularly harsh invasion crisis in the 250s that led to a territorial division of the empire as local solutions were sought for its defence.

Nevertheless, the invasions were a protracted process, and they were not always more significant for Rome than the rivalry with Persian-based empires, which tends to be underplayed in military history. Defeated at Hormozdgan in 224 by Ardashir, the Parthians were replaced by the Sasanian empire. Ardashir's son, Shapur I, beat the Roman Emperor Gordian at Misiche in 244 and defeated and captured the Emperor Valerian at Edessa in 260. As with many battles in antiquity, there are no reliable details. Shapur also inflicted a major defeat at Barbalissos near Aleppo in 252. For a long time, however, the Romans were successful in recovering from attack. Thus, Shapur was defeated in 260 when he tried to exploit his victory by advancing into Anatolia.

The Romans came to rely increasingly on a defence in depth based on mobile field armies designed to confront invaders, although also offering force for political purposes with generals regularly contesting power. Cavalry became more significant, and, partly to that end, the use of Germanic auxiliaries. The extent to which the Romans maintained their traditional formation of one main battle line, with the infantry in the centre flanked by cavalry, and with a reserve in the rear is unclear, but late Roman infantry was probably deployed as a phalanx, which was an aspect of the system's capacity to change. As a result, it is not helpful to refer to the Roman way of war, as that changed in strategic, operational and tactical ways.

Defence took a variety of forms, including governmental ones. While abandoning Dacia, the Emperor Aurelian (r. 270–5) brought a measure of recovery and, thanks to him, Rome itself in the 270s received a new multi-towered wall, while many other cities were also fortified. Diocletian (r. 284–305), a warrior emperor who was typical in coming from a military background, sought to provide delegated leadership by co-opting colleagues, creating a system of two senior and two junior emperors. However, this system eventually led to a permanent division between the eastern and western parts of the empire. The centre of power moved to the new capital of Byzantium (later Constantinople), founded by Constantine I in 330. He had converted to Christianity in 312 after defeating his rival Maxentius at the Battle of the Milvian Bridge, a conversion followed by the downgrading of paganism. This conversion, which like Japanese Westernisation in the late nineteenth century, involved considerable tension, greatly disrupted notions of continuity, and the divisiveness that resulted weakened the empire when it should have been concentrating on external threats. Well protected by its mighty walls and its peninsular location from generals who might seek to rebel, Byzantium became the capital of the Roman empire that was to survive the crises of the fifth century.

The less wealthy and populous West proved less able to cope with 'barbarian' attack, especially because mistrust helped prevent the East from supporting the West. The failure to hold the Rhine and Danube frontiers led to a serious defeat at Adrianople in 378, with the death of the Emperor Valens, and to pressure on Italy, pressure that was difficult to meet as so much of the army was committed to the frontiers or to other provinces. The crisis began far from the Mediterranean, but it hit the latter hard as 'barbarian' groups moved to its shores in search of wealthy targets, especially cities.

Under pressure from the Huns further east, the Visigoths under Alaric invaded Italy in 401, sacking Rome in 410 after the city, whose wall had held off Alaric, was starved into submission. Italy was then extensively ravaged by invaders: Goths, Huns and Vandals, the last a Germanic tribe who, having advanced via modern France and Spain, conquered modern coastal Algeria and Tunisia, plundered Rome in 455 and seized Sicily in 468. Roman Britain fell victim to invaders, principally Angles and Saxons, although Roman officials and Romanised élites put up significant opposition, and notably so in the fifth century. One of these figures may have been the model for the legendary King Arthur.

Alongside conquest, there was a process of turning for assistance to Germanic auxiliaries who were given lands within the empire and then became more powerful. Indeed, depending on the part of the empire, there was a degree of transition through synthesis and synthesis in transition, one accompanied by the conversion of many of the 'barbarians' to aspects of the late Roman world, notably Christianity. Thus, in Gaul (France), the Romans made arrangements with particular groups of 'barbarians', including some of the Franks, originally Germanic peoples, who provided troops to help against invasion; but this in effect led to a longer-term process of 'barbarianisation'. Always unstable, the terms of this relationship changed in the fifth century, as the Roman governmental presence began to decline in northern and central Gaul.

There was also, however, a continual interaction of cooperation, as in 451 when Franks fought alongside Romans against Attila's Huns, defeating them at the Battle of the Catalaunian Plains after the Huns had sacked Metz and Reims. In the end, Gaul did not so much succumb to the Germanic invaders of the fifth century as become transformed by them.

CHAPTER 9

The 'Dark Ages'

The comparison, in book 19 of *City of God* (426) by the Church Father St Augustine (354–430 CE), of Alexander the Great of Macedon with a company of thieves – 'in the absence of justice there is no difference between Alexander's empire and a band [*societas*] of thieves' – was a moralist's vain attempt to argue that intentionality, not scale, was the crucial issue. In accordance with Christian history and teaching, and notably of the example of the Roman persecution of Christ and the early Christians, sovereignty was not seen as a legitimator of slaughter. Instead, 'just war' was presented both as desirable and as a phenomenon that could be defined by the Church.

Separately, there was a world of disorder, one that was the product of Man's Fallen State and of the agencies of evil. For example, the reference to theft brought out the key role of looting in motivation, a role that continues in some cases to the present, both at the level of individual soldiers and with regard to their states and/or commanders seeking to seize resources.

Points similar to that of Augustine were made by later writers, both political commentators and others. The comparison of the ethics of 'the state' with that of 'criminal groups' can be seen in Shakespeare's *Antony and Cleopatra* with regard to pirates and in Friedrich Schiller's 1781 play *The Robbers*, not least in the 1921 version by the director Erich Ziegel, which used modern guns as props, included allusions to industrialisation and dressed the actors in contemporary military uniforms.

Ethics, however, were not to the fore in the post-Roman era, which was to be depicted from the fourteenth century as a Dark Age. With sovereignty a matter of seizure and legitimacy presented as the product of success, states were defined by victory, although that was scarcely new.

There can be a tendency to regard those who assaulted settled states as 'barbarian', but this underplays the organisation of their military systems, or, conversely, overplays the organisation of the settled states' military systems; and certainly underplays both overlaps and interactions between the two types of system. There was a predatory character to these assaults (as there had been with those of the settled states), notably when advancing and attacking in response to poor harvests, but that does not mean that organisation was lacking on the part of the 'barbarians'.

The degree of organisation in the military systems of the half-millennium after the fall of the Western Roman and Han empires is a matter that is largely unclear. The numbers involved are uncertain, as are the details of preparing for, executing or mopping up the recorded episodes of conflict. The locations and dates of many battles are themselves open to discussion, as are the relative importance of battle, as organised by leaders, opposed to, first, other forms of planned conflict, second, spontaneous violence between social groups that did not become part of memory or record and, separately, assimilation and co-existence leading to no conflict at all.

Yet, although the sources and analysis employed to argue for continuity from the Roman period and for a measure of sophistication have been criticised, there was certainly the ability to deploy forces and campaign, and, accordingly, to develop and sustain systems to produce and sustain armies. Moreover, assembling significant forces for siege warfare, as in tenth-century Germany, assumed a logistical burden that could be met, although, on these and other occasions, there could be issues over the theft of food from local farmers, leading to resistance.

'Barbarian' invasions were seen across Eurasia, from China to Western Europe, where the last Roman emperor was deposed at Ravenna by Odoacer, a Germanic leader, in 476 CE. The first waves of attackers created states such as Merovingian France and Visigothic Spain, that competed with each other leading to a degree of instability in Europe greater than that during most of the Roman empire. Moreover, there were new 'barbarian' challenges. Thus, for China, the Avars, who had been a sixth-century threat, were followed by Turkic peoples.

In Italy, very differently, the Byzantines (Eastern Roman Europe) recovered much ground in the sixth century, showing the potential of the later Roman military system in the right circumstances. Destroying the Vandal realm, and driving back the Ostrogoths and Visigoths, the Byzantines recaptured North Africa, much of Italy and southern Spain in 533–51, victories that gave them control over the papacy. These campaigns, in which the key general was Belisarius, revealed the need for an extensive range of skills. Amphibious capability was a prerequisite for the Byzantine campaigns, as also, differently, for the 'barbarian' invaders of Britain, while siegecraft was also necessary, as shown by the capture of Palermo (535) and Ravenna (539). Victory in battle required the ability to gain the initiative and to maintain pressure on the enemy, as demonstrated against the Vandals at Tricamarum (533), a struggle decided by Byzantine cavalry charges.

Nevertheless, the Byzantine position in Italy was challenged from 568 by the Lombards, another 'barbarian' people, while the Visigoths drove the Byzantines from Spain by 624. Byzantium was also put under pressure from Sasanian Persia, which in 611 conquered Syria, a long-standing Sasanian goal, as seen in Shapur's campaigning in the third century, and, in 616, Egypt. In turn, the conquerors were pushed back, the Sasanids being defeated by the Emperor Heraclius in 628 and Egypt being regained in 629.

The nature and scale of conflict, however, were transformed by the ideology and practice of early Islam, which saw rapid expansion within, and then from, Arabia. Muhammad's forces captured Mecca in 630, and his successors, known as Caliphs, united Arabia and, defeating the Byzantines and Sasanians, both probably in 636, had conquered South-Western Asia and Egypt by 642. The crucial victory in Egypt at Heliopolis in 640 is one of many generally neglected due to the long repetition of lists of supposedly decisive battles that in practice are very Eurocentric. The seizure of Egypt led to the Arab conquest of North Africa and then, in 711, to the invasion of Spain, while other Arab forces conquered Persia. Although the nature of the sources is such that it is difficult to make authoritative statements about force structure, size, weapons and tactics, the Arabs benefited from the extent to which the earlier Byzantine–Sasanian conflict had worn down their opponents, and from their own archery, mobility and morale. Weakened by the plague and in the bitter and lengthy conflict with the Sasanians, Byzantium could not devote sufficient resources to prevent the Arab advance. Constantinople itself was besieged by amphibious Arab forces in 674–8 and 717–18, but the defenders, with their strong walls, were helped by 'Greek fire', a combustible compound emitted by a flame-throwing weapon, and the city did not fall.

Arab soldiers were dominant up until the conquests of Egypt and Persia, but it then became the practice for Arab leaders to use converts from the most recently conquered regions in order to move further: Persians into Central Asia, Egyptians into Tunisia, Tunisians into Morocco and Berbers into Spain. Most of Spain and Portugal was quickly overrun in the 710s, much more speedily so than when the Romans had invaded, and the advance pressed on into southern France, where Narbonne was captured in 719.

However, the Arabs were stopped by Charles Martel at 732 in the Battle of Tours. Details of the battle are unclear, not least as to location, course and consequences, but the Franks apparently took up a phalanx formation on high ground and saw off the Arab cavalry attacks before the death of the Arab leader led to the Arab retreat. The effective sword and spear combination of the Franks appears to have been important, but so also, apparently, were the chances of the battle. The death of leaders was always a key element, as with the last Parthian ruler at Hormozdgan in 224, or of Harold of England at Hastings in 1066.

The Muslims fell back after Tours, never to repeat their advance so far north, but, more generally, they helped to mould the modern world as the Muslim advance was to be reversed in relatively few areas, principally Iberia, the Mediterranean islands, Israel and the Volga Valley.

Charles Martel also defeated the Saxons and Alemanni, and restored Frankish control of Aquitaine, Burgundy and Provence. His son, Pepin III, deposed the last Frankish king of the Merovingian dynasty, and founded the Carolingian dynasty, campaigning in Germany, Italy and southern France. Under Pepin's son, Charlemagne (r. 771–814), the Franks became the key power in Western Europe, uniting most of Western Christendom by conquering northern Germany and Lombardy, crushing the Lombards in 773–4. In the former, in marked contrast to Roman failure beyond the Rhine, Charlemagne, after extensive campaigning, completely subjugated the Saxons. He also defeated the Avars in Hungary. There was a significant religious dimension to the conflicts, with Charlemagne, crowned emperor by Pope Leo III in 800, presented as a Christian warrior against the heathen, especially the Saxons. The successes of the Franks reflected an impressive military system and determined leadership, both crucial. In contrast, the Angle rulers of Mercia who were the major rulers in England in the eighth century, particularly Offa, did not have comparable success on the British scale.

Just as the Muslim world fragmented from the mid-eighth century, so the already-divided Carolingian world was further divided among Charlemagne's grandsons by the Treaty of Verdun (843), essentially into three: what became France, a middle kingdom, and also Germany. The Carolingian world also came under heavy pressure from the Magyars and the Vikings. Each achieved considerable success, but also finally failed.

The Magyars were the latest Central Asian horsed people to move westwards into Europe. Otto I, ruler of the East Frankish kingdom (later Germany), used a heavy cavalry based on his nobility to inflict a decisive defeat on the Magyars at the Lechfeld in 955. As so often with battle, this proved a key source of prestige, both for Otto and for his family.

Benefiting from their amphibious capability, Viking forces focused their attacks on sites with plentiful supplies, notably monasteries, such as Lindisfarne on the Northumbrian coast in 793 and Noirmoutier at the mouth of the Loire in 799. The Vikings also established camps or bases where they could store goods to use as supplies. These helped them deploy significant forces for major operations, such as the capture of Angers in 864 and 872-3 and Rouen in 885, and the unsuccessful siege of Paris in 885-6; although the Vikings also benefited because significant forces for them were probably only a logistical burden of three to four thousand men. They moved from small-scale attacks in the late eighth century, to larger campaigning hosts by the late ninth, and conquering armies organised by states, Denmark, Norway and Sweden, by the late tenth. In part, this transition reflected the political development that provided a different context for the use of warbands and household troops, one seen more generally in Europe.

The Vikings were defeated in England in the late ninth and early tenth centuries, first by Alfred, king of Wessex. A new, larger-scale attack led to the establishment of a Viking dynasty of rulers in England from 1016 to 1042. A later attack was defeated at Stamford Bridge in 1066. In France, the Vikings were only able to establish themselves in Normandy, and then only as vassals of the French Crown.

In the long term, the Vikings became the Scandinavian states. These dominated the Baltic until the rise of Russian power under Peter the Great (r. 1689-1725), but generally had only a limited impact elsewhere in Europe, although with Sweden important in Germany from 1630 until the 1710s. The Vikings, however, had passed into history.

CHAPTER 10

Feudal Warfare

From the late ninth century, the kingdoms of Western Europe, and notably so in modern France, Germany and Italy, found their authority increasingly challenged by landed potentates who created a new political and military system built around private castles in their own lands which paralleled that of kings in their territories. Public order was weakened and noble families became more important. So also in China in the late ninth century where regional commanders wielded effective power, and there was a splintering into regional states in the Five Dynasties period (907–60).

Narrowly defined, feudalism was a system of vassals (sworn followers) holding land in return for military service, usually in the form of knights: heavy (armoured) cavalry, who were more expensive to hire and support than infantry. Feudalism, however, can be more broadly conceived as a system of aristocratic predominance, with hereditary landholders dominating both society and state, and, as part of that, providing a key element in the military, notably as commanders but also through raising units. A shared culture of war-making and aristocracy, focused on militarism and fighting, was part of the established nature of politics. This was a situation readily seen more generally across time, occurring, for example, in sixteenth-century Japan and nineteenth-century Mexico.

Indeed, the location of many of the castles in medieval Europe was due to the considerations of local landlords seeking to control and protect their domains, and related to the particular nature of their landholdings and the threats to them. In the early fifteenth century, with English forces at the gates, Parisian citizens complained that aristocratic feuding was weakening the kingdom, only for the Duke of Berry to reply: 'We fight each other when we please and we make peace when we see fit.'

This culture created more fundamental political problems when the aristocrats vied for control over the monarchy, if not for the Crown itself, helping to cause succession wars, such as, to an extent, the Hundred Years War in France from 1337 to 1453, and, more clearly, the Wars of the Roses in England from the 1450s to the 1480s. The same pattern was to be seen in Japan from the late fifteenth to the early seventeenth centuries.

In turn, there was a tension in Europe between 'private' and 'public' military systems, although, in practice, there was always a degree of overlap. In Francia, the lands of Charlemagne, rulers relied on their own military retinues and supplemented their strength with those of their leading supporters, a pattern that went on being very significant and can be seen as the military essence of feudalism. These retinues made up a warrior élite that was very different to the locally raised militia-type infantry of the English *fyrd*; or to the professional troops under central command of some leading states, notably the slave soldiers of the major Islamic powers, or the Varangians of Byzantium. In China, Song Taizu (r. 960–76), a general who became first emperor of the Song dynasty, ended independent regional armies by bringing their best units into the palace army, which he kept under his own control, and by replacing military governors by civil officials.

Feudalism was to be associated with the rise of heavy cavalry, the basis of the later medieval knight. Traditional interpretations that the rise was due to the spread of the stirrup, which provided greater stability, and to the Christian response to Muslim cavalry as encountered in Spain and France, have long been called into question. It has been argued, instead, that cavalry was important throughout the post-Roman period, providing a degree of continuity from the Roman empire; but also that the mass, shock, charge of heavy cavalry became more significant from the eleventh century, as was seen in the Crusades.

Both the feudal system and cavalry were less formulaic and dominant than often suggested. In particular, alongside variety from the outset, the development of the money fief in the eleventh century (money, not land, provided in return for military service) helped to weaken the link between landed status and warrior ability and as part of the increasingly institutional nature of military organisation. Moreover, it is now far more appreciated in the past that European infantry played a major role in operations, and notably in sieges, and, as well, that knights frequently dismounted to fight in battle, as also did their Japanese counterparts. Thus, English victories in the Hundred Years War involved dismounted men-at-arms as well as longbowmen.

Byzantium, an empire with impressive durability, also had a combined-arms military system, and this helped it resist a series of challenges. Alongside a long-standing emphasis on heavy cavalry, and on the related tactics of a shock-delivering wedge attack, came the need for light cavalry and infantry.

Moreover, the Abbasid Caliphs (750–1258), the leading Islamic power, relied not only on infantry and light cavalry, but also on armoured heavy cavalry armed with swords, clubs and axes. In both these cases, as in others, there was also a variety reflecting the very different military environments, both physical and human, across the range of their areas of commitment and number of opponents.

The widespread importance of money in raising and supporting forces ensured a close link in many states between governmental development and military proficiency. Far from being ineffective militarily, medieval states, moreover, could deliver lasting military verdicts as in 1212, when the Christian armies of Iberia crushed the Almohad Caliph at Las Navas de Tolosa after a surprise attack. As was normal in the period, the victory was explained in terms of divine support.

Another lasting military verdict was provided in 1314, with the crushing Scottish victory under Robert the Bruce over the poorly commanded English at Bannockburn, a victory which helped ensure the independence of Scotland. In that battle, Scottish pikemen on well-chosen ground routed the English cavalry. This system was the basis of their earlier victory at Stirling in 1296. In turn, the English combined archers and men at arms successfully at Falkirk in 1297, but, at Bannockburn, in contrast, the archers were masked. Whereas there had been a quick riposte to failure at Stirling, there was none such to Bannockburn. Indeed, that was an aspect of the sequencing that is so important in establishing what appears decisive. For example, in the American War of Independence, the British were able to recover from defeat at Saratoga (1777), but not at Yorktown (1781).

Infantry played a major and increasing role in many parts of Europe, including not only Scotland but also Flanders, the Swiss cantons, Lombardy and the Czech Republic. The Lombard League resisted the Hohenstaufen emperors, defeating the Emperor Barbarossa at Legnano (1176), an infantry victory. Swiss halberds and spears proved very effective against Habsburg (Austrian) knights at Morgarten in 1315 and Sempach in 1386, and Bohemian infantry, strengthened by artillery, against cavalry attacks in the Hussite Wars of the early fifteenth century. Social changes and technological innovation both led to convergence between areas of European warfare, with Scandinavian methods for example, more similar from the thirteenth century with those elsewhere, but also divergence or, at least, contrast.

The infantry challenge was greatly enhanced with the English development of a longbow capability as part of a combination and co-operation of archers and men-at-arms. About 6 feet (2 m) long, and with a draw weight of between 81 and 185 pounds (37 and 84 kg) force, the longbow required considerable effort to use and thus much practice. As a result, practice was made compulsory.

Armour could provide some protection against the arrows, but there was vulnerability, notably the limbs and also horses.

In the Hundred Years War (1337–1453), English archers were successful against French attacks, notably at Crécy (1346), Poitiers (1356) and Agincourt (1415); while others helped John of Avis defeat a Castilian invasion of Portugal at Aljubarrota (1385), a key step in maintaining Portuguese independence. These longbowmen lacked the operational and tactical flexibility of Central Asian archers because, although they were sometimes mounted for movement on campaign, they could not fire from the saddle and tended to fight on the defensive, which ensured that they depended on being attacked, and thus on command quality or the lack of it.

Prior to the use of firearms, infantry therefore was already effective, and cavalry less dominant in Western Europe than was the case in Central Asia, not least because light cavalry was not the norm in Western Europe. This environmental contrast was at least as significant as that in the landholding structures described in terms of feudalism. Each, however, played a role in the nature of military power, with both opportunity and need being significant in each case.

Far more than weaponry and force structure was involved in success. Thus, during the Hundred Years War, Henry V of England (r. 1413–22), the victor of Agincourt, was greatly helped by an alliance with the Duke of Burgundy and throughout the conflict the successes of the English kings owed much to French allies, with the conflict in part an international dimension to a series of French civil wars. In turn, the loss of this support helped lead to total English failure by 1453.

CHAPTER 11

Castles

Castles and fortified cities were a potent display of power and an impressive force multiplier, and much warfare focused on the capture and defence of these positions. Surviving examples of castles, whether in Europe, the Near East or the Far East, provide ample illustrations of how they literally towered over, and thus physically and symbolically commanded, the surrounding countryside.

Castles were inhabited, rather than places of refuge, unlike the hill forts which had been numerous in the Iron Age, although the usage of the hill forts is a matter for discussion and they were clearly not all of the same type or in similar settings. So also with castles, many of which were private buildings and not means of public defence. Castles also had an offensive as well as a defensive function, because they provided shelter from which attacks could be mounted, and were thereby part of a military system.

Early castles were generally simple affairs of earth and timber, but stone was not vulnerable to fire, as wood very much was. Moreover, the strength of the defences posed tactical and organisational problems for attackers, especially the difficulty of providing supplies for besieging forces. Western European states tended to put more of an emphasis on stone than their counterparts in China, India and South-East and East Asia, where the emphasis, instead, was generally on the use of earth, timber and/or brick. At the same time, so-called stone castles had plenty of wooden components as an integral part of their infrastructure, and the mining of their defences by means of a fire-filled tunnel under a wall threatened the collapse of the wall. The collapse of the burning wooden support props brought the heavy masonry walls or towers above them crashing down, creating a breach. The very weight of the stone edifice could add to the vulnerability of the structure to attack by means of mining.

In terms of power and display, there was also with fortifications the issue of scale, and notably the size of fortified cities, such as Milan, Antioch, Constantinople, Baghdad or Xi'an, which were difficult targets when contrasted with the often relatively modest numbers in attacking forces. This situation helped to lead to a pattern of focusing the attack on the gates, rather than trying to attack along the walls. However, as earlier, such a concentrated focus left besieging armies vulnerable to sallies by the defenders.

Sieges often occasioned field warfare, in part due to the action of relief forces. During the Crusader siege of Antioch from 1097 to 1098, there were three major battles and numerous skirmishes. The Crusader siege of Acre during the Third Crusade lasted from 1189 to 1191, with very determined attackers supported and supplied by sea, while a Muslim field army operating against the besiegers stiffened the morale of the besieged.

Partly as a result of their cost in time and resources, and the difficulty of maintaining supplies, some leaders did not seek sieges, and certainly sought to avoid lengthy ones; although the capture of fortified positions was desirable. Much medieval strategy revolved around this goal, not least as such success was a sign of superiority that was important to the conduct and outcome of war.

Thus, as with earlier periods, fortifications and sieges were important to conflict in medieval Europe, and, as in earlier periods, this helped ensure that infantry played a major role in warfare. As always with fortifications, more than the fortresses themselves was at stake. Instead, castles, like other fortifications across the world, were particularly effective as part of a combined military system. European military history in the eleventh to thirteenth centuries in part centred on how the development of knights, infantry, castles and siege techniques enabled the rulers who employed them to extend their power, both against domestic opponents and on their frontiers. The latter forced the rulers of more peripheral regions threatened with this extension, such as those of Lithuania, Prussia, Scotland and Wales, to build castles of their own. Castles were also to be part of a combined system in Japan.

More generally, castle building was an aspect of the expansion of territorial control. Thus, in northern England, the Norman presence was anchored in the eleventh century – with the building of castles in Durham (1072), Newcastle (1080) and Carlisle (1092), Newcastle being the linguistic counterpart of Neuburg (German) and Neufchâteau (French); and the frequent use of these, and related names, testified to the significance of the construction of new fortifications. Edward I (r. 1272–1307) was also to use castle-construction to affirm and anchor his conquest of north Wales, and notably at Beaumaris, Caernarvon, Conwy and Harlech. Similarly, in Flanders in the early fourteenth century, the French sought to employ the construction of castles to advance their interests, as at Lille, a fortified position that remains significant to the present.

However, castles built to attack or defend had in Europe a radius of power of only about 25 kilometres, which was a good patrolling journey for a mounted man without exhausting his horse. The radius of power would be less on rough ground or in mountains.

Castles were built to consolidate Christian expansion at the expense of non-Christians. This was the case with the Crusades, and in Spain and Portugal during the lengthy wars with the Moors from the eighth to the fifteenth centuries. During the *Reconquista*, the Moors, in turn, built castles opposing those of the advancing Christians. Pretty much every Christian castle was answered by a Muslim one, and vice versa. For example, built in the eleventh century after the surrounding lands were reconquered, Loarre

Castle in Huesca Province is 10 kilometres from its opposing Muslim castle, each able to see the other.

In the Baltic lands, where the 'Northern Crusades' were being mounted, castles were built, notably in the lands of the Teutonic Knights. Malbork, which was selected in 1309 as the residence of the Grand Master, was then adapted and strengthened, as was the wider complex which included impressive walls and fortifications for both the castle and the neighbouring town. The physical environment could also be significant to the defences. Thus, river features played an important role at Malbork. In 1410, a Polish siege was repelled after the field army of the Teutonic Knights had been defeated at Grünwald/Tannenberg, a name that was to resonate in German consciousness, encouraging the triumph felt by the defeat there in 1914 of an invading Russian army.

The role of castles as affirming and confirming power was also seen in their being built in cities, often as citadels with a separate part of the city walls, as with the Tower of London and the castle at Exeter. The Castelvecchio in Verona in northern Italy, built by Cangrande II in the 1350s, bristled with battlements, demonstrated his power over the city, and benefited from being built along the River Adige. Indeed, the strength of castles reflected the combination of terrain features and shooting fronts. Other castles sought to use height to their benefit, as with that in Meersburg in southern Germany which was built on a rocky promontory and protected by a 14-metre moat. Alongside a 28-metre deep well and a subterranean passage to Lake Constance, this was dug in 1334 by the new Prince-Bishop of Constance, Nicholas of Frauenfeld, the papal candidate, when preparing to resist a siege by Emperor Louis IV. The fourteen-week siege failed.

As in other periods, sieges were more common than battles, which, indeed, frequently enjoy disproportionate attention in military history. In the Albigensian crusade in southern France, the Crusaders participated in at least forty-five sieges, but fought only four field battles between 1209 and 1218. The positions besieged varied greatly, from walled cities in the plains, such as Toulouse, to isolated hilltop castles. As elsewhere, in a reflection of the continuity of particular locations, some of the castles were built on historic sites: the impressively located Château de Puilaurens was on the site of a Visigothic citadel.

Siege machines and engineers in general were less important to success than luck, resolve, aggressiveness and terror. Luck, resolve and aggressiveness proved particularly significant in the seizure in 1204 of Château Gaillard, a still impressive site on a high position on the banks of the River Seine. Built by Richard I, the Lionheart, in 1196–8, it was captured from his lacklustre brother, John, king of England and Duke of Normandy, by the forces of the determined Philip Augustus, king of France. The magnificently strong individual castle was helpless if isolated from its broader political–logistical support system, and this castle was isolated by the besieging force who blocked the River Seine and prevented a relief force from reaching the castle. The castle was eventually starved into surrender. Its seizure left Normandy vulnerable to a rapid French conquest. This also was to happen in 1449–50 with other English-held castles in Normandy, although, in the latter case, French cannon played a role. Garrisons were given the chance of surrendering or fighting on and forfeiting their lives. As with many other sieges, for example in India, negotiation, not assault, also settled most of the sieges in the Albigensian crusade and in those both defensive and offensive capabilities were in large part significant in affecting the terms of negotiation.

Fortification techniques meanwhile had developed, not least with the increasing size, height and complexity of castles, especially in the thirteenth century. Raising the height of walls was important in the pre-cannon era because, alongside mining, major threats to fortifications were posed by scaling the walls, and by archers and stone-throwing weapons. Each threat could be lessened by raising the height, which also made fire from within the castle more deadly (to participants and others). Cannon changed the situation by battering away at the foot of stone walls, and thus breaching them.

Town walls were also improved and extended. Thus, in Grenoble in France, the Roman wall built at the end of the third century was extended in the thirteenth century, with a further extension at the end of the sixteenth century. At a smaller scale, a new form of walled town known as a *bastide* was being built in south-west

France in the thirteenth century, following a common design and being self-contained entities, with church, market, homes and defended gates. Many extant examples are still largely unchanged. The most active founders of *bastides* were Alphonse de Poitiers, brother of Louis IX of France, Count of Toulouse from 1249 to 1271, who built fifty-seven, and Edward I of England, Duke of Aquitaine, who sought by them to consolidate his hold on the northern borders of the Duchy. More generally, walled hill towns remained significant as a means to enhance natural defensive features, while towers within the towns, as with the Tuscan town of San Gimignano, were built as part of the feuds of the nobles.

Castles have played a key role in subsequent story-making about the period, whether novels, television programmes or films. For example, castles were central sites and images of control and/ or oppression, as in Walter Scott's novel *Kenilworth* (1821) and Beethoven's opera *Fidelio* (1814), in the various accounts of Robin Hood of Sherwood Forest, and in more recent uses of medievalism in imaginative fiction, ranging from *The Lord of the Rings* to *Game of Thrones*. In *The Lord of the Rings* (1954–5), one of the volumes is entitled *The Two Towers* and one of the central battles is the siege of Helm's Deep. So also with online war-gaming and other approaches.

Much fortification, however, was of a different scale. Thus, to the south of the forest of Fontainebleau near Paris in the fourteenth century, an area of about 1,050 square kilometres had fifty-five fortified places, roughly one for every 19 square kilometres. This included twenty-eight fortified churches, five fortified towers and four fortified manor houses. The more ordinary was often more significant because it was widespread. Moreover, the prevalence of such fortification captured the overlaps between the dangers from formal conflict and the threats from 'informal' conflict in the shape of feuding and criminality.

This factor looks towards the modern fortification of homes and offices, as with fortified glass, locks, alarms, CCTV and other security features. Indeed, the pervasiveness of defensive features reflects the extent to which defence has a much broader meaning than what is conventionally understood as conflict.

CHAPTER 12

The Crusades

The Crusades were an important and most dramatic part of the Christian counter-attack against Islamic invasions. This was a long-standing process. Thus, the Byzantines had already regained the initiative in the tenth century, not least with the recapture of Crete in 960–61, a formidable logistical achievement in which the Byzantine fleet included purpose-built ships for horse transport. More specifically, at a time when Western Europe was expanding and becoming more prosperous, the papacy proposed an expedition to recover Jerusalem.

Separately, Byzantium had taken advantage of Islamic weakness, but this was reversed from the mid-eleventh century by Turkish invasions from the steppe. The success of the Seljuk Turks was dramatic, notably a crushing victory at Manzikert (modern Malazgirt) in Eastern Europe in 1071, with the capture of Emperor Romanos IV, but Pope Gregory VII failed to muster help. However, Pope Urban II responded to a Byzantine appeal made at Piacenza in 1095, leading to the Crusades, which became a sustained effort to recapture, and then hold, the Holy Land.

Proclaimed by Urban II in 1095, in part substantiating papal claims to lead Christendom, the First Crusade fought its way across Anatolia in 1097 and captured Antioch after a long siege in 1098, before storming Jerusalem in 1099. An ability to succeed in both battle, not least due to the potency of the heavy cavalry charge, and siege, was crucial in the establishment of the initial Crusader presence. It was expanded with subsequent successes, notably the capture of Acre (1104), Tyre (1124) and Ascalon (1153), successes that owed much to naval superiority. However, despite major efforts, the Crusaders were not to gain any of the key Islamic centres in the region: Aleppo, Damascus and Cairo.

The Crusades led to the creation of four Christian states in the region: the Principality of Antioch, County of Edessa, Kingdom of Jerusalem and County of Tripoli, as well as a novel military organisation that had political overtones, the Military Orders. The Templars and the Hospitallers (the Knights of St John), warriors who had taken religious vows, had troops and castles and were entrusted with the defence of large tracts of territory and sometimes with sovereignty over it. There were other Military Orders, notably that of the Teutonic Knights, which began in the Holy Land but, from the mid-thirteenth century, focused on the eastern Baltic, the orders of Calatrava, Alcántara and Santiago in Spain, and equivalents in other states. The rationale of these orders was that of the defence of Christendom.

In a precarious military environment, the Crusaders fortified actively in order to protect themselves from larger Muslim armies and their effective siege techniques. Castle architecture reflected the role of specialists in fortification technology. The most famous Crusader castle, Crac des Chevaliers in modern Syria, was originally built to guard the route from Tripoli to Hamah. The Crusaders developed the fortifications under the Count of Tripoli, but the castle that survives was totally rebuilt by the Hospitallers after they obtained it from the count in 1142. It successfully held out against Saladin in 1188, ensuring that it was one of the few remaining Crusader castles in 1190. The defences were strengthened at the start of the thirteenth century following a devastating earthquake, and include a massive talus (sloping face) which not only increased the strength of the castle inner walls, but also made it resistant to further earthquakes. The outer wall was strengthened by semi-circular protruding towers, while the nature of the site made mining, the undermining of the walls, difficult. The complex character and interlocking strength of the layered defences ensured that, once the outer walls had been penetrated, it was still necessary to advance along overlooked corridors and ramps, exposing attackers to fire and ambush. The outer walls included shooting galleries and box machicolations (openings through which objects could be dropped) and the walkway, while the inner castle had slits in the walls and, at the top, openings for bigger weapons in the shape of large catapults.

The Muslims had become more successful from the 1140s, capturing Edessa, one of the Crusader states in 1144, and blocking the attempt by the Second Crusade to capture Damascus in 1148, as well as an attempt by Amalric I of Jerusalem to besiege Alexandria in 1167. In turn, Saladin, the Vizier of Egypt from 1169, took over the Fatimid Caliphate of Egypt and conquered southern Syria and northern Iraq. These were age-old goals of Egyptian rulers, which showed that geopolitics could lead to similar drives in successive regimes with different ideologies.

Indeed, proclaiming a jihad in 1187, Saladin and his well-deployed light cavalry crushed the Christian kingdom of Jerusalem, out-generalling its heavily outnumbered and poorly led forces under the July heat at Hattin. The destruction of the field army left most of the fortress garrisons in too weak a position to hold out. Jerusalem surrendered after its walls were undermined and breached. The fate of the fortresses indicated some of the weaknesses of castles, notably the danger of denuding them of troops in order to create a field army and the psychological effects of the defeat of such an army.

Christian efforts to reverse the results of Hattin led to important successes, notably the capture of Acre in 1191 by Richard I of England and Philip Augustus of France, the leaders of the Third Crusade. The former went on to defeat Saladin at Arsuf that year, but was not in a position to retake Jerusalem. Just as with the competition in the late eleventh century between the Seljuk Turks and the Fatimids, the Crusader position also owed much to divisions among the Muslim powers, notably between Egypt and Syria after the death of Saladin in 1193. Moreover, the Crusaders made intense efforts to achieve an alliance with the Mongols, who overthrew the Ayyubid rulers of Syria in 1260, and fought the Mamluks, an élite fighting force, mostly ethnic Turks, who had seized power in Egypt in 1250.

However, the Mamluks' sweeping victory over the Mongols at Ain Jalut near Nazareth in 1260 settled the matter. Baibars, who seized power in Egypt that year, built up an effective army and captured most of the remaining Crusader positions. Crac fell after a siege of scarcely more than a month in 1271: the defenders were sent a forged document telling them there would be no relief and advising surrender. Acre finally fell in 1291, to a determined assault after its defences had been weakened by bombardment and mining.

The Crusades fitted into a long-standing pattern in which local peoples were fought over by incomers, or their descendants, as with the Mamluks and the Crusaders. The Turkic nomadic world, with its long-standing pressures for expansion, had greater military resources than the Crusaders, and notably so once benefiting from the takeover of the wealthier lands. The Crusades indeed were in part fought in the shadow of the struggle in and around that nomadic world.

The fighting was often very brutal, and by all sides. Thus, on the First Crusade, the Crusaders massacred the populations of Antioch, Beirut and Jerusalem indiscriminately, killing not only Muslims, but also Syrian Christians and Jews without distinction of age or gender.

The Crusaders were also unsuccessful in North Africa, the Normans of Sicily being driven from their North African conquests in 1158–60. Moreover, Louis IX of France, St Louis, failed in both Egypt and Tunisia. In 1244, in response to serious ill health, he had promised to go on crusade if he survived. With papal support for Louis, the Church in France provided funds, for the cost was formidable. Leaving France in 1248, he invaded Egypt in 1249, only to be heavily defeated in 1250 at al-Mansura and have to be ransomed from captivity. In 1270, Louis mounted another crusade, this time against Tunis (en route to Egypt), only to die from dysentery, which was then very much a killer.

In contrast, the Crusaders were far more successful both else-where in the Mediterranean, capturing Crete, Sicily, Malta and the Balearic Islands, and in Iberia. These were often major achieve-ments, the reconquest of Sicily in the late eleventh century taking two decades. The conquest of Muslim areas saw Christianisation, notably with church-building and renaming. In Toledo and Seville, the cathedrals were built on the same foundations as the mosques they replaced, while that in Córdoba was built in the middle of the mosque. Victory was celebrated and used as a political tool, for example by Alfonso X of Castile (r. 1252–84). Some Muslims were expelled, others enslaved, as on the Balearic Islands conquered in the early thirteenth century, although still others continued free.

However, the failure of the Crusades left Byzantium more exposed to Islamic attack. Indeed, the Fourth Crusade (1202–4), under Venetian influence, attacked not the Muslims, but, first, in 1202, the Hungarian-ruled Catholic city of Zara, a trading rival, and then Constantinople itself. Alexius Angelus, the son of the deposed Byzantine emperor Isaac II, offered money, help with the crusade and the union of the Orthodox Church with Rome (from which it had been divided since 1054), if his uncle was removed. This was secured by the Crusaders in 1203, but the new emperor, Alexius IV, was unable to fulfil his promises and was deposed in an anti-Western rising. This led the Crusaders in 1204 to storm the city, crown Count Baldwin of Flanders as Emperor Baldwin IX, and partition the Byzantine empire between them, in a dramatic display of military power and its consequences.

However, the new situation was far from stable. In 1261, the Greeks retook Constantinople, bringing this brief Latin empire to an end. At the same time, there was a potent ideological rivalry, that between Catholic and Orthodox Christians, a rivalry encouraged by this episode. In turn, the long weakness and, in 1453, eventual fall of Byzantium, Constantine IX dying in the defence of the city,

were to expose Christian Europe to further invasion, so that by
1500, the Ottoman empire controlled modern Turkey, Greece
(except Crete), Albania, Bulgaria, Serbia, Macedonia and Kosovo. In
1480, moreover, a twelve thousand-strong Ottoman force captured
Otranto in Italy, killing or enslaving those who refused to convert;
although the Ottomans were driven out in a crusade in 1481. It was
no surprise that the painter Albrecht Dürer had a Turk as one of the
Four Horsemen of the Apocalypse (1492–1502).

Crusades were also declared against Christians judged heter-
odox and/or disobedient. These could be successful as, eventually,
against the Albigensians of southern France, or less so, as with the
Hussite wars in the Czech Republic in 1419–34. In the Hussite
wars, victories in battle for the Hussites under Jan Žižka, as at
Vyšehrad (1420) and Nebovidy (1422), proved crucial to keeping
the conflict going, and showed the limitation of cavalry in the face
of an innovative opponent able to use infantry and artillery well
with regard to the terrain. These wars looked towards those that
began a century later in response to the Protestant Reformation, a
struggle that for the papacy drew on crusading ideas, as well as
a reminder of the significance of conflict within religions, one
already seen with rivalry between Muslim powers as a context for
the Crusades.

At the same time, crusading against the infidel took on new
energy in the sixteenth century when the Ottoman Turks made
unprecedented advances, besieging Vienna in 1529 and Valletta on
Malta in 1565. The Christian responses were presented in crusading
terms, and notably so with the successful defence of Valletta by the
Knights of St John (the Hospitallers) and with the forces that
defeated the Ottoman fleet at Lepanto in 1571 and relieved Vienna
when it was besieged anew in 1683. Indeed, crusading provided a
cooperative logic in the conflict. So also repeatedly did religious
ideology, iconography and zeal for the Ottomans, whose logic was
that of fulfilling God's will by spreading Islam.

CHAPTER 13

The Mongols and Timur

Steppe armies and societies were built to live off non-agricultural land: the horses ate the grass, while the soldiers, if necessary, drank the horses' blood and milk. As nomadic herders, they were forced to move continuously, and to carry the means of survival with them. Their culture in essence moved and was part of their armies, which were accompanied by herds of horses, sheep and goats. Steppe animals were all hardy and well adapted to moving long distances with heavy loads over harsh and inhospitable terrain. The culture and lifestyle of steppe people addressed all the essential logistical requirements for large-scale, lightly armed mobile warfare: effective transport, maintenance of transport, food supply and even equipment resupply – their composite bows were made from the bones and sinews of their animals. Their collapsible accommodation could be quickly dismantled and just as quickly re-erected. Mongol logistical support was highly effective because, in the early stages of imperial conquest, it reflected and mirrored the normal nomadic state. Indeed, the integrated logistical support inherent in the armies from the central steppes was unsurpassed at the time.

The hardiness of warriors bred on the steppes also enabled operations to be carried out in winter, which more sedentary and urban opponents considered impossible, essentially because of the logistical problems it entailed. The successful Mongol campaign against the northern Russian princes was launched in December 1237 and only stopped with the spring thaw which left the terrain waterlogged.

Steppe armies could be large, but also smaller than those of agrarian societies. Partly as a result, force conservation was a major goal for steppe armies. Linked to this, the tsunami method of conquest involved invading and devastating a large region, but then withdrawing and holding only a small section of territory. As a result, troops were not tied down in garrison duty. Moreover, the creation, by devastation, of a buffer zone made it impossible to attack the Mongols and also weakened the enemy's resources.

Different methods, nevertheless, had to be pursued by the Mongols as tasks changed, not least the lengthy sieges required for the conquest of China in the thirteenth century. A density of resource was then at issue, and had to be deployed accordingly. Mongol dependence on horses meant that where the environment did not produce a sustained source of fodder there were limitations, notably repeatedly during the thirteenth century, in Syria from 1260 in conflict with the Mamluks, but also in the Dinaric Alps in the Balkans in the early 1240s. Yet, there was a fundamental flexibility in Mongol war-making.

This flexibility was also seen in the transition to city-taking conflict. In 1212, united by Chinggis Khan (r. 1206–27), a very talented leader, the apparently inexorable Mongols, having conquered the Western Xia, pressed on to invade the Jurchen Jin empire of northern China (r. 1115–1234) with two armies, each equipped with a train of camels carrying Chinese siege weapons that could be assembled on site. The Mongols, however, did not want lengthy sieges, and this ensured that, in the 1214 campaign, Chinggis Khan did not initially attack Zhongdu (Beijing), the capital of the Jurchen empire in northern China, preferring, instead, to blockade it, a key choice for attackers. However, a resumed offensive led to a focus on the city, one supported by siege weapons and engineers. With relief efforts beaten off, the city surrendered in 1215.

Largely by using Chinese expertise, the Mongols acquired skill in siege warfare during the numerous campaigns required to conquer the Jurchen Jin empire, which was finally overthrown in 1232–4, and the Song empire of southern China, campaigns that represented the most impressive use of force in the thirteenth century. The lengthy nature of the sieges was possible only because of Mongol organisation and persistence, while the ability, in part due to terror and intimidation, to elicit and coerce support was also important.

Invading the Khwarazmian empire in Central Asia in 1219, the Mongols also took the major cities, notably Bukhara and Samarqand. The local people were driven into the fort cities, flooding them with refugees and spreading terror. As at the successful siege of Kaifeng, the new Jin capital, in China in 1232, local people were also used in sieges in order to fill moats with debris and man the siege weapons. Cutting cities off from supplies could also be important, as when Karakorum/Qaraqorum, the Mongol capital, located in what is today Mongolia, was captured by Khubilai, the ruler of China, in a Mongol civil war in 1262. The empire created by Chinggis Khan had been divided into four successor states. Once captured, the walls of cities were destroyed by the Mongols in order to leave them vulnerable.

There were also stand-alone fortresses, such as the mountain fortresses in Armenia and Georgia that slowed, but did not stop, Mongol invasion in 1238. These fortresses took on much of their significance from their position, as the tactical significance of their mountainous position was given operational importance by their role in guarding the passes through which advances were funnelled. In 1256, the Mongols under Hulegu, a grandson of Chinggis, captured the castles of the Assassins. These were located in the mountainous north-west of Iran and were built on high crags in commanding positions. The Seljuks had failed to capture one of the principal castles, Lambsar, after a siege lasting eight years. However, the ferocious reputation of the Mongols persuaded the Assassins to surrender. More generally, the Mongols followed a deliberate policy of total annihilation towards those who resisted them, erecting mountains of skulls outside Baghdad and Aleppo, but were lenient to those who surrendered without a fight.

Technology also played a role. In the twelfth century, the ropes on a trebuchet, which had been pulled down by men, were replaced with a counterweight, although not everywhere or always. This development began probably in the Middle East, although it is not certain who was responsible. Possessing Persian technology from the 1220s, the Mongols took up the innovation, using these trebuchets to pound Baghdad, the capital of the Abbasid caliphate, into surrender in a week in 1258, bringing that long-lasting caliphate to an end in a key episode in Islamic history. The counterweight trebuchets are clearly depicted in illustrated Persian accounts of the siege. At Aleppo (which the Crusaders had not captured) in 1260, the Mongols focused all their trebuchets on one point, the gate facing Iraq, and broke through there.

From the Middle East, the innovation spread. For example, the Mongol ruler in Persia, the Il-Khan Abaqa, sent two engineers to his uncle, Khubilai, to help the latter in his conquest of Song (southern) China. The engineers built seven counterweight trebuchets, previously unknown in China, each able to hurl stones weighing hundreds of pounds. The effectiveness of these stones depended on the thickness and structural integrity of the walls. The cities of Xiangyang and Fancheng fell in 1273. Shayang followed in 1274 and Changzhou in 1275, with gunpowder bombs fired by trebuchets adding to the destructiveness.

Mongol flexibility was shown in battle as well as siege. Far-reaching advances brought them into contact with many different opponents. The Mongols did not always win. They could lose against fellow steppe people, including in civil wars, and were defeated by the Mamluks of Egypt, notably at Ain Jalut and Homs in 1260, Homs in 1281, Marj al-Saffar in 1303, and by the Delhi Sultanate in 1298, 1305 and 1306. Nevertheless, they were highly adaptable and the ability to defeat very different opponents was striking, as in 1241, when the

Mongols beat Polish, Hungarian and German Forces. At Mohi, the Hungarians retreated to a wagon fort after the Mongols, in part by using their siege weapons, had driven them back from their defensive position at a bridge on the Sajo River. The Mongols shrewdly left the Hungarians a way to escape their wagon fort, and the Hungarians were then destroyed in the open field while retreating, the Mongols pressing on to storm the nearby cities of Buda and Pest.

This flexibility was true of Central Eurasian nomads in general, as with Turkic peoples and leaders, notably Timur (Tamerlane, 1336–1405), who campaigned successfully from India to the Aegean in the sequential war-making that was important to his success. Timur sought to restore the Mongol empire of Chinggis Khan and claimed descent from him, a significant source of legitimacy, although, in fact, he was not a Chinggisid. Timur married Chinggisid princesses so that he could have the title. Among his feats were the conquests of Persia and northern India, the capture of Delhi, Damascus and Baghdad, the defeat of the Mamluks in Syria in 1400 and the defeat and capture of the Ottoman Sultan, Bayezid I, at Ankara in 1402. In the last, after a long struggle, Timur's army, which was mostly cavalry, was victorious, not least because much of the Ottoman cavalry defected or abandoned the field. Subsequently, in a pattern that was frequent, the Ottoman infantry was finally broken: the cavalry struggle tended to decide the fate of any battles, which increased the significance of cavalry. The battle was celebrated in Constantinople, the capital of the Byzantine empire, which was greatly under Ottoman pressure. Indeed, the Ottoman advance into Europe was delayed by Timur's victory, which was an instance of the wider strategic context for particular struggles.

Although some were of the nature of raids, Timur's campaigns were characterised by careful planning, including thorough reconnaissance. Indeed, repeatedly across history there has been an overlap between the two, and it is misleading to assume that raids are necessarily unsophisticated in their goals and/or means. Supplies were raised on the march but, rather than simple devastation, efforts were made to use existing structures by levying tribute on the basis of lists of businesses and tax registers. In captured cities, there was a systematic attempt to seize goods, rather than disorganised plunder. Indeed, Timur, who, unlike Chinggis Khan, was a child of the city, not a steppe nomad, preferred to persuade cities to surrender and then pay ransom; he only stormed them when this failed. Victory over the Golden Horde in 1395 was followed by the sacking of the capital, Sarai Serke, and Timur rerouted the Central Asian trade routes to converge on his capital, Samarqand.

When he died at Utrār, Timur was en route to invade Ming China. China's vulnerability was to be shown by Mongol attack in the mid-fifteenth century and by Manchu conquest in the mid-seventeenth, but Timur would have faced the far greater issue of a more distant base. Moreover, Manchu success took several decades of operations, as that of the Mongols in the thirteenth century had done.

At any rate, Timur's empire did not long survive. His son and successor Shāhrukh (r. 1405–1447) lacked his father's dynamism and aggression, and under his rule, based in Herat, Timurid government became increasingly sedentary.

In Iraq and much of what is now Iran, the Türkmen cavalry of the Aqquyunlu Confederacy eventually took over in the chaos that followed the death of Timur. Their army was a classic Central Asian one, armed with bows, swords and shields, and largely deployed on the battlefield in a two-wing cavalry formation. In 1469, their envoy arrived in Cairo carrying the severed head of Abū Saʾid, the Timurid ruler of Bukhara and Samarqand, impaled on a spear.

The region of north-east Iran known as Khurasan, in which Meshed was a key city, remained a Timurid dominion until it was conquered in 1507 by the Uzbeks, whose wide-ranging success in Central Asia in the 1490s and 1510s reflected the continued dynamism of cavalry. However, in turn, the Uzbeks were defeated by the Safavids near Merv in 1510. Rivalry between the two continued for over two centuries, with neither able to launch knockout blows in the distant centres of the opposing power, a situation also seen with other competing pairs, notably the Mughals and the Safavids, the latter and the Ottomans, the Ottomans and the Habsburgs, and the latter and the French. In this respect, these powers lacked the success of the Mongols and the Manchu.

CHAPTER 14

Early Japanese Warfare

Mongol power found its bounds, and one such was Japan. The Mongols took over Chinese and Korean naval capability, but invasions of Japan in 1274 and 1281 failed in large part because of storms, thus ensuring that Japan was not ruled from China.

Japan had a long history of conflict, in part because of the lack of unity that owed much to its largely mountainous terrain. About 10,000 BCE, the Japanese began to use bows and arrows in their hunting. Bows played a major role in conflict, with the compound bow in use by about 300 BCE. The Japanese first encountered cavalry when they invaded Korea and fought the kingdom of Kogūryō in about 400 CE. It proved a rude shock. Prior to that, horses had been used in Japan for food, religious ceremonies and work. By 650 CE, mounted archery was well developed in Japan, although the infantry, who used swords and spears, remained important. Their horses were fairly small, and cavalry shock action attack did not become significant in Japanese warfare.

Prefiguring the opening up to the West in the late nineteenth century, external pressures in the shape of the thirteenth-century Mongol challenge had an impact in Japan, presenting the samurai (warriors) with an enemy that relied on more sophisticated tactics and used both novel forms of familiar weaponry, such as swords, bows and armour, and completely unknown weapons, such as exploding shells. The invasions appear to have triggered changes: in styles of armour better suited to fighting on foot; in weapons, with swords now having shorter, heavier blades; and in tactics, such as the use of more coordinated infantry movements.

Yet external examples were not the sole factors in the elaborate development of a warrior class and culture. Thus, clans and daimyo (autonomous princes) built castle seats, as with Tsuruoka in northern Honshu, the castle seat of the Sakai clan. Broad moats were a major feature, as at Hagi. Stone castles were built from the fifteenth century, notably Nakagusuku (c. 1450) on Okinawa, the castle of a feudal lord. There was also a process of expansion. Thus, Himejī Castle, built in 1333, on a strategic hilltop overlooking the coastal route along the Inland Sea west of Kobe, was strengthened in 1467 with the addition of two baileys. The location of castles reflected a range of factors: aristocratic rivalry was a key element, but that does not exhaust the analysis. On the island of Okinawa most of the castles are located close to transition areas between different types of soil, which suggests that there were trading routes to control.

Power from the mid-fourteenth century was largely wielded by the shogun, the head of the government, as the emperor had no real power. The shogun's effective power over much of Japan, including the Kantō region, the crucial section of the main Japanese island, Honshu, was limited. The *shugo* (military governors) of the provinces comprising Japan were among the last remaining forces defending centralisation, largely because their principal asset distinguishing them from other powerful warriors in their provinces was their title as *shugo*, which was meaningful only in the context of continued imperial control. Nevertheless, the *shugo* were increasingly autonomous as well as affected by opposition by local warriors.

Moreover, the leading *shugo* families were hit by succession disputes that had reached the stage of open warfare. So also with the Ashikaga shogunate. In a situation that in some respects paralleled England during the Wars of the Roses or France in the late sixteenth century, the Ōnin War of 1467–77 arose from a dispute within the Ashikaga house which was exacerbated by the role of rival *shugo*, both in that dispute and in those within the leading *shugo* houses. Fighting between the contenders was the spur for what became a highly destructive war. The imperial capital of Kyoto was the principal site of much of the fighting, and suffered much devastation as a consequence, but the fighting spread elsewhere and the Ōnin War led into the local and regional conflict that characterised much of the age of *Sengoku* (Warring States) from 1467 to 1615. The Ashikaga shogunate had lost its power and the *shugo* network had collapsed in a context of general disorder with ties of vassalage increasingly broken in a society that was very much in flux. Moreover, from 1485, peasant armies began to appear.

Alongside the continued cultural unification provided by the person of the emperor, warrior chieftains emerged, these daimyo (literally 'big names') coming largely from the former vassals of *shugo*. The daimyo were far more independent of shoguns than the constables had been. The authority of daimyo rested on successful conflict, and this proved the way to retain the support of vassals. The idea that the latter should be loyal to daimyo who inherited their position meant little if the daimyo could not win victory and the lands and prestige that came with it. The need for such success helped ensure that betrayal was central to the politics of daimyo conflict; and, as a result, treachery played an important role in both battles and the seizure of fortresses. Operations were partly designed so as to display strength, and thus induce surrender and deter treachery.

From the late fifteenth century, repeating a tendency seen in the civil warfare of the fourteenth century, as the pace of warfare within Japan accelerated, there were a series of major changes in Japanese warfare including larger armies, a greater preponderance of infantry, sophisticated tactics and command structures, and changes in weaponry, especially the spear and armour. The combination of larger armies and an emphasis on infantry was linked to a move away from the largely individualistic style of fighting hitherto followed and, instead, towards a focus on massed formations with a corresponding increase in the importance of command skills.

Spears were the key infantry weapon, paralleling the role of the pike in Western Europe and underlining the extent to which mass formations, unit fighting and discipline were not necessarily linked to firepower, whether archery or handguns. In response to spears, as earlier to arrows, body armour sought to combine flexibility with protection, but the effectiveness of armour was affected by the introduction of firearms.

From the first half of the sixteenth century, effective guns were introduced in Japan as a result of trade: firearms of Western provenance with modifications that had been applied to them in South-East Asia. As an instance of the general degree to which the diffusion of new technology was dependent on more than receptivity, these handguns were widely copied and rapidly so as Japan's metallurgical industry could produce them in large numbers.

Firearms certainly played an important role in war after the Battle of Shinano Asahiyamajo (1555), although, as elsewhere, the extent to which they changed tactics has to be handled with care: in many respects, firearms mostly just replaced bows one-for-one. The guns were still very expensive and in relatively short supply, which would argue against wholesale changes to tactics. But the desirability of owning firearms probably accentuated the trend towards political consolidation into larger units, since smaller daimyo would have had difficulty affording firearms, and would not have been able to acquire them in sufficient numbers to make much use of them.

The use of firearms added a new element to combined arms operations, as handgunners had to be protected when they reloaded. As a result, they were integrated with spearmen and archers, the former offering protection while the latter maintained firepower. Thus, in terms of weaponry, combined arms had differing consequences to the situation in Western Europe where the combination was of pikemen and musketeers. The importance of guns was shown operationally, as well as tactically, as Oda Nobunaga, a leading daimyo who rose to power in the 1560s, seized control of major gun foundries at Sakai and Kunitomo.

Alongside his drive, ambition and skill, Nobunaga benefited from the extent to which other leading daimyo had exhausted their forces to a considerable extent in campaigning in the 1550s and early 1560s. Nobunaga's rise to prominence owed much to a victory over Imagawa Yoshimoto at the Battle of Okehazama in 1560. Nobunaga was outnumbered, by roughly five thousand to twenty thousand troops, but, rather than respond defensively to the invasion of his territory, he took the initiative in a surprise attack, allegedly benefiting from a very heavy downpour, after which he launched the assault in which Yoshimoto was killed. This victory showed the value of command skills, fighting quality and the tactical offensive; and also made Nobunaga's reputation. The value of surprise reflected the ability to take and exploit the initiative, which was an ability that owed much to tactical flexibility. Rigid formations and fighting methods were generally incapable of this flexibility. Nobunaga also facilitated the mobility of his forces by building pontoon bridges and improving the road system.

Like other commanders, Nobunaga used fighting as a key component of a politics of alliance and betrayal and, partly as a result, was reluctant to engage in battles in which losses might be heavy. Instead, the taking of forts was a preferred way to display power and advance interests. However, as with the Italian Wars in Europe (1494–1559), changing sides frequently did not prevent hard-fought battles. Furthermore, a bitter struggle for control between rival daimyo encouraged the search for comparative advantage.

The Battle of Nagashino (1575), in which Nobunaga defeated the Takeda, provides a key instance of the role of revisionism in affecting our overall account of military history. Conventionally, the emphasis was on the role of three thousand musketeers in the army of Nobunaga, which used volley fire to smash the repeated charges of Takeda cavalry, winning a decisive victory. Placing musketeers in the front of an army meant giving them the position traditionally occupied by the bravest, often mounted, samurai. Now, however, the account of Nobunaga lining gunners up in ranks and having them shoot in volleys is contested. That idea was originally based on a screen painting produced more than a century after the fact, and there is good physical evidence to indicate that the conventional account would have been impossible under the conditions on the battlefield at the time. Instead, it is pointed out that the Takeda had almost as many gunners at Nagashino as Nobunaga did, and that victory for the latter was obtained by outnumbering the Takeda almost two to one and by fighting from behind pretty elaborate field fortifications that the Takeda could not see, because of heavy rains, until they were too deeply committed to the battle and almost on top of them. Moreover, Nobunaga tricked his opponent into letting one wing of his forces get encircled by a Nobunaga ally who pretended to be willing to defect.

Increasing army size, as a result of better daimyo organisation and mastery of logistics, was probably more important than changes in weaponry. By the mid-sixteenth century, handgunners were being drilled and organised in ways that had never applied to archers, but the earlier extent of tactical change was limited. This serves as a useful qualification of the general tendency to treat changes in weaponry as revolutionary and also indicates the value of counterpointing developments in different regions, not least in order to assess cause and effect with caution. In Japan, the most important consequence of gunpowder appears to have been from cannon, which, while in short supply and not all that heavily used, did result in fundamental changes to castle construction.

The extent of instability and civil warfare in the sixteenth century encouraged the building and maintenance of fortresses. Japanese castle building responded to gunpowder by combining thick stone walls with location on hilltops of solid stone, which gave the fortresses height and prominence, and blocked mining. Unmortared and angled stone block at the base guarded against earthquake damage as well as besiegers. Toyotomi Hideyoshi, the unifier of Japan in the 1580s and 1590s, proved successful in siege-craft, as with the fall of Odawara and other Hojo fortresses in eastern Honshu (the main island of Japan) in 1590. Cannon became more important from the 1580s, but Hideyoshi's success in sieges owed much also to other factors, notably the use of entrench-ments to divert the water defences offered by lakes and rivers, a technique also employed by other powers, for example the Mongols (successfully) against Baghdad in 1258. These entrenchments threatened fortresses with flooding by rising waters, or with the loss of the protection by water features on which many in part relied. This reliance was true of many fortresses, not least because of their role in protecting crossing places across rivers.

Power was also spiritual. In oriental cultures, the understanding and use of space had a spiritual character in the shape of geomancy, or feng shui, and the specific positioning of fortifications, as with other buildings, was important to their effectiveness. Thus, fortifi-cations could take the place of missing hills to produce a geomantic pattern that was effective in defence. The enhancement of the envi-ronment for defence, and to harm opponents, was regarded as a key component for both feng shui and martial arts. Mountains and water were essential elements to ensure the proper martial posi-tioning and circulation of energy to help achieve success. Thus, in Japan, it was thought necessary to appreciate local geomantic configurations.

In a pattern that continues to the present, symbolism is more generally significant in war, not least in order to maintain morale. It is normal to regard one's own symbolism as reasonable, and that of others as quaint and a foolish distraction, but that is not a helpful attitude from a military historian. The symbolic character of Japanese warfare did not lessen its lethality or rationality. The key change that was to occur was an abandonment of foreign war from the end of the 1590s until the 1870s.

CHAPTER 15

Warfare in the New World to 1500

An area of great extent and geographical variation, discussion of the Americas is made even more difficult by the need to rely on archaeology, without there being the written sources seen in much of the world hitherto discussed. There was certainly an enormous variety, from the Eskimos of the Arctic and the hunter-gatherers of Amazonia to the more imperial state systems, notably the Inca, but also the Aztecs and others. Common to all, however, was warfare without horses, gunpowder, iron metallurgy, wheels or writing. Yet, despite these limitations, successive empires showed what could be achieved by infantry-based armies and stone technology.

There were no empires across most of the Americas. Population densities were low, indeed often very low, and both settlement and authority were dispersed. Conflict, however, was frequent. Thus, in northern Canada, the Dorset culture of the Palaeo-Eskimos of the eastern Arctic was overwhelmed from about 1000 CE by the Thule people of northern Alaska, whose kayaks, float harpoons and sinew-backed bows made them more effective hunters of whales.

On land, the Thule gained mobility from dogsleds. The Dorset people were killed or assimilated. In contrast, the Viking impact in North America was perfunctory, while the longer-lasting Viking settlements in Greenland established in the tenth century ended in the fifteenth century, possibly due to conquest by the Inuits, or intermarrying, or climate change, or some combination.

Further south, in southern Ontario, the most populous area of modern Canada, because it was warmer, it was possible to cultivate crops. The spread of settlement led, by 800, to the construction of villages protected by palisades, and eventually by double palisades, which created a series of defendable cul-de-sacs that increased the risks for attackers, and had similarities with Maori *pās*. These agricultural societies fought: in about 1300 CE, the Pickering people conquered and assimilated the Glen Meyer, while, in the fifteenth century, the Huron conquered the St Lawrence Iroquois. In North America, there was 'public' warfare, in the form of conflict between tribes, but also 'private warfare': raids with no particular sanction, often designed to prove manhood.

The effort devoted to fortification indicates the extent to which concern about conflict was widespread prior to the permanent arrival of Europeans from the 1490s. Some forts reveal traces of sophisticated defences, such as the Inca fortress of Sacsayhuaman near Peru's capital of Cusco built in about 1440 CE. Bastions have been found in Brazil, Mexico and Peru. In North America, the fortifications built in about 1100 CE at Cahokia in Illinois contained what have been presented as projecting bastions, which provided opportunities for archers to provide flanking fire on attackers. So also with the Crow Creek site on a steep bluff near the Missouri River which was protected by a bastioned wooden palisade fronted by a ditch. Further south, in the Mississippian culture, Etowah, a 54-acre site occupied from about the 1100s to the 1600s, had a large encircling ditch protecting the town, inside which was a wooden palisade which contained rectangular bastions or towers located at regular intervals. So also with defensive structures at Ocmulgee, a settlement that thrived between 900 and 1150. The journals of the Spaniard Hernando de Soto, who travelled around the region in 1540, mentioned a number of such sites. Such fortified positions were frequently to pose problems for European forces.

Fortification, however, was not necessary to conflict. Thus, the sequence of peoples in the West Indies was not peaceful, for evidence of the last stage, the spread of the Caribs from 1200 CE, indicates that they killed or enslaved the Arawaks where they encountered them.

Identity was bound up in conflict. Thus, the remains of the Colima culture, which thrived in west Mexico from 100 BCE to 300 CE, show that its shamans (religious figures) communicated with the gods on behalf of the people, and were also great warriors depicted with the heads of the defeated. The treatment of the defeated in this fashion was a way to gain their potency and magic, and to demonstrate victory over the living and the dead.

Terror was important to this process. Thus, finds from the Veracruz culture of eastern Mexico include a head with a serpent helmet of about 300–900 CE; while, from the Maya, there comes a terracotta standing warrior depicted wearing armour and a removable mask bearing an image to create terror, and holding an axe and a circular shield.

The most wide-ranging of the empires, and yet again one that was the creation of force, was that of the Inca. It began in the central Andes mountains in Peru as a small state in the thirteenth century, and became significant as a result of expansion under Pachacuti (1438–71) and his successors. Under Túpac Yupanqui (r. 1471–93), there was an expansion, not only to the north, defeating the smaller empire of the Chimú in 1476, but also far to the south, into central Chile. In part, this was thanks to the utilisation of a sophisticated governmental system able to deploy considerable numbers. An extensive road system helped hold Inca territories together and subject peoples were used to provide the porters that ensured the logistics of their far-flung campaigns. The Inca used spears, bows, clubs, slings, swords and battle axes, but made of wood, stone, bronze or copper, and not iron. Conscription raised armies, with most of the troops from subject peoples, which was a way in which war fed war, but which also led to much variety in fighting technique and weaponry. Large numbers were raised in this manner. The chiefdoms to the south of the Inca core area, the area of major expansion, could not field comparable forces and were assimilated into the Inca system by becoming subject peoples with their sacred objects taken into Inca control, which was a means of recognising the superiority of Inti, the Inca sun god. South of the Maule River in Chile, however, the Mapuche blocked Inca expansion, just as, from the mid-sixteenth century, they were to block the Spaniards.

The Incas also benefited from the extent to which the farming villagers in the tropical forests to the east of the Andes did not pose a military challenge, any more than the nomadic hunter-gatherers to the south-east. Equally, the Inca did not try to extend their power far into these areas, especially the former, and this limitation represented a sensible response to their environment. In an instance of the wider pattern of environmental adaptation, the forest people used bows and archers, while the Incas, coming from treeless uplands, did not, and this contrast gave the former a marked advantage in conflict. Equally, these forest people did not seek to conquer the uplands.

The Aztecs in Mexico did not match the Inca in scale but, from 1427, expanded across Mexico from the Gulf of Mexico to the Pacific. Huitzilopochtli, the god of war, was their patron deity, and human sacrifice played an important part in Aztec culture. Control over otherwise autonomous city states was expressed through tribute payment, and this was sustained by a high level of military activity. An élite corps was available year-round, but the bulk of the manpower was of a lower status. In their conflicts, the Aztecs used a variety of techniques. Thus, in the defeat of the Huaxtecs in about 1450, a feigned retreat drew the pursuing enemy into an ambush, a tactic used around the world. Neither Aztecs nor Incas, both of whom had their centres far from the coastlands, deployed naval forces, and those of the Maya were limited. The Atlantic was to be a thoroughfare for pressure from east to west, and not vice versa.

Nevertheless, the strong and sometimes successful resistance faced by the Spaniards was a testimony to the vigour of native fighting techniques and to native determination. The Caribs and Arawaks of the Guianas thwarted Spanish attacks, and mounted counter-raids with fast, manoeuvrable shallow-draft boats carved from tropical trees. Indeed, the Caribs of St Vincent kept the Spaniards out.

Nor was there necessarily an easy arrival on the coasts of the mainland. When the Spaniards first arrived in Florida in 1513, they had been obliged to withdraw by Timucua and Calusa archers, while Pánfilo de Narváez's expedition of 1528 was repelled there by Apalachees and Autes, whose accurate archers used arrows capable of penetrating Spanish armour. A smaller Spanish force under Francisco Hernández de Córdoba left Cuba in 1517 to seek new lands and, in particular, slaves, finding, after a storm, the Yucatán coast with the first major urban centre encountered by the Spaniards in the New World. Initially, the Mayas met the expedition with ten large canoes that were equipped with oars and sails. The Spanish expedition suffered from a shortage of water, and that led to later landings. Beaten in battle by Maya warriors equipped with quilted cotton armour, and carrying bows, slings, stone-tipped spears and flint or obsidian-edged swords, all deadly, the Spaniards fled, naming the area 'the coast of the evil battle'. The survivors reached Havana where the wounded Hernández died.

These were not the sole demonstrations of Native American fighting ability. Thus, in their subsequent conquests, including of the Aztec empire, of Guatemala and of northern Yucatán, the Spaniards, like the Inca in their expansion, benefited greatly from local support. This was a classic form of imperial expansion, one seen for example with both the Mughals and the British in India, and one that offers a qualification to any attempt to juxtapose clear-cut fighting methods.

CHAPTER 16

African Warfare

The vast size and diverse geography of Africa helped ensure, as in Asia, a striking variety in warfare, but the sources for this are far less good than in parts of Asia. Moreover, there is no central narrative, but, instead, as elsewhere in the world, major divides in physical geography and state formation.

The impact of physical geography was very varied. Thus, the tsetse fly helped ensure that the southward spread of the horse was stopped in the massive jungle belt of mid-Africa, contributing to a major divide between the Sahel, the savannah belt to the south of the Sahara which, like the coastal lands north of the desert, was suitable cavalry terrain, and the jungle lands that essentially were infantry country. Moreover, there was no equivalent to the use of elephants in Ceylon and South-East Asia: the larger African elephant is less manageable and is a creature of the savannah further south. Reliance on cavalry increased the dependence of operations on the availability of water and fodder, but also made it possible to expand what became far-flung empires in the Sahel.

As in South America, there was the contrast between the areas where such empires could develop and the jungle regions where they were not seen. Thus, in the valley of the Niger, there was the eleventh-century kingdom of Ghana, and the Malinke empire of Mali created in the thirteenth century; while, in East Africa, a mountainous core provided the basis for a long-standing Christian state in Abyssinia (Ethiopia), and in South-East Africa, there was the plateau-based state of Great Zimbabwe.

At the same time, there were many areas in which there were no such polities, for example South-West Africa, where, in a difficult environment with low rainfall, there was a low density of population. There is a strong tendency to write military history in terms of the states, both because they appear more significant and because the limited sources are far more sparse for any other type of society, but that risks leaving the military history of much of Africa poorly covered, if not neglected.

The emphasis on the local scale of most polities, added to the limited population of much of Africa and logistical problems, presumably meant relatively small-scale forces. In contrast, trade could lead to a commitment over distance, with trans-Saharan trade routes and those focused on the Swahili port cities on the Indian Ocean, such as Malindi and Kilwa, particularly important. Inland states could reach to the coast, with the Mali empire doing so in West Africa. However, there are no signs of long-distance naval activity by them nor, despite their coastal trading, by coastal polities, such as Kwa, in the region of Dahomey in the late first millennium CE.

Fortification was affected by both the political basis for resource availability and the environment. Where timber was common, the focus was on wooden palisades, but where stone was workable, as in Abyssinia and Zimbabwe, it was utilised. Stone-walled enclosures, with long, high, thick and impressive walls, were important in Great Zimbabwe, especially in the thirteenth century; but sun-dried mud bricks were used in the Niger valley, notably in what is now Mali and northern Nigeria.

Earlier, Africa had seen significant population moves, especially the spread of the Bantu from 2000 BCE, as well as the southward diffusion of the Iron Age. From the seventh century CE, there was the expansion of Islam, at first rapid along the North African littoral and then slower across the Sahara and in the Horn of Africa.

Alongside these and other developments, came, as in Asia, the long-standing systemic pressure of nomadic herders on settled peoples. Thus, the kingdom of Ghana was destroyed by the Berber Almoravids in 1076, while, in the thirteenth century, the Banu Marin advanced from the fringes of the Sahara to overrun Morocco. Abu'l-Hasan, the 'Black Sultan' (r. 1331–51), of the Marinid dynasty of Morocco went on to conquer the Maghrib, taking Tunis in 1347.

Understandably given the scale of Africa, different types of forces operated. Whereas the Fatimids successfully invaded Egypt from Tunisia in 969 with an army largely of black slave infantry, the Christians of Nubia (northern Sudan) used horse archers to preserve their independence from Egypt until they were conquered by the Mamluks in the late thirteenth century.

The spread from North Africa to the Sahel, from at least the fourteenth century, of larger breeds of horses, new equestrian techniques and new tactics of cavalry warfare, increased the capability of cavalry-based states, which focused attention on the supply of horses. The warfare of the period fuelled the slave trade, which was very large-scale before the arrival of European traders keen to supply the new colonies in the Americas. The Islamic states in the Sahel, such as Kanem, Bornu and Tunjur, raided south in the jungle belt, and the slaves they acquired by war or purchase were sent for sale northwards across the Sahara to the Islamic world of the Mediterranean.

In the late fifteenth century a new Sahel empire emerged in the Niger valley, that of Songhai based on the city of Gao. Sonni Ali (r. 1464–92), the leader of Songhai expansion, fought every year of his reign. Some of his campaigns, most obviously against the Tuaregs of the Sahara, who used raiding to benefit from the wealth of settled societies, can be characterised as defensive; but war was central to the Songhai state, not least for maintaining control over tributaries, and gaining the resources of subject cities, such as Jenne and Timbuktu.

As part of the full range of factors, economic interests were among the causes and means of war, with control over fresh water, grazing land and human labour all significant. Thus, Idris Alooma, ruler of Bornu (r. 1569–c. 1600), an Islamic state based in the region of Lake Chad, made careful warlike use of economic measures, attacking crops or keeping nomads from their grazing areas in order to make them submit. So also in conflict in the Sahel in the early 2010s, notably in Darfur in west Sudan, but, by the late 2010s, more general, and particularly so across the expanses of Mali and into Niger and Nigeria. Yet again, however, the physical geography takes effect in large part due to changes in its human counterpart, notably the dispersal from Libya, following the overthrow of the Gaddafi regime in 2011, of troops and weapons.

Outside powers played a long-standing role in North Africa, notably with the Roman empire. Having conquered Egypt in 1517, the Ottomans intervened in the struggle between Adal and Abyssinia in East Africa, a religious as well as political struggle. In 1541, the Portuguese dispatched four hundred musketeers to the aid of Abyssinia and, with their aid, the Abyssinians defeated Imam Ahmad in 1541. He then turned to the Ottomans, who provided him with nine hundred musketeers and ten cannon with which he defeated his opponents in 1542, killing two hundred Portuguese, including their commander, Christopher da Gama. Thus, the conflict in Abyssinia, hitherto the land of the mythical Prester John for Christian Europeans, had been integrated with global military relations. Ahmad, in turn, was defeated and killed in 1543 at the Battle of Soina-Dega on the shores of Lake Tana. The Abyssinians rewarded Portuguese musketeers with land in order to retain their services, a variant on the idea of military colonies; and these musketeers and their descendants continued to play an important role into the following century.

The struggle, however, continued. A new Ottoman territorial unit on the Red Sea, the *eyelet* of Habes, established in 1555, was designed to focus resources for the conquest of Abyssinia and Massawa was captured in 1557. An Ottoman invasion of Abyssinia in 1557 was driven back to the coast, but, in 1559, Ahmäd's nephew, Nūr, led the forces of Adal on a fresh invasion in which the Abyssinians were beaten and the ruler, Galawdewos, killed. External pressure exacerbated divisions within the Abyssinian royal family and élite, and these divisions further encouraged intervention with Bahr Nagash Ishaq, a leading Tigrean noble, proving a key Ottoman ally. In 1562, Ottoman cannon fire helped decide the battle that temporarily determined the conflict over the Abyssinian throne, but a renewed Ottoman attempt to dominate northern Abyssinia was defeated in 1579.

The southward direction of Ottoman interest tends to be underplayed and, despite concerns with protecting Egypt and the Hejaz, was certainly not central to Ottoman activity. Nevertheless, action around the Red Sea was an important indication of the Ottoman ability to operate in several directions simultaneously. So also were Ottoman moves into the Indian Ocean.

As a far more minor sphere for operations, the Ottomans also advanced up the Nile valley, although there is relatively little information on the struggle with the Funj kingdom to the south, the rulers of which converted to Islam. The Ottoman frontier moved to the First Cataract on the Nile near Aswan around 1555, and, by the early 1580s, to the Third Cataract. A number of fortresses garrisoned by Bosniak troops marked the advance of Ottoman power.

This is a long way from the military history to which we are accustomed, but the last four paragraphs capture the role of outside powers and the extent to which it was not necessarily the Western Europeans who were dominant in coastal Africa. Indeed, the sixteenth century saw the Spaniards fail, most spectacularly, at Algiers in 1541, Djerba in 1560 and Tunis in 1573, and the Portuguese likewise in Morocco, with king Sebastian defeated and killed in 1578. The direction of African history was to be that of Western rule by the mid-nineteenth century but, even then, African forces were capable of formidable opposition, as in Abyssinia in the 1890s, and there is need for care before assuming that an outsider's ability to operate successfully in coastal and near-coastal regions is the narrative that should come first. So also with India, where the Europeans established coastal bases from the 1500s, but did not become an appreciable power in any inland region until after British victory at Plassey in 1757 was confirmed by further victories at Buxar and Patna in 1764.

Indeed, in terms of decisiveness, the Battle of Alcácer Quibir, also known as the Battle of the Three Kings, in 1578 was one of the most decisive of the age and of African history. Sebastian intervened in a Moroccan civil war, but the Moroccan cavalry proved successful in encircling the Portuguese, and this helped ensure a total defeat. No European force campaigned again into the Moroccan interior until 1844, when the French successfully did so as a prelude to their conquest of Morocco in the early twentieth century. This leads to questions of coverage in military history, for Morocco is not alone in having a military history that is readily accessible, but that is apt to be underplayed or ignored.

The same for example is the case with Madagascar, where again the European presence was very much limited to a few coastal enclaves until French conquest in the 1890s. Prior to that, Madagascar had supported powerful states. For example, in the seventeenth century, the kingdom of Merina was given cohesion by a sacred monarchy, force by firearms and purpose by warfare for slaves. In 1719, the crew of a Dutch ship recorded their surprise at the skilful use of muskets by the army of Menabe and in 1722 another Dutch commentator was impressed by that of Boina which, by 1741, had an army about fifteen thousand strong with plentiful firearms obtained from Western traders in return for slaves. Much of the island was conquered by the Merina in the 1820s, although, aside from resistance, disease, hunger and fatigue were major hindrances to operations, especially in the dry lands of the south. Moreover, rebellions were touched off by demands for tribute and forced labour.

Firearms could be important, for example in the Battle of Azezo in Abyssinia in 1769, but so could other factors, such as shock tactics, as at Sabarkusa in Abyssinia in 1771. This contrast underlines the need to consider battles as a whole, rather than looking at only one battle, whether supposedly decisive or not, in isolation.

The need for a multifaceted approach to military history appears readily apparent both in the case of Africa and if adopting an African perspective on global military history.

CHAPTER 17

Australasian and Oceanic Warfare

The overlap between hunting animals and fighting other tribes typical of hunter-gatherer societies was particularly the case across Australasia and Oceania, with, at the same time, adaptation to specific physical and human environments. The former included the proximity of other islands and the nature of the terrain and vegetation, which was very varied in terms of tree cover. The latter included the size and geographical range of tribes, with population density an important overall factor. Alongside the absence of gunpowder, iron metallurgy, horses, beasts of burden and wheeled transport, there was variation in weaponry and fortification, although there can be problems with the dating of archaeological finds.

As far as weaponry was concerned, there was an important distinction between the use of projectiles such as sling and stones, and contact weaponry. The Hawaiians tended to use the former, but the Tongans and Maori of New Zealand made use of contact weapons, including clubs from whalebone and jade timber, and adzes made from jade. Shark teeth were also used to edge swords, spears and daggers. Coconut fibre could be used for armour, as on Kiribati, where it was worn by the key warriors, and thus became a way to differentiate among the troops.

There was also strength on the water. War canoes, many of which had two parallel hulls, were a formidable sight for the painter William Hodges when, accompanying the British naval explorer James Cook, he saw them at Tahiti in 1776. They also came out to challenge Cook off New Zealand. Canoes could have shields, as with the Iatmul people of Papua New Guinea, where they protected the lead warriors, but were also part of the symbolism in which the shield itself was part of a prow representing the ancestral crocodile.

Fortifications were widely used. In New Zealand, fortified *pā* settlements, as opposed to *kāinga* or open settlements, spread, especially on the North Island, and their number suggests serious competition for the resources of land and sea. They were fortified with wooden palisades. Many would not have been occupied at the same time, but over six thousand *pā* sites have been found, and it has been suggested that there may have been about twice that number. In contrast, the Samoans adopted forts with high stone walls and a protective ditch or moat. Hawaiians did not build fortified villages, but relied mainly on natural features for defence.

War greatly affected social relationships, bringing status or the stigma of defeat, with the weak seeking shelter with stronger kinsmen or, if captured, being incorporated into the victors' kinship network. Religious belief was important to the understanding of warfare. Thus, in the Tahitian archipelago, 'Oro, the god of fertility and war, was a formidable figure who received offerings of dead men. Overpopulation, there and elsewhere, was linked to conflict, with rival clans competing over farming areas. The defeated could expect slaughter and the destruction of their traditional temples. The clan war of 1768 over who would be paramount chief of Tahiti led to genocide for the defeated and a wall of skulls built by the victor.

Maori mythology focused on the demigod Māui, under whom the islands of New Zealand allegedly originated. The assertion of a relationship to Māui was important as part of a process of winning and asserting divine support in the frequent conflicts between tribes. War dances and priestly incantations celebrated the power of gods and ancestors, and the latter in turn warred.

Explanations for military developments can be contentious. For example, on East Timor, in the East Indies to the north of Australia, in 1100–1700, there was a major shift towards fortified settlement sites in the shape of stone-walled structures on hilltops and clifftops. Research has linked this to climate change in the shape of the El Niño–Southern Oscillation, with decreasing and unpredictable rainfall the key context leading as it does to an emphasis on granaries and their defence. At the same time, as a reminder of the dynamic nature of research, there has been scepticism about climate-based accounts. Instead, there has been an argument for the redating of sites and for the possibility that the profits of sandalwood exports and other external factors were crucial in the process of fortification. This underlines the difficulties of developing and adopting global models of development and the problematic nature of supposedly definitive accounts. Thus, in contrast to East Timor, the focus in the Pacific Northwest of North America was on coastal positions where salmon congregated.

None of the coastal states became powers across the Pacific, but the situation changed with the establishment of Western bases from the sixteenth century, including Lima and Manila. Moreover, firearms came to be significant with the Western presence in the vast region. In the sixteenth and seventeenth centuries, this presence was limited as far as the islands were concerned, although sometimes violent, as in 1595 when a Spanish expedition reached the Marquesas. In the late eighteenth century, the pace of contact increased with HMS *Dolphin* arriving in Tahiti in 1767 only to clash with the population and fire grapeshot at menacing canoes from which stones were being fired by means of slings.

In turn, obtained through trade, the local employment of firearms was linked to the use of often sizeable combined forces in order to pursue operational, indeed strategic, goals. One with a lasting effect was the unification of the Hawaiian archipelago. Replacing or at least supplementing spears, clubs, daggers and slingshots, Kamehameha, who dominated the west coast of the island of Hawaii, a coast frequented by European ships, and whose army increased in size to about twelve thousand men, used guns and cannon to help win dominance of the island of Hawaii in 1791, and of those of Maui and Oahu in 1795, with the key engagements, notably Nu'uanu in 1795, occurring on land. Nu'uanu, or in Hawaiian *kaleleka'anae*, which means the leaping mullet, refers to the defended Oahu army being driven back to a cliff edge where they were pushed over the 1,000-foot drop. In 1796 and 1803, difficult waters and disease ended Kamehameha's plans to invade the island of Kauai, but in 1810 Kauai submitted rather than risk invasion.

This unification was part of the more widespread process of state formation in Oceania. In the same period, the Pōmare dynasty benefited from Western mercenaries and firearms in order to unify Tahiti in 1788–1815, subordinating the previous independence of the clan chiefs.

Firearms also served Western expansion, as with the Russians in the Aleutian Islands in the 1760s, with cannon effective against the Aleut villages, while massacres and European diseases were also significant. However, the Tlingits in the eastern Aleutian Islands proved more formidable as a result of acquiring British and American firearms, and in 1802 destroyed the settlement of New Archangel on the island of Sitka. Paralleling the situation in north-east Siberia, where resistance long persisted, resistance to Russian rule in Alaska continued until it was sold to the United States in 1867.

Firearms were introduced to New Zealand by European traders, and then used extensively by the Maori in inter-tribal warfare in the early nineteenth century. They helped make the Maori with their *pās* formidable opponents for the British, whose eventual success in the wars between 1845 and 1872 depended in large part on support from some of the Maori tribes.

In contrast, the less numerous Australian Aborigines proved easier to subjugate after the British had established a penal colony there in 1788. The Aborigines used spears against the muskets of British settlers and troops, and learned new tactical methods in order to lessen the dangers posed by the muskets – not least guerrilla warfare, which included raids on farmhouses. To a degree, ritualised inter-tribal warfare was downplayed in favour of tribal co-operation. Rather than firepower alone, the British were helped in Australia by numerical superiority, which was accentuated by the impact of Western diseases on the Aborigines, as well as by tactical developments, notably the use of light infantry, especially in night-time encirclements of Aboriginal camps. The net effect was a total change in control over a large area.

Over the following century, the same was to be the case over the whole of Oceania. Thus, Tahitian resistance to French control was crushed in 1844–6. In Samoa, civil wars between rival factions in 1886–94 and 1898–9 provided an opportunity for Western expansion. The Hawaiian interest in Pacific expansion in the 1880s, including an unsuccessful attempt in 1887 to intervene in the Samoan conflict, ended when America took over Hawaii. Hawaii indeed next entered military history in 1941, when it was attacked, as America's leading Pacific naval base, by the Japanese in the Pearl Harbor operation, thereafter serving as a key American base in the subsequent war.

It would be all too easy to leave Australasia and Oceania out of a book with space constraints. Indeed, most histories of war do so, or restrict mention to the idea of a primitive 'other', one that essentially enters the picture in order to be conquered by the imperial powers and then to provide the setting for the War in the Pacific in 1941–5. That is a misleading approach, and at a number of levels. It is based on the idea that there is a key strand of development, one moreover closely related to social development and economic capability, with the world ranked accordingly. Instead, it is more helpful to think in terms of fitness for purpose, with adaptation to circumstances being a crucial dynamic. From this perspective, Australasia and Oceania saw both success and enormous variety. The remote valleys of highland New Guinea were a very different environment to Polynesian atolls, and the density of population on the North Island of New Zealand contrasted with that on Australia; and so on. Thus, to even group the whole as a region is misleading, and to provide an overall evaluation accordingly is problematic. The best conclusion is one that works with this variety, and presents conflict as fundamental and protean, rather than an activity with clear characteristics that can be readily evaluated.

CHAPTER 18

Gunpowder on Land

The genesis of gunpowder weaponry was a long one. First developed in China, where the correct formula for manufacturing gunpowder was discovered in the ninth century, an established arsenal to produce gunpowder existed by the mid-eleventh, effective metal-barrelled weapons were produced in the twelfth, and guns were differentiated between cannon and handguns by the fourteenth, although each of these processes in practice involved many stages. Prior to cannon, gunpowder played a role in Chinese sieges, attached to devices such as balls and sticks, fired from siege engines, or used for sapping under the walls. Gunpowder was employed as an incendiary device, both against fortified positions and, conversely, from their walls in order to destroy wooden ladders and towers used in siegecraft.

The ability to harness chemical energy was a valuable advance, and cannon have been referred to as the first workable internal combustion engines, but gunpowder posed serious problems if its potential as a source of energy was to be utilised effectively. It was necessary to find a rapidly burning mixture with a high propellant force, while an increased portion of saltpetre, which was not easy to obtain, had to be included in order to transform what had initially been essentially an incendiary into a stronger explosive device, which was thereby easier to weaponise.

From China, the use of gunpowder spread westward, eventually, via Europe, to the Americas and Australasia, and via Europe and the Ottoman empire to sub-Saharan Africa. There was no independent development of firearms in these regions, which, in large part, reflected a lack of the appropriate resources and economies, and the relevant production techniques, but also an absence of need.

The effectiveness of cannon remained limited by their inherent design limitations throughout the fifteenth century. Large siege bombards were extremely heavy and cumbersome to move and position, and presented all armies that used them with a major logistical problem. The use of a separate breech chamber to hold the powder and the shot made them slow to load, and the requirement to cool down after firing limited their rate of fire. Great skill was required by the gunsmiths to hammer lengths of wrought iron together to ensure that the seams were able to withstand the pressures generated within the barrels, and, in 1460, James II of Scotland died while laying siege to English-held Roxburgh Castle when one of his Flemish bombards exploded beside him, as the wedge holding the breech chamber in place was blown out. The first use of any gunpowder weapon on an English battlefield was at St Albans the following year.

The employment of improved metal-casting techniques and the use of copper-based alloys, bronze and brass, as well as cast iron, made cannon lighter and more reliable. They were able to cope with the increased explosive power generated by 'corned' gunpowder, which was developed in Western Europe around 1420. The gunpowder was produced in granules which kept its components together and led to it being a more effective propellant, providing the necessary energy, but without dangerously high peak pressures. Furthermore, the use of potassium sulphate, rather than lime saltpetre, possibly from about 1400, helped limit the propensity of gunpowder to absorb moisture and deteriorate. As a result of these changes, the military possibilities offered by gunpowder were to become increasingly apparent in Europe in the mid-fifteenth century.

Improved metal casting also allowed the introductions of trunnions that were cast as an integral part of the barrel. This gave improved mobility, along with higher rates of fire. The introduction of more powerful and stable 'corned' gunpowder and iron cannonballs, supplemented by canister, or grape shot, combined with the advances in casting and metallurgy, made cannon more flexible and effective. In 1494–5, Charles VIII of France took with him an impressive artillery train when he invaded Italy.

Handguns had greater penetrative power than either longbows or crossbows. This was particularly important as, thanks to quenching rather than air-cooling in manufacture, improved armour was produced in sixteenth-century Europe. However, detailed tests have suggested that handguns were less effective than is sometimes claimed. They were cheaper than bows, but handguns had a limited range and a low rate of fire, and were, as with the performance of other weapons and troops, affected by bad weather as rain doused burning matches, affecting ignition, and also damped powder. Handguns were also harder to make than bows, and more dangerous to use (a bow cannot explode while you hold it), needed a supply of powder and shot, and were not easy to use from horseback, and certainly if firing other than at a close range, that itself brought vulnerability. At Fornovo in 1495, the artillery duel at the start of the battle between French and Italian forces was ineffective as rain had dampened the powder.

Aside from problems rooted in the mechanical properties of handguns and in the chemical nature of the gunpowder reaction, for example the lack of consistency in purity of the chemical reagents, there were also characteristics of the weaponry that interacted with a poor use that was understandable under the strain of combat. Maladroit shooting, notably a lack of steadiness in igniting the match to fire the powder, was one of these. Gunpowder-driven projectiles have markedly higher velocity than earlier weapons, and arrows are much closer to hand-thrown spears in terms of velocity than projectiles fired from handguns. Thus, guns are much dead-lier than earlier weapons, but they were also less accurate, shorter range and slower than the composite recurved bow, and could not be so easily fired from horseback as bows.

Gunpowder led eventually to the supplanting of earlier missile weapons, the crossbow and the longbow, but not that of other weapons, notably the pike which, having become more important from the fifteenth century, continued to play a major role on the European battlefield until the close of the seventeenth century. Hand-to-hand combat and cold steel remained important in both infantry and, even more, cavalry fighting. In infantry combat, it was combined-armed forces that were most effective.

The use of the arquebus, the first effective hand-held firearm in Europe, spread from the 1460s. This spread appears to have been due not to an instant acceptance of overwhelming capability, but to the use of the arquebus in a particular niche and by a specific group: militia who guarded city walls, a protected role that compen-sated for their battlefield vulnerability. From this, the use of the arquebus spread, but it is no accident that the weapon was most effective in the Italian Wars when employed in concert with field fortifications that protected the musketeers from attack, notably while they rearmed, as successfully by the Spaniards against French attack at Cerignola in 1503. Organising infantry deployments to provide pikemen to protect musketeers was part of the same process.

Looked at differently, new weapons, techniques and tactics worked best when they could be fitted into existing military prac-tices and structures, and certainly so without transforming the socio-political structure. Thus, field fortifications had a long back-ground before being used to anchor firepower.

Firearms eventually replaced bow weapons as their potential was grasped, but this learning curve also entailed learning to appreciate the limitations of firearms, both as individual weapons and tactically on the battlefield. Problems with the availability of muskets, powder and shot were important in helping ensure that mounted archers remained more significant across much of Asia;

while, separately, interlinked issues over range, accuracy and killing power guided the tactical use of handguns. Effectiveness was seen to depend on volume of fire, not individual accuracy and lethality. This emphasis lessened the need for lengthy training, which, in turn, increased the ease of use of muskets. However, to provide a volume of fire and thus compensate for individual inaccuracy, musketeers were grouped together, creating, alongside their slow rate of fire, serious problems of vulnerability which ensured that pikemen had to be deployed alongside them for protection. Similar problems affected the use of cannon, and underlined the need for combined arms forces, a need that was also to be seen with other weapons systems and in other tactical environments, as in World War Two, with the use of tanks alongside artillery rather than on their own, and the provision of fighter escorts for bombers.

The 'Gunpowder Revolution' may have been important for the Spanish conquests in the New World in the early sixteenth century, which were achieved with very few Spaniards, but the role of gunpowder weaponry was still limited in these conquests which were not in principle very different from other cases, both earlier and contemporaneous, of warriors conquering agricultural societies with much larger populations. Gunpowder weapons were employed in only some of these conquests and were not a precondition for them: gunpowder neither set the goal, nor was the agent that explains all. Instead, the Spaniards benefited from exploiting inter-tribal hatred.

So also with Ottoman expansion. Thus, at Mohacs in 1526, the attack by the Hungarian cavalry was stopped by Ottoman firepower, notably about 240 to 300 cannon, but the battle, which was crucial to the conquest of Hungary, was also won by greater manpower and better generalship, while, more generally, the Ottomans benefited from rivalries between the Christian powers. Five years later, Imam Ahmad of Adal (centred on modern Djibouti) benefited from his cannon in defeating the Ethiopians at Antika, but had also hired a force of Arabian archers.

Sixteenth-century developments in the West made gunpowder weaponry normative, which is to say that drill, tactics and assumptions were all increasingly focused in a particular way, while remaining far from identical. Yet, elsewhere in the world, alongside the diffusion of firearms, as in North America and West Africa, the focus could be different and the standardisation less pronounced. To treat this contrast as failure may be pertinent from the perspective of the late nineteenth century, but is far less helpful if judging sixteenth-century forces on their own merit. Indeed, tactical flexibility in some contexts meant a mix of weaponry very different from that of leading Western armies. In particular, volley fire from densely packed formations could be particularly inappropriate in many environments and against many opponents.

The Western weapons and tactical system continued until the end of the seventeenth century, when the spread of bayonets attached to muskets ensured that there was not a separate need for pikemen. As a result, infantry firepower increased. This was enhanced further with the replacement of matchlock muskets by the more reliable flintlocks.

The battles of the eighteenth-century West focused on lines of infantry firing volleys, with cavalry usually on the wings. This, in particular, was the standard deployment of John, 1st Duke of Marlborough, the leading British general of the 1700s, and of Frederick II, 'the Great', of Prussia (r. 1740–86). Each took existing forms of fighting to new heights of success, though neither transformed the possible. Success in battle owed much to command abilities, particularly reading the battlefield and also knowing when to feed in reserves, as well as to fighting quality, notably fire discipline and unit cohesion in conflict. Effective commanders, such as Marshal Luxembourg in the early 1690s and Marshal Saxe in the 1740s for the French, made a big difference, but wars were also exercises in alliance dynamics, and the possibilities and tensions involved. Marlborough benefited from the Grand Alliance with Austria and the Dutch against Louis XIV of France, and Frederick from a lack of coherence between his opponents, notably Austria, France and Russia in the Seven Years War (1756–63).

Aside from the combination of effective Prussian commanders, flexible tactics and fighting quality, Frederick's forces also benefited from their new attack in oblique order, so as to be able to concentrate overwhelming strength against a portion of the linear formation of the opposing army. Frederick devised a series of methods for strengthening one end of his line and attacking with it, while minimising the exposure of the weaker end. This formation depended on the speedy execution of complex manoeuvres for which well-drilled and well-disciplined troops were essential, and benefited from the greater mobility provided by the move from matchlocks and pikes to flintlocks and bayonets. Such attacks helped to bring victory at Hohenfriedberg and Soor in 1745 and, initially, Leuthen in 1757. Marshal de Saxe, the leading French commander, claimed in 1749 that the Prussian army was only trained to attack. By retaining the tactical, operational and strategic initiative, it was able to do so.

CHAPTER 19

The New-style Fortress

> We are now so close to the enemy at every point, that we
> could have shaken hands with them.
>
> Francisco Balbi di Correggio, one of the
> defenders of Malta in 1565

Fortifications were often a continuation of earlier works. At Bari in southern Italy, Spain added bastions to a Norman fortress built over a Roman fort and strengthened in the early thirteenth century by Emperor Frederick II. At Milazzo in Sicily, the castle built by Frederick II on the site of a Greek acropolis was enlarged by Charles V in the early sixteenth century.

Cannon initially were not very much more effective against stone walls than earlier siege machines, although they could be very effective against wooden (ship) walls. Aside from a slow rate of fire, a short range and recoil, cannon suffered from the poor casting techniques that led both to frequent accidents and to the need to tailor shot to the specifications of particular guns. Indeed, the notion that cannon brought the value of medieval fortifications to an end requires qualification. Cannon failed more often than they succeeded, and many times a castle fell to treachery or negotiation rather than bombardment, while stormings rather than sieges were also important, as when the French stormed Venetian-held Brescia in 1512. Despite subsequent improvements in the design and manufacturing techniques of guns, other factors were still the main determinants of the outcome of sieges, although, with the demise of the siege tower and the battering ram, siege operations in 1550 were different to those of a century earlier. Thus, the introduction and effects of gunpowder weapons were gradual processes, more akin to evolution than revolution.

Similarly, in response to gunpowder, the anti-cannon fortifications of the new style, since referred to as the *trace italienne*, were introduced: bastions, generally quadrilateral, angled and at regular intervals along all walls, to provide gun platforms able to launch effective flanking fire against attackers, while defences were lowered and strengthened with earth. Yet, there were a number of much cheaper ways to enhance existing fortifications than such a rebuilding, and these other methods were used much more extensively.

As with other aspects of conflict such as the use of pikes, the discussion of fortifications in, and after, the Renaissance looked back to classical sources. Thus, Guillaume Du Choul's study of Roman fortification and military discipline, first published in Lyon in 1554, appeared in new editions in 1555, 1556 and 1567. Mathematics was also a key element in the design of fortresses. Publications were important in developing and strengthening the consciousness of a specific military tradition. Printing spread techniques far more rapidly than word of mouth or manuscript, and permitted the sharing of information, and, therefore, a degree of standardisation.

In his *Arte della Guerra* ('Art of War', 1521), Niccolò Machiavelli (1469–1527), a one-time senior Florentine official, notably in organising a militia for the republic in 1506–12, sought to revise classical military thought, not least to take note of the lessons

offered by the Italian Wars which had begun in 1494. The impact
of artillery was a major theme:

> Towns and fortresses may be strong either by nature or by art ...
> those situated upon hills that are not difficult of ascent, are
> deemed weak since the invention of mines and artillery. Hence,
> those building fortresses in these times often choose a flat site
> and make it strong by art.
>
> For this purpose, their first care is to fortify their walls with
> angles, bastions, casemates, half-moons, and ravelins, so that no
> enemy can approach them without being taken in both front and
> flank. If the walls are built very high, they will be too much exposed
> to artillery; if they are built very low, they may be easily scaled.

Machiavelli correctly argued the need for a multi-sector defence
in the shape, in particular, of covering the gates with ravelins
(outworks with two faces forming a salient angle), and also, on a
long-standing pattern, keeping the area beyond the fortifications a
bare firing zone.

Adopting a wider perspective, in his *Il Principe* ('The Prince'),
written in 1513, but not published until 1532, Machiavelli addressed
the question of the usefulness of fortifications as a means of maintaining control, and emphasised the importance of circumstances
and, in particular, the value of popular support:

> Princes, in order to hold their dominions more securely, have
> been accustomed to build fortresses, which act as a curb on those
> who may plot rebellion against them, and which provide a safe
> refuge from sudden attack. I approve of this policy, because it has
> been used from the time of the ancient world.

Having then discussed three cases of rulers destroying fortresses,
Machiavelli continued:

> So we see that fortresses are useful or not depending on circum-
> stances; and if they are beneficial in one direction, they are

harmful in another ... the prince who is more afraid of his own people than of foreign interference should build fortresses; but the prince who fears foreign interference more than his own people should forget about them ... the best fortress that exists is to avoid being hated by the people. If you have fortresses and yet the people hate you they will not save you; once the people have taken up arms they will never lack outside help.

Sieges were frequently determined not by the presence of wall-breaching artillery, but, instead, by the availability of sufficient light cavalry to blockade a fortress and dominate the surrounding country. In doing so, the cavalry took a crucial role in a war of posts and raiding. Supply issues, however, were not simply a problem for defenders. Sieges accentuated the logistical problems that were so difficult for contemporary armies, as besieging forces had to be maintained in the same area for a considerable period, thereby exhausting local supplies as well as exacerbating risks of disease.

Whereas the besieging army faced problems in order to maintain a close line of control around the city under siege, combined with a heightened state of alert for either a break-out or a break-in by a relief force, the besieged, who had to maintain their force in a state of alert, faced a less taxing process. Many sieges ended not with a fight to the finish, but with a surrender in the face of a larger besieging army. This was a relationship that could be almost ritualistic in its conventions, although conventions varied and surrender was encouraged by the risk of slaughter if the fortress was stormed.

Individual sieges indicate some of the factors that were at play. In 1529, the Ottomans failed when they attacked Vienna, the walls of which were 300 years old. Niklas von Salm conducted a vigorous defence, showing how fortifications could be rapidly enhanced and expanded at times of need. The energy and skill with which this was done was a key element in any successful defence and should not be detached from discussions of fortifications or treated as inherently secondary. Salm blocked Vienna's gates, which were the most vulnerable points in any fortified position, reinforced the walls with earthen bastions and an inner rampart, and levelled any buildings where it was felt to be necessary. This defence exacerbated the problems posed for the Ottomans by beginning the siege relatively late in the year, which was a consequence of the distance that Ottoman forces had to advance from Constantinople, a distance far greater than that to Belgrade in 1521, let alone to Rhodes, which fell the following year. Having successfully withstood the assault in part with an improvised defence, the Habsburgs afterwards constructed massive, purpose-built, encircling fortifications for Vienna. These long retained their value and were instrumental in the successful defence of the city against Ottoman attack in 1683.

In 1565, Malta, which was a dominion of the Knights of St John, the Crusading Hospitaller Order, was invaded by Ottoman troops in a campaign in which the strength of defensive positions, some recently enhanced, proved a key element in their failure. Most notably, it took over a month (as well as heavy casualties) to capture Fort St Elmo, a secondary fortress, and not the anticipated three days. And yet, there were many other factors, not least poor and divided command (which contrasted with the attack on Rhodes in 1522, for which Süleyman the Magnificent had been present), and the determination of the defence of the fortress of Valletta. The close proximity of Sicily and the presence of Spanish troops and galleys there was a crucial moral factor as they held out the possibility of relief. Two relief forces landed, the first at a vitally important time, on the day Fort St Elmo finally fell. With good leadership and the luck of a fortuitous mist, the force of forty-two knights, twenty-five gentlemen volunteers and six hundred veteran Spanish infantry entered Valletta without loss. Their arrival so disheartened the Ottoman commander that he offered the Grand Master terms, which were refused. Due to bad weather and the caution of the Spanish fleet commander, the second relief force, nine thousand-strong, did not land for another six weeks, but it proved decisive in lifting the siege.

Yet, as a reminder of the need for caution in reading from one example, the Ottomans proved very successful in sieges of positions recently fortified in accordance with new ideas, as in Cyprus in 1570–71 and Tunisia in 1574. Moreover, that the Ottomans did not have an equivalent fortification re-evaluation, in expenditure or style, was not so much due to a failure to match Western advances, as because the Ottomans were far less under attack in this period, a point also true of China. The Ottoman emphasis on field forces and mobility, as well as their interest in expansion, ensured that they were less concerned with protecting fixed positions. As so often, fitness for purpose was a key context for evaluating capability; and that remains the case.

The cost element in fortresses makes this particularly so, as they required not only construction, and on a particular site, but also garrisoning, and the support of that garrison. Thus, the opportunity costs were frequently considerable, not least if opponents did not choose to fight where, or as, the fortress planners wanted. At the same time fortresses fulfilled a purpose when they obliged opponents to consider how best to respond to them and thereby pushed up the hazard and cost of the offensive.

This certainly helped Louis XIV of France (r. 1643–1715) when opposing a powerful coalition in the War of the Spanish Succession (1701–14). His reign saw extensive fortress building by Vauban, with works that can still be seen today, for example at Lille which only fell in 1708 after a long siege by the British under John Churchill, Duke of Marlborough. Toulon repelled an Austrian siege the previous year. The French fortification programme ultimately provided a necessary defence-in-depth, which enabled Louis XIV to survive the consequences of repeated defeats for his armies.

Later in the century, major fortresses fell to attack, as when the French took the Dutch ones of Bergen op Zoom (1747) and Maastricht (1748), but, again, this consumed a lot of campaigning time. Sieges were also very important to European operations overseas. Indeed, success was often a matter of gaining key positions, as with the British capture of Louisbourg on Cape Breton Island from the French in 1758, and of Havana from the Spaniards in 1762. However, sieges were frequently dependent on battle, as in 1759 with the British capture of Quebec. In all these cases, the victories were ultimately a product of British naval power, which provided both lift and vital firepower, as well as preventing the re-supply of opposing forces.

Sieges generally played a smaller role in warfare in the second half of the eighteenth century: while true of the American and French Revolutionary wars, this was already the case with the Seven Years War of 1756–63. Nevertheless, they played a role in each of these conflicts.

CHAPTER 20

Naval Reach Transforms the World, 1400–1763

Naval warfare was altered by the development of long-range, sail-powered warships using navigational systems that made it easier to move safely away from sight of land. Transoceanic navigation was not begun by the Europeans, but they took over from earlier practitioners, notably the Chinese, who had successfully sent large fleets into the Indian Ocean in the early fifteenth century but had not persisted in this deployment. This was not due to any defeat, but as a consequence of a refocusing in the 1440s on a revived and effective Mongol threat.

Whereas galleys, which had a low freeboard, were vulnerable to high waters in poor weather, sailing ships with higher freeboards were better suited to operate in the Atlantic, and such ships were developed by the Europeans and enabled them to cross that ocean and to sail into both the Indian and the Pacific oceans. A wider geopolitics was also important in the development of Portuguese and Spanish expansion, which was initially intended to help secure resources for warfare with Islam. Thus, this expansion, which had begun with the Portuguese seizing Ceuta in Morocco in 1415, was a continuation of the driving of the Moors out of Iberia. The latter, in 1492, saw the fall to Spanish forces of the kingdom of Granada, the last independent Moorish state in Iberia. Prior to that, both powers had already established themselves in the islands of the eastern Atlantic, Spain after a conquest of the Canary Islands, while the Portuguese had created bases down the Atlantic coast of Africa and also established themselves in Madeira, the Cape Verde Islands and the Azores.

The 1490s transformed the situation, with the Portuguese reaching India via the southern Atlantic and the Spaniards the Caribbean, these serving as the basis for two very different types of empire. Portugal established one, focused on the Indian Ocean, of naval power and coastal bases, with key victories over the fleets of Indian states in 1503, 1513 and 1528, and of an Egyptian fleet in 1509, and with subsequent conflict in the Indian Ocean with the Ottomans after they had taken over Egypt in 1517. The Portuguese warships benefited from being more heavily gunned, while their cannon came to be fired from the side of the vessel, a change that owed much to the development of the gun ports just above the waterline and of waterproof covers for them. Portugal's fortified naval bases included Goa, Malacca, Mombasa and Muscat, the last two until 1698 and 1650 respectively. The Portuguese did not have comparable success in Chinese waters in the 1520s, but it was the Portuguese and not the Chinese in the Indian Ocean.

Spain, in contrast, created a territorial empire, one focused on its ability to defeat and replace the Aztec and Inca empires. This success owed much to point-of-conflict advantages, notably in firearms, steel swords and horses, but also to the political ability, as with other conquering empires, for example the Mughals in India from the 1520s, to exploit existing divisions in order to gain backing. Local support provided crucial fighting power, intelligence, supplies and porterage. Disease, notably smallpox, was also very significant in weakening resistance, especially with the Aztecs. Conversely, disease hit the Europeans very hard in sub-Saharan Africa.

A major contrast was that of conflict at sea. The Portuguese continually faced this in Asian waters, as, once established, opposing states such as Atceh and Oman deployed impressive navies. The situation in the Atlantic was very different. Sub-Saharan African polities had effective inshore navies, essentially large canoes, that could thwart deep-draft Portuguese ships in shallow coastal waters, but there was no force able to mount deep-sea opposition other than the Moroccans with their long-range privateers. The Spaniards found that the Caribs and Arawaks could also deploy coastal canoes in Caribbean waters, but faced no deep-sea opposition, while the New World empires, the Inca and Aztecs, did not have navies and, unlike the Ottomans, had not acquired a naval capability.

Spain faced the consequences of overthrowing the Aztec and Inca empires in quite settled areas with the resources locally available for conquest, but elsewhere in the New World the situation was generally less propitious. Alongside difficult terrain and vegetation, there could be intractable opposition, as the Spaniards faced in northern Mexico and central Chile. Operating in Venezuela, Panama and Colombia from the 1580s, Vargas Machuca recorded both the dangers posed by traditional native weapons and tactics, such as poison arrows, rocks rolled down from on high, ambushes and pits, as well as the native ability to respond to Spanish capability and limitations, such as profiting from the damaging impact of rain on gunpowder. Native opposition and disease hit the Portuguese hard in Angola and Mozambique, ensuring that they faced heavy casualties in unsuccessful attempts at expansion into the interior.

The Portuguese and Spaniards were swiftly to be followed in the mid-sixteenth century by European competitors, with the French seeking to establish themselves, notably in Brazil and Florida; and the English trying to break into Portugal's trade in West Africa and Spain's position in the Caribbean. The resulting conflicts indicated the difficulties of establishing an infrastructure in order to sustain power projection. Helped greatly by storms, the English were able to defeat a Spanish invasion fleet, the Armada, in home waters in 1588, but found the support of expeditions to the Caribbean very difficult. Spanish defensive precautions showed considerable resilience, while attackers were hit hard by disease, which was to be a continuing pattern, as with the unsuccessful English/British attacks on Hispaniola in 1655 and Cartagena (in modern Colombia) in 1741, and even with the successful attack on Havana in 1762. In the sixteenth century, the French were driven from Brazil and Florida by Portugal and Spain respectively.

Both England and France were essentially to succeed by claiming lands beyond the Spanish empire. By 1630, the French had developed a position in the St Lawrence valley, as well as on some of the islands in the Caribbean, and the English in the latter and also in Newfoundland, Massachusetts and Virginia. The Dutch, after rebelling successfully against Spain in the late sixteenth century, had established themselves in the early seventeenth in the East Indies and the Hudson Valley, and had begun in 1630 an attempt to drive Portugal from Brazil, one that was to fail in 1654 after major efforts. The Portuguese also succeeded in regaining mid-century losses to the Dutch in Angola and West Africa, but not those in coastal regions of Sri Lanka and Malaysia.

The net effect was to enhance the contrast between an Atlantic world, in which the Iberians remained significant, and that of the Indian Ocean, where they had been largely superseded or bypassed in the seventeenth century, not least as the English became more important in India and the Dutch in the East Indies (Indonesia). There is a tendency to think in terms of a decline of Spain in the seventeenth century, but most of the empire was retained and, after a branch of the Bourbons replaced the Habsburgs on the throne in 1700, so also with the eighteenth. In the Treaty of Paris of 1763 that ended the Seven Years War, it was France, not its ally Spain, that lost territory heavily to the British, notably what the French then controlled in Canada but also islands in the Caribbean and positions in West Africa. Indeed, the Spaniards and Portuguese (in Brazil) maintained their position in the New World until the eventually successful rebellions of the early nineteenth century. In the meanwhile, they expanded their control over native peoples, the Spaniards for example suppressing the last Maya state, in the Yucatán in 1697 and moving into California in the eighteenth.

In India and the East Indies, expansion was largely at the expense of European rivals prior to the mid-eighteenth century. Thus, the Dutch replaced the Portuguese in coastal Sri Lanka from 1656 (only to be replaced in turn by the British from 1796). Thereafter, expansion was also at the expense of native forces: the British succeeded in conquering internal Sri Lanka in 1815, which the Dutch had failed to do. Earlier, in mid-century, the British made major gains in India and the Dutch in Java.

This was a very different context for military activity to that prior to the 1490s, when powers were limited to one hemisphere, and this new situation was to help provide crucial resources, first bullion and later food, to Atlantic states when they fought elsewhere, both in Europe and further afield. Indeed, infrastructure, in the shape of bases, shipping and escorts, were put in place in order to protect these trades, as with the impressive fortification of Havana by Spain between 1577 and 1630. The Iberian gain from the New World encouraged envious competition from other Western powers and brought more benefit than that obtained by Russia as it spread its power at the expense of local people across Siberia, establishing bases such as Tobolsk in 1587. So also, subsequently, with the British gain from India.

The Europeans proved beneficiaries of the lack of sustained East Asian naval activity. From its stronghold in Manila in the Philippines, established in 1571, Spain established bases on Taiwan, at Keelung in 1626 and Tamsui in 1629, in between which Philip IV of Spain claimed the island in 1627. In turn, while they failed to overrun these positions in 1641, next year a Dutch expedition of eight warships and 690 men, and not a Chinese one, forced the vulnerable Spanish positions to surrender by placing cannon on commanding positions. Their capture was part of the global Dutch assault on the Hispanic world, an assault that, at once, greatly contributed to the widespread crisis that affected the latter while also being a product of a longer-lasting situation of wide-ranging commitments and vulnerabilities on the part of Spain and Portugal, and of the potential for naval power projection, amphibious operations and profitable long-distance maritime commerce developed by the Dutch. This assault also testified to the geopolitical possibilities for offshore European activity that were accentuated by China's own mid-seventeenth-century crisis in the shape of the decline, and then collapse, of Ming power.

In the face of attack from China in 1661, the Dutch presence on Taiwan was not sustained, but, further from East Asia, the Europeans were successful in establishing a strong presence, the Dutch in the East Indies and the Spaniards in the Western Pacific, in so far as a strong presence can be used to describe, particularly in the latter case, a position in such vast bodies of water. Moreover, the Dutch role in the East Indies rested in large part on a willingness by the local powers to trade, a willingness in which coercion played a part, but alongside mutual profit and also the use of local powers of the Dutch presence in order to advance their own interests. The Spanish position in the Philippines proved far more secure than that in Taiwan. A Chinese expedition from there to the Philippines in 1673 failed, while, although the Japanese considered an attack on Manila, none was launched. Moreover, the Spaniards were able to extend their position in the Philippine archipelago, for example capturing Zamboanga on the coast of Mindanao in 1635. A strong fortress was then constructed there under the direction of the Jesuit missionary-engineer Melchor de Vera. In the Western Pacific, Spanish power was established in the Mariana Islands in 1668 and in the Caroline Islands in 1696.

More significantly, trans-Pacific trade developed between Manila and Acapulco on the Pacific coast of Mexico to the extent that, although the trade was relatively small-scale in volume, Mexican silver dollars became the international currency of the region and had a major impact on the economies of China and Japan. This was a Western-dominated oceanic world very different to that of the 1480s, and that was not to change until the twentieth century.

CHAPTER 21

The Place of Battle

> Throughout the region the tangled undergrowth, broken
> ground and ever prevailing damp made movement off the
> track difficult and arduous in the extreme.... Beyond Nauro
> the track is inches deep in mud while whole leeches abound
> everywhere.
>
> General Thomas Blamey, Australian commander in
> New Guinea, July 1943

The pervasive impact of geography on war can be seen most clearly at the tactical level, and it is that which engages the overwhelming majority both of participants in conflict and readers about war, and notably so when the latter are concerned with 'the face of battle'. Fighting, killing, risking death and dying all take part in particular locations.

The influence of geography on battle can be far more significant than appears at first glance to the modern observer, or earlier counterparts, not least because much of it is not apparent to the eye. In part, this is because much of the geography is sub-surface, affecting, for example, past drainage patterns, and these are not simply matters of long-distant episodes. Thus, in World War One (1914–18), geology and terrain were important when trench systems were dug, as the geology influenced their strength and vulnerability and the terrain helped determine their placement. Both deep and surface geology were at issue.

Terrain features, such as hills, valleys and slope profiles, survive most clearly from past physical geography, but combatants also recall other aspects of geography, both physical and human. The former range from surface features, most significantly vegetation and drainage, to weather, particularly temperature, rainfall and wind. The human aspects include the farmed and built environments, as well as interventions in drainage patterns, as well as the extent and nature of worked and (very differently) non-worked woodland, but also local resources, communications and the presence of civilians with the many issues they pose.

These and other factors help provide a geographical context for fighting, but the military (as well as irregular forces) are no passive recipient of influence. Instead, there is also an impact on, and from, geography, one reflecting the needs, means and attitudes of the military, whether driven by the pressure of immediacy, or a consequence of doctrine and/or experience, or a mixture of all of these. The processes by which experience of the environment, and of how best to respond to it, are acquired, understood and then disseminated, have understandably left little evidence for most of history. Linked to this, training was always essentially on the job. Yet, basic tactical principles would not have required much consideration.

The most obvious geographical feature, and the easiest to plan for, was the slope, which offered visibility, height and dynamism, as with the Athenians hemming the Persians in at Marathon in 490 BCE. Each factor was significant, but very variously so, and each depending on particular circumstances, notably the tasks and requirements of individual commanders. Visibility provided an awareness of the location of forces, but was also a question of display and a means thereby to encourage supporters, influence the undecided and intimidate the enemy. Each of these was significant. Indeed, the tactics of display and intimidation were a major feature in the struggle over morale that is integral to conflict.

The importance of height to fighting drew together natural features and those added to the landscape by settlement, by fortification, permanent or temporary, or by the use of animal mounts. In using missiles, whether stones, javelins, slingshots, arrows or shot from firearms, height gave greater range, aided aim, made it easier to fire on the rear ranks of opponents, and reduced air resistance. As far as stabbing and slashing weapons were concerned, height potentially provided much greater impact, which was a factor in the use of cavalry.

Moreover, dynamism was given by the real and apparent advantages of advancing downhill with a greater speed and force obtainable for the effort expended, as with the Christian army under John Sobieski of Poland defeating the Ottoman army outside Vienna in 1683. As a consequence of these advantages, major efforts were made to gain and use particular hills in battles.

Conversely, those firing or advancing uphill, as with the British at Bunker Hill outside Boston in 1775, or, alternatively, defending against those attacking with the advantage of slope, were at a disadvantage in each of these respects. This helped explain William the Conqueror's use at the Battle of Hastings in 1066 of the Saxon advance forward of their shieldwall from the commanding hilltop, although there is debate about how far this use was planned and how far expedient. Attacking firepower, as with the Norman archers at Hastings and the English cannon against the hilltop Scots at Flodden in 1512, was one way to confront this defensive potential of height.

The overall situation only really changed when the range and volume of firepower increased to the point that those higher on the slope were more vulnerable due to their visibility, which was very much a consequence of the greater use of artillery in the Napoleonic period, and caused heavy casualties for the Prussians at Ligny in 1815. To avoid the risk, the British increasingly deployed their forces on the reverse (back) side of slopes and/or lying down in

order to minimise the impact of preliminary French bombardment. Wellington repeatedly used this technique, and with great
success, as at Bussaco (1810) and Waterloo (1815). Indeed, he grew
to be particularly skilful in moving his troops forward at the right
moment.

Direct fire, that along the line of sight, as opposed to indirect fire,
was the key element for cannon on both land and at sea until the
early twentieth century; in the air there was no fundamental change
from direct fire until the development of heat-seeking missiles.
Linked to this focus on direct fire, there was considerable emphasis
in the mapping of the French Revolutionary and Napoleonic wars
(1792–1815) on depicting 'strong ground': terrain that could play a
part in conflict, notably as giving a basis for firing positions; and
this emphasis reflected the importance of relief and slopes, not only
to help or impede advance, but also for determining the sight lines
of cannon.

Similar techniques to that of Wellington were to be seen in the
two world wars, with defensive positions in World War One on
reverse slopes. On Iwo Jima (1945), the Japanese used reserve-slope
positions in order to lessen the impact of American firepower. So
also with the use of tanks during that war and subsequently, as
hull-down positions, in which only the turret was exposed, reduced
exposure to opponents' fire.

The problem of terrain varied as combatants altered their
methods. For example, writing about Somaliland, a British intelligence report of 1919 noted that 'Dervish rushing tactics', as with
the attack on a British infantry square at Dul Madoba in 1913, had
been superseded by a stress on the defence that was related to
changing weaponry:

> The large increase in the number of rifles in the Mullah's posses-
> sion and the consequence discard of the spear . . . We may expect
> the Dervishes to take up defensive positions which they will
> defend stubbornly behind cover without exposing themselves.
> We must be ready to carry out attacks against most difficult posi-
> tions and up narrow and steep-sided valleys, to employ covering

fire and frequently to capture the heights or the key to the position before it will be possible to make any headway. It will also be necessary to employ artillery, firing high explosive-shell, if the various Dervish strongholds are to be captured without very heavy casualties. In short, whereas in the past the training of troops in Somaliland could, in the main, be carried out with a view to meeting one form of savage warfare, namely the Dervish rush in bush country, troops must now be trained to readily adapt themselves to a more varied form of fighting which will, in some degree, resemble hill warfare in India.

At the strategic level, the place of battle reflected what was seen as important in the definition of priorities that is so crucial to the deployment and use of troops. No two wars were identical in their goals, contexts and contingencies; and the course of events forced a need to reconceptualise goals. War is crucially not so much a planned activity but one that is shaped by a process of competition that is uncertain in its course and consequences.

In the late twentieth century, cities became more significant as a setting for combat. This had already been seen during World War Two, notably with the bitter fighting in Stalingrad in 1942 and Berlin in 1945, but became more so as states faced internal resistance ranging from mass demonstrations to terrorist movements. So, even more, with both of these factors in the early twenty-first century. Thus, in 2020–21, the attempt to overthrow the authoritarian Belarus regime focused on the capital, Minsk.

CHAPTER 22

The Ottoman Powerhouse

Things are different today from what they were thirty or forty
years ago. Back then we talked about the Turks as if we were
talking about the Antipodes, but now they come so close ... it
is normal for their fleet to sail by this island every year.

Viceroy of Sicily, 1557

When Mehmed II captured Constantinople in 1453, the last
Byzantine emperor dying in the unsuccessful defence, he served
notice of a great change in the military balance. So did his
grandson, Selim I, in 1517, when taking Cairo from the Mamluks,
and his great-grandson, Süleyman the Magnificent, in 1526, when
capturing Budapest from the Hungarians.

With an empire that lasted more than half a millennium, the
Ottomans were the most successful of the several Turkic peoples
who played such a major role in Eurasia's military history. There
had been no empire ruling Anatolia, Syria, Egypt or the Balkans
since Byzantium (the Eastern Roman empire) at its height in the

seventh century. The Ottomans combined the classic fluidity of Asian light cavalry tactics with, from the late fourteenth century, an effective use of infantry and finally artillery. European rivals were defeated in battle, notably the Serbs at Kosovo in 1389 and the Hungarians at Varna in 1444 and Mohacs in 1526. Handguns became more important for the Ottomans from the late fifteenth century, and helped lead to victory at Başkent in 1473 over the Türkmen cavalry of the Aqquyunlu of Iraq. However, in the 1510s, most of the Ottoman infantry still carried bows.

It is all too easy to forget the human cost. Thus, in the Peloponnese in Greece in 1460, after his troops were repulsed in their first attack on Kastrion, Mehmed II addressed them, promising 'splendid rewards to those who should fight well, and stated that the fortress would be pillaged'. The women and children were indeed enslaved. Two years later, one-third of the population of captured Mitylene in the Aegean was enslaved and distributed to the soldiers, and all the captured Italian defenders killed.

Religion could impart particular enthusiasm to campaigns against both Christian nations and Shi'ite Persia under its Safavid dynasty. Its founder, Isma'il, was seen as having divine attributes and deserving absolute obedience, being regarded as the reincarnation of Imam Ali, Muhammad's son-in-law and the founder of Shi'a Islam, or as 'the Hidden Imam', a millenarian figure. Conversion to Shi'ism helped provide coherence to the tribes supporting Isma'il, while the conquest of Iraq brought the prestige of gaining control over major Shi'a shrines, notably Karbala. In contrast, Sunni shrines were desecrated and prominent Sunnis slaughtered.

In addition to the general challenge to the Sunnism of the Ottoman sultans, support among the peoples of eastern Anatolia for the Safavids and their millenarism threatened Ottoman control and security and their sense of religious identity. Moreover, in 1505, Isma'il claimed Trebizond, and thus a coastline on the Black Sea. Attacking Persia in 1514, Selim I obtained a fatwa declaring his opponents heretics. The resonance in recent conflict in the region, between Sunni and Shi'a, and notably over Iraq, is striking.

Cannon helped in the defeat of the Safavid cavalry at Chaldiran in 1514, moving the Ottoman frontier to the east, and Selim then turned against the Mamluks. As so often with battles, it is possible to cite a number of reasons for success. At Marj Dabiq in 1516, the battle that decided the fate of Syria, Selim won in part due to the use of firearms, but other factors were also significant, notably disunity among the Mamluk commanders and troops. As a reminder of the uncertainty of conflict, this was very different to the Ottoman–Mamluk War of 1485–91.

In 1517, Selim pressed on to the victory at Raydaniyya that gave control over Egypt. From there, the Ottomans extended their power along the coast of North Africa, ultimately to the frontier of Morocco, and also gained overlordship over Mecca and Medina which strengthened the claim to be the protector of Muslim ortho-doxy. Syria and Egypt produced about a third of the empire's income, and the Arab influences they encouraged led the Ottomans to become more clearly Muslim in their practice of statecraft.

Ottoman strength was based upon the resources of a far-flung empire, especially of Egypt and the Middle East, on an ideology which saw war against the non-believer as a duty, and on a society structured for the effective prosecution of a war. Its troops were deployed in accordance with a grand strategy based on a consid-ered analysis of intelligence and policy options and drawing on a formidable and well-articulated logistical system. The most valu-able of the regular troops were the janissaries, recruited from the *devshirme*, a tribute originally of children levied in the Balkans. Converts to Islam, they were a trained élite corps, paid from central funds and partly armed with firearms, and their availability less-ened the potential independence of the Türkmen cavalry. The janissaries achieved levels of military professionalism unmatched in Europe or elsewhere in the Islamic world.

The true value of the janissaries lay in the fact that they were a full-time, regular professional force who owed their allegiance solely to the sultan, as opposed to the traditional feudal and regional troops that made up the bulk of the Ottoman armies. Their discipline, especially when on the march and when in camp, was commented on by numerous Christian observers who witnessed their operations. They were also quick to adopt hand-held firearms and during the siege of Malta (1565) their accuracy with them was considered by the Knights of St John to be superior to those of the Christian troops. In Christian Europe, the cost of maintaining a full-time body of soldiers long proved prohibitive, although the French monarchy tried to establish and maintain the *compagnies d'ordonnances* from the middle of the fifteenth to the middle of the sixteenth centuries. The janissaries never wore armour, and this meant they suffered heavy casualties when attacking during major siege operations, such as Rhodes (1522), Malta (1565), and Famagusta (1570). However, their administration and organisation of the *devshirme* was such that a steady stream of new recruits was always available in the cadet schools to replenish the combat units, and this ensured that they remained at the core of all Ottoman armies, and to a lesser extent their navies when on campaign.

Succeeding his father Selim, Süleyman the Magnificent (r. 1520–66) discovered another reason for war bar the sense of mission: seeking and gaining victory provided a way to satisfy the army, and gain the loot and fame that served as the lubricant of obedience. By capturing Belgrade (1521) and Rhodes (1522), he succeeded where Mehmed II had failed, and, by such comparative success within the dynasty, established his success and call for respect and obedience. Hungary fell victim as a result of a total victory at Mohacs in 1526, but the advance on Vienna in 1529 was thwarted by a determined defence, logistics and the onset of winter.

The Ottomans also developed a significant naval capability in the Mediterranean, and, from the 1520s to the 1570s, this provided them with the amphibious capability to take Cyprus as well as Christian bases in Greece and North Africa. The headline facts are the failure of the expedition against Malta in 1565 and the serious Ottoman naval defeat at Lepanto in 1571; but this can lead to an underrating of the Ottoman success in dominating the eastern Mediterranean and in retaining their acquisitions of Algiers, Tunis and Cyprus against Christian counter-attacks. Lepanto, in which more than 100,000 men took part, with possibly close to forty thousand killed and 125 galleys sunk, demonstrated the extent to which triumph in battle did not necessarily lead to success in war: the Christians won but failed to recapture Cyprus.

The general focus on the European operations of the Ottomans has led to a failure to devote sufficient attention to the other fronts, notably against the Safavids, especially in 1578–90, but these often received more attention from the Ottomans. Under sustained Ottoman pressure, the Persians felt obliged to negotiate a peace, which gave the Ottomans what they had conquered in Azerbaijan, the Caucasus and western Iran. As a result, the Ottoman empire reached its greatest extent territorially. War with Persia resumed in the early seventeenth and early eighteenth centuries.

Meanwhile, war with the Austrians had resumed in 1593–1606, 1665–6, 1683–99 and 1716–18, but no clear Austrian superiority on land was to be demonstrated until the defeats of the Ottomans in the 1680s, 1690s and 1710s. The Ottoman empire is generally noted in histories of seventeenth-century warfare for its failure to take Vienna in 1683 and for the subsequent loss of Hungary, culminating in the overwhelming victory of the Austrians under Prince Eugene of Savoy at Zenta in 1697. These were important episodes, but they need to be set against examples of Ottoman resilience, including the recapture of Baghdad from the Persians in 1638 (after unsuccessful sieges in 1625–6 and 1630), the conquest of Crete from the Venetians in 1645–69, the successful invasion of southern Poland in 1672 and the ability of the Ottomans to regain the initiative in the Balkans, at least temporarily, in 1690 and 1695–6. Other Ottoman successes included the reconquest of the Peloponnese (southern Greece) from the Venetians in 1715, and of Belgrade from the Austrians in 1739, and the ability to defeat rebels in Egypt in 1786. Separately, although there were only small-scale clashes, there is no reason to suggest in the late seventeenth century that European war-making was superior to that of the Manchu of China and Mughals of India.

However, by the eighteenth century, the strength of Christian infantry firepower, and the value of its ability to operate in a disciplined fashion on the battlefield, were increasingly apparent, both against the Ottomans and in India. Certainly, Ottoman war-making no longer had an edge in battle, especially so in the case of Russia, which very much became the key power in Eastern Europe, sending forces moreover into Germany in 1716–17, 1735, 1748, 1759–60 and 1813–15, and into the Netherlands and Switzerland in 1799. Russian failures against the Turks in the 1680s, 1695 and 1711 were succeeded by victories in the wars of 1736–9, 1768–74, and 1787–92 and, in the latter two conflicts, the Russians advanced south of the Danube, although the consequences for the Ottomans were less serious than when the Goths had done so at the expense of the Romans in the late fourth century.

The Russians were also able to annex the khanate of Crimea in 1783, and to defeat an Ottoman attempt to regain Crimea in 1787, pressing on to fresh successes against the Ottomans in the wars of 1787–92, 1806–12 and 1826–8. The Russians were increasingly effective in battle and on campaign, with column formations employing both firepower and bayonet charges, and more flexible supply systems, which permitted better operational planning. An absence of new conquests and success in battle acted as a powerful constraint for the Ottomans, causing a loss of prestige as well as a lack of pillage and fresh land to distribute, which reduced the sultan's control over the army.

In the major Ottoman naval clash of the century, the Russians also heavily defeated a fleet at Çeşme off Chios in the Aegean in 1770: the closely moored fleet of twenty ships of the line and at least thirteen galleys was outmanoeuvred, and almost totally destroyed by fireships with about eleven thousand Turks killed.

Fitness for purpose is a crucial concept when judging the applicability of military system. The Ottomans made attempts at improvement, but these did not serve to recover the vigour and success of the centuries of Ottoman expansion. Comparative advantage had been lost, and was not recovered.

CHAPTER 23

Japan and China Clash

Japan moved from civil conflict to external war in the late sixteenth century. In 1577, Oda Nobunaga (see chapter 14) deposed the shogun, becoming the leading ruler in the country, only to be forced by Akechi Mitsuhide, a rival general, to commit suicide in 1582. One of Nobunaga's protégés, Toyotomi Hideyoshi, rapidly defeated Mitsuhide before fighting another major commander, Shibata Katsuie, the following year. As with Nobunaga, Hideyoshi's mobility was a key feature in these campaigns, which led in 1583 to the suicide of Katsuie during the Battle of Shizugatake.

In 1587, Hideyoshi pressed on to invade the island of Kyushu, the southern of the main islands of Japan. There, as at Shizugatake, firepower led to a stress on defensive tactics: in Kyushu, Hideyoshi's forces were deployed behind entrenchments. Finally, in 1590, Hideyoshi, with fifteen thousand troops, attacked the Hojo who controlled the eastern part of the main island, Honshu. Japan was now largely united, with a successful campaign in 1591 bringing the north-east under control. Already, in 1588, after the Shimazu clan had been defeated in southern Kyushu, Hideyoshi had demanded the surrender of all weapons held by farmers. This monopolisation of the means of violence was matched by the policy of systematically destroying the fortifications of defeated rivals.

In a pattern similar to Alexander the Great and Persia, Hideyoshi then decided to conquer China, an invasion that would provide new lands and tasks for his warriors and enable him to keep his control over them, a key element in many conflicts. Continual success, moreover, had led Hideyoshi to lose a sense of limits while the cult of the warrior, anyway, discouraged an interest in limits. He planned to advance via Korea, a Chinese client state, and to rule the world from the Chinese city of Ningbo. From there, Hideyoshi intended to conquer India. He also demanded that Taiwan and the Philippines submit to him, an ambition that reflected his maritime hopes. In 1593, Hideyoshi was to press for equal status with the Wanli emperor of China (r. 1573–1620), which was a major challenge to Chinese views of the world.

Korea refused to transfer its allegiance to Japan, while the Wanli emperor had no intention of heeding his demands. A Japanese invasion of Korea, with about 168,000 men, mounted in 1592, was initially successful, helped by a weak resistance. Having taken the fortress city of Pushan on the south coast, defeating its large garrison, the Japanese rapidly won victory at Ch'ungju, using their handguns and bows to great effect. They then captured the abandoned capital, Seoul, and advanced north to the Yalu River. King Sŏnjo had already fled towards China.

Korean naval resistance helped alter the situation. The Japanese fleet had been initially successful, but was defeated by Yi Sun-shin in a number of battles, more particularly the Battle of Sacheon. The Korean fleet included some of the more impressive warships of the age: 'turtle ships', oar-driven boats equipped with cannon, and possibly covered by hexagonal metal plates in order to prevent grappling and boarding. They may also have been equipped with rams, but they were essentially for coastal waters. Yi Sun-shin, who had a good understanding of the coast and its tides and straits, won a series of further victories in 1592. In addition, Korean guerrilla tactics on land undermined Japanese control and, like other invading powers, the Japanese were also seriously affected by logistical problems.

Worried about the frontier, in a way that prefigured its position in 1950 when American forces advanced north towards the Yalu River during the Korean War, the Chinese committed large forces to Korea in January 1593 and the Japanese were driven back.

Japanese sources emphasised the size of the Chinese army in explaining their defeat, although its technology was also important, notably the use of cannon in the field. This use was significant because the effectiveness of the Chinese was affected by the extent to which their northern forces, configured to fight the threat of attacking cavalry from the steppe, were confronted in Korea by the Japanese, who had themselves developed infantry, equipped with spears and firearms, and driven cavalry from the field. Although the use of firearms in their army had spread, the Chinese also deployed large numbers armed with traditional weapons: bows, lances and swords.

The Sino-Korean allies benefited from having stable land and sea lines of support from China. The Japanese, while being able to get some supplies from the homeland, were stymied by guerrilla efforts on land and by the Chinese and Koreans at sea from supplying their armies on the western side of the peninsula. They also failed to extract the expected resources from the Korean countryside, mirroring their supply woes in China during the Second World War. As with the South Koreans in 1950, the Japanese, who evacuated Seoul on 9 May 1593, were pushed back to a bridgehead on the southern coast around Pushan, but the Chinese were unable to destroy the bridgehead.

In 1597, the year of a smaller-scale Spanish invasion scheme against England, a fresh invasion of Korea was mounted by 140,000 Japanese troops. However, the Chinese, and the Koreans in particular, although affected by factional strife, were now better prepared for attack. Despite initial successes, the Japanese were unable to repeat their success of 1592, even though the Chinese were affected by grave logistical problems. The Japanese advance was stopped south of Seoul and the Japanese moved onto the defensive.

In 1598, the Koreans were supported by a Chinese fleet under an artillery expert, Ch'en Lin. The Japanese had rapidly deployed cannon on their warships, but their tactics remained focused on boarding and their fleet was defeated by Yi Sun-shin at the Battle of the Noryang Strait. In this battle, the Koreans and Chinese navies made more extensive use of cannon and firearms and sank over two hundred Japanese ships, although Yi was killed in the battle.

Hideyoshi had died of illness on 18 September 1598, having already decided to withdraw from Korea. The Japanese forces withdrew in the spring of 1599, and Hideyoshi's plans against China were not pursued by his successors, which was an important moment in East Asian and, thus, world history.

The Chinese had benefited greatly because Mongol power had declined after the death of Altan Khan in 1582. Indeed, the end of the Mongol threat and the defeat of the Japanese were aspects of the late Ming vitality seen under the Wanli emperor. As yet, the Manchu were not a major threat to China. Partly as a result, the sixteenth century closed for China with an impressive display of force in a way that failed to indicate the military challenges of the following century, challenges that focused on Manchu attack and major domestic rebellions.

Far from invulnerable, China was to fall to Manchu attack in the 1640s, which raises the question of whether the Japanese could have succeeded earlier. Despite the problems the Japanese faced in securing their sea lines of communications, and the resource and logistical strains of invasions of East Asia (a strain also seen during the Russo-Japanese War of 1904–5, and then again when the Japanese invaded, first, Manchuria and, then, all of China between 1931 and 1945), the Japanese, like the Chinese, had the manpower and agricultural resource base necessary for operations in the 1590s and, had they continued, the 1600s. This capability was especially the case if the Japanese were not diverted into internal conflict, a factor contributing to international power in this period that was more generally important than administrative development. However, the Japanese did not have the comparative advantage over the Chinese provided by the mobility, flexibility and firepower of the Manchu mounted archers, a force the Chinese could not match as they lacked a comparable supply of horses. Many Chinese commanders were ready to turn to the Manchu.

Hideyoshi's position in Japan was taken by Tokugawa Ieyasu, a daimyo whom Hideyoshi had never trusted. His rise to power was resisted by a rival league of daimyo, but Ieyasu had undermined his opponents by secretly winning several of them over, and this led to victory at the Battle of Sekigahara in 1600. As with many battles, betrayal proved a key element, with Ieyasu benefiting from bringing over about fifteen thousand troops from the 82,000-strong opposing army. Ieyasu then established the Tokugawa shogunate, which lasted until 1868. Hideyoshi's son, Hideyori, was defeated when Osaka Castle was successfully besieged in 1614–15 by Ieyasu's 200,000 strong army. The need for fortresses then fell as cohesion and unity were imposed. The official prohibition on the bulk of the population bearing weapons ensured that fencing became an élite marker, while the absence of war meant that it became a cultural form, and not a practical means of combat.

The seventeenth century saw Japan withdraw from all long-distance maritime activity. Domestic political developments were highly significant to this withdrawal, as groups that had maritime interests appeared a threat to Ieyasu, who founded the Tokugawa shogunate in 1603. Shimazu, of the powerful Satsuma clan, had obtained permission to restore the profitable trade with China via the Ryukyu Islands, but his invasion of the latter in 1609 in order to impose Satsuma suzerainty was seen as a threat by Ieyasu and he ordered the destruction of all large ships in south-west Japan. Moreover, there was a more widespread restriction on the military activities of Japanese adventurers. As a result, there was no repetition of the rogue attempt to conquer Taiwan in 1616. Mounted by a merchant-adventurer, this was a failure: thirteen junks filled with warriors were wrecked by a storm; only one ship reached Taiwan, and the local population killed the crew. In contrast, adventurers were given more leeway by European rulers in the first half of the century, and were, indeed, crucial to the system of military entre-preneurship by which troops were raised.

In Japan, the shogun's fear was in part also of domestic disorder fuelled by the contending rivalries of the recently arrived European missionaries and traders. By the 1630s, these were mostly expelled, as were the Portuguese in 1639. Links with the Dutch were curtailed in 1641. Although the Japanese had traded with South-East Asia in the sixteenth century, in the 1630s they were forbidden to travel overseas.

In 1792, a Russian request to open diplomatic and commercial relations led a hostile Japan to order the establishment of coastal defences, but the Russians did not pursue the approach. Conflict in eighteenth-century Japan was a matter of revolts, all of which were suppressed, stemming from social pressures largely due to a rising population. There was no foreign conflict.

CHAPTER 24

The Age of Fighting Sail, 1588–1827

The Age of Fighting Sail extended from the English defeat of the Spanish Armada in 1588 to the Anglo-French-Russian defeat of the Turkish fleet at the Battle of Cape Navarino in 1827, a key stage in the freedom of Greece. Warships were developed as cannon-carrying platforms able to provide ship-devastating firepower, and the use of sail-power as opposed to oars freed up more manpower to service the guns. Earlier changes in ship construction and design in the fourteenth and fifteenth centuries, especially the increase in the number of masts, the number of sails per mast, the variety of sail shapes and the spread of the sternpost rudder, increased sea-keeping capabilities. Early cannon fire was not broadside fire but, instead, firing from fore and aft. Broadside fire, which provided far more firepower, reflected the ability to build ships capable of safely carrying cannon lower down, without risking capsizing or the sea coming in. Subsequent improvements in firepower were also crucial, not only with cheaper cast-metal cannon but also more effective gunpowder.

There was also the need to operate a fleet as more than a number of individual ships. In part, certainly in the case of the English, the line formation reflected a transfer of military models to sea, as commanders with experience of combat on land sought to apply its lessons and to devise a formation that permitted control and co-operation during the battle. There was not a clear division between different 'services'. In practice, however, the nature of conflict at sea, not least variable skill in responding to the demands of the weather, made it very difficult to maintain cohesion once ships became closely engaged. Nevertheless, fighting instructions and line tactics helped instil discipline and encouraged a new reliance on maximised broadside power.

At the same time, as so often with military history, there is a need to appreciate that battle was the least typical of activities, not least because weaker forces tended to avoid battle. Smaller-scale clashes, escort duty, blockades and operations against the coastline were all also significant. Supporting invasions was a key task, as with William III of Orange's successful invasion of England in 1688.

Naval battles between Western powers occurred in the period 1588–1651, for example the defeat of the Armada in 1588, and the heavy Dutch defeat of the Spaniards in the Battle of the Downs in 1639. However, they were relatively uncommon compared to the more intense nature of large-scale naval clashes in 1652–92, as England, the Dutch and France vied for naval superiority and built warships and constructed infrastructure accordingly. Proximity was a key element, as also for Japan, Korea and China in the 1590s.

In Europe, specialised bases were developed, including Brest for France and Plymouth for England. Funded by governments, these were some of the more formidable sites of the period, with docks matched by storage facilities. Cannon-carrying warships were the product of complicated supply chains and manufacturing processes.

The three Anglo-Dutch wars between 1652 and 1674 were of particular significance. With larger ships, the English fleet proved stronger than the Dutch in the first war of 1652–4. In contrast, in the second, that of 1665–7, the English were handicapped by French support for the Dutch, while the Dutch were strengthened by a major shipbuilding programme in which they built warships as large as those of the English. In the third war, that of 1672–4, the Dutch confronted both England and France and fought a successful defensive war, largely because they were able to deny their opponents the possibility of invading the Netherlands by sea, which had the potential to deliver a knock-out blow.

The English (British from the 1707 Union with Scotland) proved particularly good at broadside firepower, with discipline and training contributing to the strength that went with having the largest fleet in the world from the mid-1690s until surpassed by the Americans in 1943–4. Political emphasis was significant, with France and Spain, Britain's principal rivals, putting a greater stress on army strength, and the French crucially not focusing on their navy after its major defeat by the English at Barfleur in 1692, instead devoting much more attention to the army which was under great pressure in Belgium.

Moreover, the size of the mercantile marine ensured that Britain had a greater reservoir of trained seamen. Good naval leadership was combined with impressive administration, and expenditure on maintenance, dockyards and equipment, indeed a continuous pattern of support, facilitated improvements in operational practice and tactical effectiveness.

Key victories in 1692, 1747 and, even more, 1759 over the French combined with successful amphibious operations enabled Britain to transform the geopolitics of the Western world. Naval success was not due to superior weaponry, as neither the ships nor their equipment were substantially different from those of the Bourbons (France and Spain) or, indeed, the Dutch. Instead, there was an effective use of the warships of the period in the context of an ethos and policy that combined the strategic and operational offensive with tactical aggression. Failure could lead to disgrace, as with Admiral Byng who was court-martialled and shot after he did not prevail over a French fleet off Minorca in 1756. This encouraged bold command in the two key battles of 1759: Lagos and Quiberon Bay, the British in the second pursuing the French in a very high wind into dangerous coastal waters.

In the American War of Independence (1775–83), the British were able to sustain their forces in North America, but naval victory over the French off the Îles des Saintes in the Caribbean in 1782 came too late to make a key impact on the war. So also in the French Revolutionary War, with successive victories, at the Glorious First of June (1794), St Vincent (1797), Camperdown (1797) and the Nile (1798), more important in enabling Britain to maintain naval dominance than in countering growing French control of Western Europe. The Napoleonic Wars saw a more sustained struggle, but 1805 brought the abandonment of French invasion plans and a major defeat of a Franco-Spanish fleet at Trafalgar.

Britain was able to maintain an effective convoy system that helped it increase its proportion of global mercantile shipping, and also to deny access to world markets to France and its allies. Moreover, the strength and nature of British naval power and maritime resources enabled Britain to resist Napoleon's attempt to isolate it commercially from the Continent, to support army campaigns in Portugal and Spain, and to capture French and allied overseas bases. This led to a global span for British amphibious power, with, for example, the capture of Cape Town in 1806, Martinique in 1809, Réunion and Mauritius in 1810 and Batavia (Jakarta) in 1811. There were failures, notably the attacks on Buenos Aires in 1807 and New Orleans in 1815, the latter during the Anglo-American War of 1812 (1812–15), but these were British attacks on foreign bases, and not the opposite. Naval blockades, which, despite the strength of American frigates in ship-to-ship clashes in 1812, became effective from 1813, hit the American economy as well as American naval operations. A British force was able to capture Washington in 1814 and to approach Baltimore bombarding Fort McHenry and forcing expensive defensive preparations on the Americans.

British guns rang out over much of the world, and the limitations of naval technology could not prevent both the reality and the perception of power. These were driven home anew in 1816 when the bombardment of Algiers led to an agreement to end the taking of Christian slaves.

British capability rested more deeply on the unique Western experience of creating a global network of empire and trade, which was based on a distinctive type of interaction between economy, technology and state formation, and on the specific strength of the liberal political systems, pre-eminently that of Britain which, like the Netherlands, could elicit the co-operation of capitalists (who benefited from naval commerce-projection), producing a symbiosis of government and the private sector that proved both effective and especially valuable for developing naval strength. China, Korea and Japan were able to build many ships, and their economies and level of cultures in the seventeenth century ranked with those of the West, but in those three states there was no lasting interaction between economy, technology and state formation. Their merchants were not involved in government, while the nobility saw overseas trading as below them.

Britain remained the great naval power in the nineteenth century, its self-image focused on the sea to a degree not matched elsewhere. As a result, the technological transformation of the move to power by steam, not sail, and to construction with iron, not wood, was successfully made without overturning Britain's leading position. In part, this was a reflection of Britain being the key country in the Industrial Revolution.

Although the transformation took time, steam power replaced dependence on wind, making journey times by sea far more reliable, predictable and short. Thanks to steam, warships were able to manoeuvre in calms and make headway against contrary winds. This made it easier to operate inshore and in hazardous waters, to attack opposing fleets in harbour, to mount landings, and to remain on a blockade station over an extended time. The ability of steamships to work with confidence close inshore affected the tactical, operational and strategic potential of naval power. Coal supplies became a major issue, although, as the ability to use sail reduced this need, most steamships retained their sailing rigs for a while. Nevertheless, whereas the warships of 1815 were not too different, in construction, propulsion, manning or weaponry, to those of a century earlier, the situation was very different a century later.

CHAPTER 25

China, Russia and the
End of the Steppe

In the early seventeenth century, two very different epics saw the Russians extend their power across Siberia to the Pacific, while the Ming, who had driven the Mongols from China in the late fourteenth century, were in turn conquered by Manchu (Qing) invaders benefiting from Ming weaknesses. This was another victory for steppe forces, and one that suggested that such victories were far from over. Indeed, in the late eighteenth century, the British historian Edward Gibbon felt it appropriate to ask whether 'barbarians' could conquer Europe anew, although he came to the conclusion that the Westernisation of Russia under Peter the Great (r. 1689–1725) provided an insuperable barrier.

The Manchu, once successful conquerors, went on to sinicise, presenting themselves as Chinese. They also created a hybrid form of warfare that gives them a particular effectiveness. They were able both to operate successfully on the steppe and to draw on the resources of China in a new version of the military system established by the Mongols when they took over China in the thirteenth century, including a naval capability that enabled the Manchu to take over Taiwan in 1683.

The Kangxi (r. 1661–1722) and Qianlong (r. 1735–96) emperors were the most successful exponents of the new system. The first suppressed the Revolt of the Three Feudatories (1673–81), a dangerous rebellion by warlords-generals who were provincial governors, one of whom proclaimed himself emperor in 1678. This was the largest-scale rebellion of the century.

Thanks to both the Kangxi and the Qianlong emperors, control was established over Tibet and the Zunghar confederation, the last of the great steppe empires. This was an epic struggle. In 1687, the Zunghars, under Taishi Galdan Boshugtu (r. 1671–97) expanded from western into eastern Mongolia, bringing them into direct confrontation with China which was challenged both by this advance and by the collapse on the steppe of any balance of power that they might manipulate.

In 1690, the two armies clashed at Ulan Butong, 320 kilometres north of Beijing. Galdan's defensive tactics, not least sheltering his men behind camels armoured with felt, limited the effectiveness of the Chinese artillery, but the Chinese drove their opponents from the field. Unable to mount an effective pursuit due to a shortage of food and because their horses were exhausted, the Chinese commander was happy to negotiate a truce.

In 1696, the Kangxi emperor, a determined figure, advanced against the Zunghars, north across the Gobi Desert with converging columns, a serious test of logistical capability and 'near-run thing' which led his advisers to urge him to turn back before the army starved. The Chinese coped far better than the Russians had in their unsuccessful advances across the steppes against the Crimean Tatars in the later 1680s, and the Zunghar army was destroyed in battle at Jao Modo. Underlining the need, as so often, for a multi-faceted explanation, success owed much to support for the Chinese from the rebellious nephew of the Zunghar leader. Yet, Chinese effectiveness also reflected the strength of the army including an underlying impressive logistical system ensuring that the wealthy agricultural zone of lowland eastern China could be tapped to support campaigns to the north and west closer to the frontier. The combination, under the Manchu, of steppe and Chinese forces and systems, had proved crucial in ensuring that the frontier was overcome, a process underlined when settlement was undertaken in conquered areas in order to stamp control and provide resources to support the army. This was a long-standing pattern in Chinese history.

The crucial factor in Chinese military capability against the Zunghars was not weaponry, but the ability to deliver and sustain considerable power at a great distance, having made preparations. This situation matched that within the Western world where organisational developments, range and capability were more important than military technology and tactics (which Western powers shared, notably at sea), and in terms of both absolute and relative power. The Chinese exploited their victory in 1696 by extending their control in Mongolia and intervening in Tibet, thus helping to ensure the shape of modern China. In 1717, the Zunghars, in turn, advancing across very difficult terrain, conquered Tibet, but they were eventually driven out when the Chinese counter-attacked in 1720, after a first response was defeated in 1718.

In the early 1730s, the Chinese were less successful in conflict with the Zunghars, but, in 1755, they benefited in a renewed offensive from divisions in the Zunghar élite due to a serious succession dispute. Chinese success in 1755 was followed by rebellion, but that was suppressed. The Zunghar population was hit hard by smallpox and massacres.

The logistical achievement was important to the Chinese management of steppe warfare. In the 1750s, building on their earlier system, the Chinese established two chains of magazine posts along the main roads on which they advanced in Central Asia against the Zunghars. Supplies were transported for thousands of kilometres, and the Mongolian homelands controlled by their eastern Mongol allies provided the horses and plentiful fodder, each crucial to operating on the steppe. These improvements in logistics – due partly to a desire to keep the troops from alienating the populace and partly to the latter's lack of food in a very arid region – ensured that the Chinese armies did not disintegrate as Napoleon's did in 1812 when he encountered serious problems in invading Russia, despite advancing over a shorter distance. Comparisons are difficult, not least because Napoleon faced greater resistance than the Manchu armies had done in 1755, but the contrast in the supply situation was very important. It is clearly inappropriate to put the Europeans to the fore in logistical discussion.

The application to military purposes of the great demographic and agricultural expansion of China during the century was related to the extension of arable farming in Gansu and, in order to ground the new conquests with the establishment of colonists, shifting the focus in these areas from animal husbandry. In order to wage war with the Zunghars, there was a massive transfer of resources from eastern to western China, and, as with other instances of Chinese war-making, this capacity reflected both administrative capability of the state and the extensive resources of well-developed mercantile networks. The Manchu conquest of Central Asia, which continued in 1759 beyond the Zunghar world with the conquest of Hotan and Yarkant, succeeded in part because they successfully solved the logistical problems of operating on the steppe which no previous dynasty could surmount, although other factors were involved, notably civil war and defections among the Zunghars and also devastating smallpox. The combined Manchu, Mongol and Han, infantry, artillery and cavalry forces, discovered how to manage steppe warfare, because that was considered the central strategic threat by all Chinese dynasties, while they were much less successful on the Burma, Sichuan, Vietnam southern frontiers both because that was not of central strategic interest and because the physical environment was quite different, not least in the shape of the disease that badly hit operations in Burma in the late 1760s.

Thanks to its victories, China became both a contiguous empire of great size and also a state where the heavily populated core in eastern China was given considerable strategic depth other than from attack by sea, as occurred between 1839 and 1945. Moreover, important elements among the Kazakhs accepted tributary status and remained under Chinese influence until it was supplanted by that of Russia in the nineteenth century. However, the Chinese faced opposition, notably the Dungan Revolt of 1862–77 by Muslim areas, and Tibetan desire for independence which was de facto from 1912 to 1951.

The Chinese were able to drive the Russians from the Amur valley in the 1680s, but in general the two powers avoided rivalry until Russian expansion from the late 1850s. In the meantime, Russia had expanded greatly at the expense of the steppe people, while also driving back the Turks. The Crimean Tatars saw off earlier Russian attacks, notably in the 1680s, but these became more significant from the late 1730s and Crimea was annexed in 1783. As a result of this success, and of Russian defeats of Turkish forces, notably in the wars of 1768–74 and 1787–92, in each of which Russian forces advanced south of the Danube, the Black Sea ceased to be a Turkish lake. Further east, the Russians made significant gains, but did not take over much of Central Asia until the late nineteenth century: Tashkent was stormed in 1865 and Samarqand taken in 1868, Khiva following in 1873 and Merv in 1884. These were significant achievements given both the difficulties of operating in the area and earlier failures, as well as those of the British in Afghanistan, notably in 1842.

Russian expansion was a topic of wider concern from 1791, when Britain came close to war, a process that eventually led to the Crimean War of 1854–6. Russia survived this peripheral threat, while it crushed the more central challenges from Charles XII of Sweden in 1708–9 and Napoleon I of France in 1812, the two most significant army operations in Europe in the long eighteenth century. In each case, the invading army was destroyed and its leader forced to flee for his life. These failures were in many respects not so much instances of the so-called modernity of the period, but rather a continuance of long-established patterns of conflict, not least with a relatively brief invasion commanded by a sovereign.

In each case also, Russia made long-term territorial gains, notably, from 1710 (confirmed by treaty in 1721) a long Baltic coastline that was held until 1918 and, from 1772, and even more, 1813, control over most of Poland until 1915. As a result, Russia became the dominant power from the Baltic to the Pacific and the central topic of concern for those interested in Eurasian geopolitics.

CHAPTER 26

The Collapse of European Control in the New World, 1775–1825

British redcoats moving forward across sun-dappled meadows soon to be shot down by brave Patriots: that is a standard image of the American Revolution (1775–83) and one that helps make its outcome appear inevitable. That, of course, was not a luxury enjoyed by contemporaries, and there was no sense of inevitability until after the surrender of a British force at Yorktown, Virginia, in October 1781. Instead, we have to turn to the specifics of the episode and without any view that revolutionary forces were bound to defeat counter-revolutionary ones. Indeed, the total failure of the 1775–6 American invasion of Canada underlined the strength of the British military system.

The two major shifts in global territorial control over the last quarter millennium were those of 1775–1825 and 1943–91, the first focused on the New World and the second on the Old. In each case, international conflict interacted with civil war, and what in hindsight appeared inevitable was certainly not so to contemporaries. Some insurgency struggles had succeeded, most obviously giving rise, between 1300 and 1600, to Swiss, Scottish and Dutch independence, and to driving the Mongols from China; but most had failed. And unsurprisingly so given the value of the military resources, notably weaponry, organisation and training, enjoyed by professional armies, and the difficulty of defining lasting political identities around rebellion.

Indeed, it is an appreciation of the difficulties of the task that leads to a realisation of the absence of inevitability in 1775–1825. A key factor was the international dimension. The British had conquered Canada from France in 1758–60, and war with France in 1778 greatly distracted British attention from suppressing the American Revolution. In particular, the French challenged the command of the sea required to support and supply specific British operations, leading to British defeat at Yorktown, Virginia, in 1781 by an American-French force. This was part of a massive pressure on the British empire which, by 1781, included war also with Spain, the Dutch and, in southern India, Mysore. The British were under pressure in the Indian Ocean region, the Mediterranean, West Africa, North America and the West Indies, and, in 1779, there was an unsuccessful invasion attempt of England by a Franco-Spanish force, an attempt that made the defence of home waters a priority throughout.

The international dimension tends to be underrated in insurgency struggles, not least because it does not match narratives of national success, but it was important throughout. Thus, British opposition made it impossible for France to sustain its resistance to the Haitian revolution of 1791–1804, and prevented the French from supporting Spain in overcoming revolution in Spanish America.

Yet, that was only one of the relevant factors. Indeed, push and response elements were both significant. The politicisation of much of the American public and the motivation of many of their troops were important in encouraging a determination to keep going, a factor also seen in the other New World revolutions. However, the revolutionaries' war effort was close to collapse by early 1781, and the erosion of British resolve after Yorktown was a key factor, as otherwise the Americans could not force the British to end a war.

The British ministry lost the support of Parliament in the spring of 1782 and was replaced by a new ministry pledged to end the war by negotiation. This factor of political resolve was/is always significant in war and most significantly so in counter-insurgency struggles.

On Haiti, the army Napoleon sent in 1802 compromised any chance of success by terrible brutality. However, the army was also weakened, as so often with counter-insurgency conflicts, by its own deficiencies as well as the strengths of the opposition. The French suffered from poor leadership and planning, from the distance from France, from a lack of troops, money and supplies, and from the British attitude. The last was important as the resumption of war between Britain and France in 1803 left the French vulnerable to British naval superiority. In turn, the Haitians benefited from their ability to work with the environment, from their use of irregular operations, and from the serious impact of yellow fever on the French. Indeed, disease operated as a major killer for European forces in the Caribbean and Africa, although it alone did not stop them operating. The ultimately successful Haitian revolution was a more important precedent for twentieth-century insurgencies than the American Revolution, particularly given the significance of racial issues.

Taking place over a far larger area (Mexico to Chile) than the War of American Independence, and very much lacking the military and political coherence of the latter (for there was no equivalent to the Continental Congress or the Continental Army), any description of the Latin American Wars of Independence risks becoming a confused account with rapid changes of fortune. Major mountain chains and the problems posed by disease, such as yellow fever on the eastern coast of Mexico, accentuated the problems of operating. As in the War of American Independence, or in Europe, where in the 1790s and 1800s insurgency forces were defeated in the Vendée, Calabria and Tyrol, there was no automatic success for the revolutionary forces, and they were not inherently better at combat than their opponents.

Instead, both sides adapted to the issues and problems of conflict across a vast area in which it was difficult to fix success or, indeed, in relatively poor societies, to arrange logistical support. These problems helped ensure the significance of local and regional dimensions. The result, as in Mexico, could be the fragmentation of the insurgency. The same was true of the army, whose units engaged in counter-insurgency operations with little central supervision, while their commanders tried to build up local power bases. Logistical needs helped compromise the popularity of both sides, while the seizures and looting involved in obtaining supplies inflicted much damage on society.

Meanwhile, the royalists were also badly hit by shifts in government and policy within Spain, shifts which alienated support in Latin America and indeed culminated in a civil war in Spain in 1823. Moreover, like the Western European empires facing anti-imperial rebellions after World War Two, Spain had been greatly weakened by the French Revolutionary and Napoleonic wars, as had been its major ally since 1700, France, and this weakness made it difficult to overcome revolution.

At the same time, the fighting ability and command skills of the rebels, especially those of José de San Martín in Chile in 1817–18, and of Simón Bolívar in the more intractable struggle in northern South America and the Andean chain in 1813–25, were important in wearing down the resistance of the increasingly isolated royalist forces.

Despite royalist successes, notably in Venezuela in 1806, 1812, 1816 and 1818, in Bolivia in 1811 and 1815, in Chile in 1814 and in Mexico in 1815, it proved impossible to bring the struggle to a close. Insurgents withdrew to more isolated regions from which resistance continued. The royalists, furthermore, failed to devise an effective strategy for reconciliation, and their emphasis on repression, including, in Venezuela, the forcible relocation of civilians into camps, proved counter-productive. Ultimately, the royalists were defeated in battle in Peru, a bastion of royalism, in 1824, that of Ayacucho proving decisive. Antonio José de Sucre, with 5,780 troops, defeated the viceroy, José de La Serna, and his 9,300 troops by repelling attacks, before using his reserves of infantry and cavalry to break through and encircle part of the opposing force.

The loss of many of the senior royalist commanders, including the captured viceroy, in this battle left the royalists leaderless.

Crucially, Spain was in no position to mount a renewed struggle after this defeat. In part this reflected the domestic divisions that had led to civil war in 1823 and was to resume in the 1830s with the First Carlist War, a civil war. In addition, Spain lacked foreign allies and faced continued opposition from Britain. This opposition did not involve conflict but entailed backing for the rebels, notably diplomatic and economic support. Moreover, Spain's supporters in Latin America had been weakened by the long conflict, while many had accommodated themselves to the new regimes.

In a different process, and far more rapidly, Portugal lost control of Brazil. Subsequently, separatist revolts in Brazil were suppressed by the new state, in large part because they did not provide a united challenge and could be overcome sequentially. As a result, they were less serious than the Taiping rebellion in China in 1850–64 and the Southern one in the United States in the civil war of 1861–5.

In contrast, Mexico was to fail to overcome a separatist revolt in Texas. In part, this reflected the peripheral nature of Texas to the Mexicans, but serious divisions within Mexico were also significant, while the Mexican leader Santa Anna mishandled his advance in 1836, so that the Texans were able to surprise, defeat and capture him.

Rather than remaining independent, Texas was subsequently to unite with the United States in 1845. This serves as a reminder of the degree to which, in contrast to the relatively fixed nature of boundaries in the decolonisations of the twentieth century, there was no fixed character or boundaries for New World states after the end of European rule. Instead, warfare played a major role in the shaping of the post-independence landscape, as with the War of the Pacific in 1879–83 in which Chile defeated a Bolivian–Peruvian alliance and was able to annex coastal areas from its opponents. This situation remained the case until Paraguay defeated Bolivia in the Chaco War of 1932–5, which was the last major conflict in South America and, again, one that has established a border lasting to the present.

CHAPTER 27

Napoleonic Warfare

In Egypt, I found myself freed from the obstacles of an
irksome civilisation. I was full of dreams ... I saw myself
founding a religion, marching into Asia, riding an elephant,
a turban on my head and in my hand the new Koran that I
would have composed to suit my needs. In my undertakings
I would have combined the experiences of the two worlds,
exploiting for my own profit the theatre of all history.

Napoleon

The repeated successes of Napoleon between 1796 and 1811, with
Austrian forces repeatedly defeated, but also victories over Prussian,
Russian and Turkish ones, helped define warfare in the Western
tradition. This was because of the need of other powers to oppose
his military system and as a result of the subsequent commentary
upon the period offered by Clausewitz and Jomini, the most influential Western commentators on land warfare. In practice, however,
Napoleon, who was driven from power by invading forces in both

1814 and 1815, was a failure, prefiguring German war-making in the two twentieth-century world wars. This was because his ability to win tactical and operational advantage was not matched by an adequate grasp of strategic issues, not least in terms of converting battlefield advantage into political acceptance.

Napoleon was a figure who became increasingly common in the widespread instability of the late eighteenth century: a general who used his military position to exploit the 'people's warfare' of the period and to seize power, although there was a long pedigree, as with Sulla, Julius Caesar, Augustus and the Barracks emperors in Rome. That was not to be the course in the United States, where generals who became presidents, from George Washington in 1789 to Dwight Eisenhower in 1953, did so as a result of constitutional means. However, that was not the usual pattern. Instead, with the army frequently the most organised force in the state, and a focus of centralisation and identity, it was often generals, in Napoleon's lifetime from Thailand to Haiti and the newly independent states of Latin America, who were the key beneficiaries of division and instability, as well as frequently being a cause of such instability.

Born in 1769, a Corsican who had become a Second Lieutenant in the artillery under Louis XVI, Napoleon's career took off as a result of the French Revolution, which provided many opportunities for talented opportunists, notably the transformation of patronage criteria and networks, and a major war that began in 1792 and subsequently broadened out. Making his name in 1793, when his successful command of the artillery in the siege of Toulon played a key role in driving off British forces, Napoleon helped suppress a royalist demonstration in Paris in 1795, with a 'whiff of grape-shot' that was part of the internal war by which the regime maintained power. Given command of the Army of Italy, he developed and demonstrated in 1796–7 his bold decisiveness at the tactical and operational levels, not least swift decision-making, rapid mobility and the ability to grasp and use the initiative. At the same time, there was also brutal exploitation and the harsh repression of the resulting popular opposition, as in Lombardy in 1796, Cairo in 1798 and Spain in 1808–13.

Napoleon's seizure of power in 1799 from the Directory government of the French Revolution reflected also the militarisation of nationalist ideology that became more common. Yet Napoleon transformed the Revolution into an empire, crowning himself emperor in 1804 and launching France into a process of seemingly ineluctable expansion that was the very opposite of the nationalist republicanism of 1792–9.

This quest for new horizons was already apparent in Napoleon's expedition to Egypt and the Near East in 1798–9, an expedition in which he crushed the Mamluks at the Battle of the Pyramids, a victory over shock tactics for defensive firepower, the sound of the latter described as 'like a boiling pot on a fierce fire'. At one level, this expedition was a 'modern' response to the developing geopolitical prospects arising from the increased importance to Western powers, particularly Britain, of routes to the Indian Ocean, and the possibilities for expanding strategic range accordingly. The French hoped to encourage opposition to Britain in India, notably by Tipu Sultan of Mysore, and the expedition was a response to the British capture of Cape Town from France's Dutch ally in 1796. Yet, Napoleon also imagined himself in Egypt as another Alexander the Great.

There was subsequently to be a distinctly traditional imperial theme to his reign, as if Napoleon were a latter-day Charlemagne, indeed the first emperor of the Franks since him. Moreover, the militarism of Napoleon's system had a neo-feudal character. Dominions were given to family members, his brother Joseph being made king of Spain after Napoleon seized it in 1808, honours and lands to his officer class, and military service was preferred to all other criteria. The wearing of uniform became the norm. Combined with the conscription introduced under the Revolution with the *levée en masse*, this ethos and practice helped make France more similar to Prussia, the acme of German militarism, than either was prepared to accept.

The standard account of Revolutionary and Napoleonic France emphasises the causes of repeated victories from 1792 to 1809, and France's success in replacing Prussia at the apparent cutting edge of military achievement and progress, Prussia having won this position through repeated victories in 1741–2, 1745–6 and 1756–63, notably over Austria, but also over France at Rossbach in 1757. That approach is ironic because, like Germany in 1918 and 1945, Napoleon was to collapse in failure, repeatedly in 1812–14, leading to his enforced abdication in 1814, and then again in 1815 when he returned to power, with Prussia, alongside Austria, Britain and Russia, among the victors in each case.

The key to France's earlier success was in part due to tactical emphases, notably attacks in columns. These provided a way to take advantage of the large number of poorly trained conscripts, as well as of the possible vulnerability to shock attack of a defending line of infantry relying on firepower, as with the defeat of the outnumbered Austrian force at Jemappes in 1792, which was the prelude to the rapid French conquest of Belgium. Organisational factors were also valuable, especially an effective artillery and the development with divisions and a corps system of combined arms units able to operate independently. The last was ably articulated by an impressive staff system.

These much-described factors helped deliver repeated victories, but there has been a tendency to underplay the defeats suffered by the French, particularly at Austrian and Russian hands both in the 1790s and after Napoleon had seized power, as well as the ability of France's opponents to mask her advantages, especially by developing relevant counter-tactics. In part this was a matter of closing the capability gap, which so often is a key element in military history, as for example with the German and Japanese defeat in World War Two. In addition, French generals were not always able to execute their supposed system well. Moreover, many battles became a confused mêlée in which a degree of muddling through was important to success, as for Napoleon at Marengo in 1800 and Jena in 1806, at the expense of the Austrians and Prussians respectively.

There was also a decline in Napoleonic skill. The famed triumph of the Ulm–Austerlitz campaign of 1805, in which the Austrians and Russians were totally outmanoeuvred on both campaign and on the battlefield, was replaced by the serious failures in both respects during Napoleon's invasion of Russia in 1812, as with the bludgeoning but costly victory at Borodino, and in his Leipzig operation the following year. Already, in 1807, he had found it difficult to defeat Russia and in 1809 Austria.

France profited from the divisions among its enemies rather than the supposed military genius of Napoleon, more especially the difficulties of ensuring an alliance of Austria, Prussia and Russia against France. Thus, Prussia left the war against France in 1795, rejoined it in 1806, left again in 1807 and did not rejoin until 1813. Austria, like Prussia, cooperated with France in 1812 in invading Russia, which itself fought France only in 1798–1800, 1805–7, 1812–14 and 1815. The mutual suspicions and competing interests of these powers, especially in Eastern Europe, where Austria, Prussia and Russia partitioned Poland out of existence in 1772–95, helped give the revolutionaries and Napoleon the advantage of sequential campaigning. The situation at sea was very different as Britain was the most consistent opponent of Napoleon, only briefly at peace with him in 1802–3. Moreover, although French conquests and alliances peeled off the other major naval powers from Britain, their co-operation with France could not produce success, as the British defeat of the larger Franco-Spanish fleet at Trafalgar in 1805 demonstrated.

The different situation on land ensured particular problems for France when a major alliance was assembled and sustained against France, as in 1798–9, 1813–14 and 1815. So also for Germany in 1942–5, as opposed to 1939–41. In 1813–14, in his now difficult situation, Napoleon proved unwilling in negotiations to surrender control of territories as part of the price for a peace that left him in control of France. This reflected his bellicosity, but also lack of skill, as Louis XIV (r. 1643–1715) proved better able to divide the opposing coalitions.

Defeated in 1814, Napoleon was exiled to Elba, a small island in the western Mediterranean, which became a principality under his rule. In 1815, he easily regained power in France, but was totally defeated. The 1815 campaign showed many of Napoleon's characteristics. His risk-taking and decisiveness got him back into power in France and, once he faced renewed war, he took the initiative. In doing so, Napoleon sought to defeat the nearest armies of his opponents, the British and Prussian forces in Belgium, so that he could then turn on the more distant Austrians and Russians. He was able to fight the British and Prussians separately, at Quatre Bras and Ligny on 16 June, but, although inflicting serious losses on the Prussians, failed to defeat either decisively. They were able to cooperate at Waterloo two days later, British fighting quality winning a defensive victory against determined but poorly executed French attacks to break through the British position, before the Prussian arrival meant that the British and Prussians could go on to win a striking offensive victory. Fleeing back to France, Napoleon did not find the support in defeat he had previously enjoyed in victory and, as a result, there was no guerrilla war against the occupying Allies comparable to that the French had faced in Spain in 1808–13. The invading forces captured Paris. Having surrendered, he was then imprisoned on the distant British South Atlantic island of St Helena until his death.

Any emphasis on French capability needs to note the problems encountered by opposing two powers that would have liked to reach an agreement with France: Britain and Russia. Each was more impressive than France as military powers because of the range of their tasks. Thus, Russia in 1805–14 fought France, but also the Turks, Sweden and Persia; while Britain also fought in India and North America. Ultimately, therefore, a focus on Napoleon is one that is Eurocentric, rather than global, and concerned with failure rather than success. There are parallels with the quest for domestic and international power of non-European rulers, such as Agha Muhammad of Persia (r. 1779–97), but the French were not able to prevail on a world scale. As such, the focus on Napoleon provides an instance of the way in which the losers too often get not only to be the topic but also to a degree to write the account, a process also seen with the Confederates in the American Civil War and the Germans in World War Two.

CHAPTER 28

Wars within the West, 1816–1913

State-making and state-preserving were the key results of the near-century between the end of the Napoleonic wars in 1815 and the outbreak of World War One in 1914, all against a background of swiftly rising population and rapid industrialisation. The most important states made by war were Germany and Italy, and those preserved by the suppression of rebellion were America, Brazil and Austria-Hungary. In turn, Italy and Germany went down to total military failure in 1943–5, less than a century after their unification. Given the longer-term significance of the United States in global history, it is the American Civil War of 1861–5 that focuses attention, not least because it captured both the military and the political side of war, the latter always of particular significance in civil wars, but not only of them.

Many civil wars arise from attempts to take over a state as a whole, and this was the case with the Taiping Rebellion in China in 1850–64, the largest-scale conflict of the century. Civil wars tend to be win or lose, notably separatist struggles, as either a new state will gain independence or it will be suppressed. There have been peaceful solutions, as when Norway broke away from Sweden in 1905 or, more clearly, Czechoslovakia split up in 1994 into the Czech Republic and Slovakia, but these are far less common. Indeed, some lengthy wars arose from such struggles, as with the Dutch Revolt against Spain of 1566–1609, and the Portuguese War of Independence from Spain in 1640–68, both of which were eventually successful.

North America saw two such wars, that of independence in 1775–83 and the Civil War of 1861–5. However, a diachronic comparison, one between events very different in time, can be problematic. Thus, in 1861–5, there were ironclad steamships, railways, telegraphs, barbed wire and percussion cap guns, none of which were present in the former struggle, while America's population was far less located in coastal regions and thereby vulnerable to amphibious attack than had been the case in 1775. Yet, such contrasts can themselves be valuable as throwing attention on the importance of these factors, as in 'Was the North (Union) victorious because it used the railway successfully?' Aside from technological progress as a factor, there is that of resources. Here, attention is generally devoted to the undoubted strength of the North.

Yet, there was also the extent to which, as with the failure of Brazil's regional risings in the 1820s–40s, that strength was not offset by external intervention on behalf of the South (the Confederacy). In contrast, the Americans, up against Britain, the world's leading mercantile power in the War of Independence of 1775–83, benefited from France, Spain and then the Dutch joining in on their side.

Resources apparently provided a clear explanation for Northern success in the Civil War. The North had far more people, agricultural production, mineral wealth, industrial strength and transport infrastructure than the South. These disparities were exploited by financial and economic mobilisation, as with the purchase of government bonds and the creation of US Military Railroads as a branch of the War Department. There was also an accentuation of the contrast due to the economic and financial dislocation in the South stemming from the increasingly effective Northern blockade, as well as the systemic weakness of a Southern central government saddled with the incubus of 'states' rights'. Thus, the very cause of the rebellion helped lessen its chance of success.

This imbalance in resources had direct military consequences. Northern resources made it easier to equip the large number of troops raised, as well as a significant navy. Thus, nearly 1.5 million Springfield rifles were manufactured, a total that reflected the capability of contemporary industry, and one which the South could not match. Moreover, supply factors played a role in particular campaigns, with Robert E. Lee and the Army of Northern Virginia invading the North in 1862 and 1863, in order to gain supplies, to secure Virginia's grain from Northern attack, and to capture the Pennsylvania coalfield.

Resources were obviously an important part of the equation, but it is misleading to push them to the fore at the expense of other elements, for there was a fundamental asymmetry in goals. The South only had to preserve the independence it had claimed, while the North had to conquer the South: it was necessary for Northern forces to capture Southern cities such as Atlanta, Charleston and Richmond, but not vice versa. At the same time, as for the Americans in the War of Independence, the Southerners could not stop the North persisting in the struggle. Instead, by continuing to resist, a situation dramatised by moving north in 1862, 1863 and 1864, they had to force the North to rethink its goals. This approach to war, one that does not assume the need for complete victory, was, and remains, more common than is often appreciated.

The position of the South was eased by the continuation of constitutional government in the North during the war, and by the extent to which the opposition there, the Democratic Party, did not support President Abraham Lincoln. This was especially so from 1862 and more particularly 1863, with Lincoln abandoning conciliation towards the South and, instead, pursuing the end of slavery. Thus, for the South, campaigning that might help the Democratic Party to success in the 1862 mid-term elections or, more plausible, the 1864 presidential one, was a sensible war-goal. Indeed, Lincoln feared defeat in the latter, while his victory in it was followed six months later by the end of the war. To Lincoln, the course of the conflict was important to his electoral success, just as, in far less difficult circumstances, it helped President Franklin D. Roosevelt in World War Two with the presidential election of 1944. Resources therefore did not dictate the outcome of the struggle, and Southern strategy was not without point even if it failed to trigger supportive intervention by Britain and France as had appeared possible in 1862.

The Civil War involved not only the North having to defeat Southern armies in the field, notably successfully ending Lee's invasion at the Battle of Gettysburg in 1863, but also considering how best to end Southern resistance. Political leadership and generalship both played a role, as did crippling morale through inflicting collective punishments. The North became committed from 1863 to the emancipation of the slaves in those parts of the South still in rebellion, a measure seen as a way to weaken the Southern economy and thus war effort, as well as providing a clear purpose to maintain Northern morale, and a means both to assuage the sin that was leading a wrathful God to punish America and to make America new. The 1865 song 'Marching Through Georgia' proclaimed:

> So we made a thoroughfare for freedom her train,
> Sixty miles in latitude, three hundred to the main;
> Treason fled before us, for resistance was in vain
> While we were marching through Georgia.

The previous year, General William T. Sherman, to whose army the song referred, having captured Atlanta, had the civilian population moved out and destroyed much of the city. Rather like Allied bombing of Germany and Japan in World War Two, his devastation of the Confederate hinterland in Georgia and South Carolina in 1864–5 increased the resolve of some Southern soldiers, but helped destroy Southern civilian faith in the war, and made the penalty for, and limitation of, guerrilla warfare apparent. By making territory his objective, Sherman moved beyond the unproductive nature that that goal and method frequently entailed, instead using its occupation to fulfil his aim of psychological mastery.

This was one of the major ways in which the South was hit by the uncertainty of war. So also with General Ulysses S. Grant, the commander of the main Union army in 1864–5, who mounted frequent attacks in Virginia, providing a tempo of operations that applied pressure and, as with Sherman, forced the South to experience risk in a highly damaging fashion, as well as leading to the eventual capture of Richmond, the Southern capital.

The South had not turned to radical solutions, such as utilising slave soldiers (which many slave societies did) nor, more plausibly, turning to guerrilla warfare, as Jefferson Davis, the Southern president, recommended. Such warfare was antipathetic to the generals' understanding of military and social order. As a consequence, the most bitter episode in American history came to a more abrupt end than might have been anticipated.

However, as an indication of the complex nature of war, Southern opposition switched in 1865 to widespread resistance to Reconstruction, the attempt to push through radical Union goals, notably rights for African Americans. Armed Southern whites, organised in bodies such as the Ku Klux Klan, used violent intimidation, in particular attacking militias supporting Reconstruction. Moreover, the remaining federal troops in the South were withdrawn in 1877, so that the Southern whites, having lost the struggle for independence, preserved their tarnished 'rights'.

Located in very different political contexts, insurgencies tested military systems in different ways. There was the urban street fighting seen in Paris in 1830, 1848 and 1871, the first two successful in overthrowing successive regimes, but not the third. Urban street fighting in Brussels in 1830 led to the overthrow of Dutch rule. This was not the same as the repression of Bosnian insurgent opposition by the Austrian occupiers in 1878. From the perspective of the present day, such episodes appear more significant than the interstate warfare of the period that dominated attention until the end of the Cold War, which is part of the pattern in which later conflicts appeared prefigured by what was under consideration.

The prime ideologies at stake in Western warfare in 1816–1913 were nationalism and sectional division, the latter variously proto-nationalist, as in Poland and Hungary, social-class, and sectarian-political. Rivalry between liberals and conservatives was crucial to civil wars in Italy, Spain, Portugal and Latin America. In practical terms, many conflicts, once begun, acquired a military and political dynamic of their own. As more generally, morale, experience, surprise, terrain and numbers were crucial in battle, while strategy, morale and generalship were shot through with political considerations.

These constants were more significant than the changes in weaponry towards more firearms with greater lethality, range and rate of fire, or the development of General Staff systems based on a Prussia/German model, although those factors helped to affect the move towards less dense battle formations and the planning for future conflict respectively. It is possible to emphasise technology, as with the successful French intervention against Austria in Italy in 1859. Rail transported French troops to Mediterranean ports from which they could move by steamship to Italy. In the battles of Magenta and Solferino, the new French rifled cannon destroyed their Austrian smooth-bore counterparts. But, in practice, as with most battles, there was no such clarity. The Austrian infantry had technically advanced rifles, but had not been adequately trained in range-finding and sighting and, as a result, the French were able to close and use their bayonets. On both sides, there was a lack of adequate planning and of coherence in command. Tactics as a result were piecemeal and the battles became attritional. For the cost involved, more success was achieved by Giuseppe Garibaldi who, with a small force, overthrew the Neapolitan Bourbons in Sicily and southern Italy in 1860 in a rapid campaign that benefited from a degree of popular support, including urban uprisings.

The tendency to consider the period in terms of the imminent world war is understandable but unhelpful, as such a sustained and wide-ranging conflict did not seem possible until shortly before it began in 1914. Instead, conflicts within Europe were generally short, as with the mid-century wars of German and Italian unification, and the Balkan wars of 1912–13, wars that did not have the wider implications of the struggle that broke out in the Balkans in 1914, as Austria sought to reduce Serbia to control. Politics was crucial, as foreign intervention by one power, for example France in Spain in 1823 in support of the conservative king, and France in Italy in support of Piedmont against Austria in 1859, did not lead to a wider conflict. With alliance systems coming into play, the situation was to be totally different in 1914.

CHAPTER 29

Nineteenth-century Imperialism

Village fighting ... desperate ... we took two sepoy prisoners
the other day and they were blown away from the guns: the
stink of fresh flesh was sickening in the extreme, but I have
seen so many disgusting sights and so much bloodshed that
I have grown quite callous.
  Lieutenant Hugh Pearson, British army, Indian Mutiny, 1857

The near-complete swallowing of Africa by European powers was
an 'achievement' in this period, and a similar process was seen in
South and South-East Asia and Oceania. This provides us with an
opportunity to consider both how imperialism operated and why
it succeeded. Fighting played a key role in the conquests, but other
significant elements included the adaptation by local people to
the arrival of new rulers. Indeed, co-operation was an important
theme in conquest, one very much the case with the major role of
locally raised forces in imperial armies, a process seen back into
antiquity, as with the Roman empire.

In the nineteenth century, the ambition and capability of European states for imperial expansion in Africa and sub-Siberian Asia increased. This shift was emulated by states that Europeanised at least their armed forces, notably Egypt and Japan. Long-standing imperial powers greatly increased the intensity of their territorial ambitions.

Indeed, while much of the warfare of this period arose from the worldwide expansion of European power, it would be misleading to suggest that the sole expanding powers were European or that most of the warfare of the period involved Europeans. Prior to the 1840s, the European impact on much of Asia was limited, and this was also the case in much of Africa before the 1880s. In fact, the list of expanding powers in the nineteenth century included, in Africa, Egypt, Lunda, Abyssinia, Sudan under the Mahdi, and the Zulus, as well as a series of personal empires in West Africa, notably that of Samori Touré (*c.* 1830–1900), the 'Napoleon of the Sudan', a term employed by Europeans in order to win glory from his eventual failure. Touré, a Guinean Muslim cleric, created, in 1878, the Wassoulou empire in West Africa, resisting the French from 1882 until his capture by them in 1898.

The context and character of such expansion varied greatly. For example, the jihad launched by Usman dan Fodio in West Africa in 1804 was directed against other Africans, especially the – in his eyes – insufficiently rigorous Islam of Hausaland. The result was the creation of the Sokoto Caliphate. In contrast, for a short while, Mehmet Ali of Egypt (r. 1805–49) must have been one of the most successful conquerors of the century. He was motivated by a drive to create a powerful 'modern' state and a new dynasty. Egyptian power was extended into Arabia, Sudan, Israel and Syria. In turn, Egypt was defeated by Britain in Syria and by the jihadist Mahdi in Sudan. In Asia, China was still able to intervene effectively in Nepal in 1792, and the list of expanding states there would include Burma, Punjab under the Sikhs, Siam (Thailand) and Japan.

Any emphasis on adaptation by, and to, local people means that the many wars of imperial conquest have to be put in their varied contexts. In suppressing the Indian Mutiny of 1857–9, the British benefited from the loyalty of many of their Indian regiments and from assistance by the rulers of Hyderabad, Kashmir and Nepal, so that the British outnumbered the rebels in many of the battles in 1858.

Western weaponry could be dramatic. The British naval bombardment of Alexandria in 1882, including the fire from the four 16-inch guns on HMS *Inflexible*, drove terrified, half-trained gunners from their posts on land. However, the bombardment did not do enormous damage, and it was landing parties that did the real work. It is not enough simply to refer to advantages in weaponry, important as they could be. The weaponry that helped the British conquer what are now Myanmar and Nigeria did not mean that Afghanistan fell. This is a point that is more generally pertinent.

Indeed, if technology is to the fore, then it is technologies other than weaponry that were also highly significant. Those of movement, supply and communication were particularly important, and the steamship, tin can and telegraph all changed the situation. Improvements in logistics proved of particular value when campaigning in the Tropics: the invention of canned meat, dried milk powder, evaporated milk and margarine in the 1840s to 1860s, all highly significant due to the lack of refrigeration, changed the perishability and bulk of provision, making it easier to operate for longer periods between revictualling. Margarine derived in 1869 from a competition by Napoleon III of France to find a non-rancid substitute for butter for his army.

Mechanical water distillation was also important, and helped overcome the major problem of drinking untreated local water, a problem that had led to damaging consequences for Napoleon I's army in Russia in 1812. Medical and hygiene advances were important to campaigning in the Tropics.

As far as movement was concerned, railways were vital to the protection of empire as well as for their economic value. Faced by the rebellion of the Métis (mixed-blood population) in Manitoba and Saskatchewan in 1885, the Canadian government sent over four thousand militia and their supplies west over the Canadian

Pacific Railway, achieving an overwhelming superiority that helped bring rapid victory. This display of capability was followed by a new increase in government subsidy for the railway that enabled its completion that year. Similarly, the railways the British built in India helped ensure that troops and their supplies could be moved to areas of difficulty, as in 1897 when they were sent to the North-West Frontier (of modern Pakistan) to assist in overcoming resistance among the Waziris. Railheads, notably Peshawar and Quetta, played a key part in British planning both on that frontier and with regard to power projection into Afghanistan, and, in turn, these railheads and the routes from them had to be protected; while an anxious eye was kept on the development of the Russian rail network. The construction by Russia of the Trans-Siberian Railway encouraged Halford Mackinder, the founder of the formal subject of British geopolitics, to suggest in 1904 that dominance over land routes was becoming more important than their maritime counterparts.

As a reminder of the need not simply to focus on the 'cutting edge', a simpler technology than that of railways, namely roads, remained highly significant. Usage in the nineteenth century did not yet focus on vehicles equipped with internal combustion engines, but the construction and maintenance of roads required certain techniques, such as cambering, to increase their durability and thus resistance to weather and wear and tear, while the technological element rested with the equipment used for construction and maintenance. The high explosives that helped disrupt and move large quantities of rock, as in tunnel construction, were important. Furthermore, the relevance of roads in the late nineteenth century was not a case of a residual significance in the gaps between new railways, for many new roads were built. For example, road construction was crucial in New Zealand in the 1860s, when British troops were used to extend the Great South Road from Auckland over the hills south of Drury in the face of Maori opposition. By 1874, a road had been finished between Tauranga and Napier, separating two areas of Maori dissidence. This was part of the process by which the Maori were overcome through marginalisation.

Steamships also changed power projection and logistics, as well as making inshore operations easier. Early versions suffered from slow speed, a high rate of coal consumption, and the space taken up by side and paddle wheels and coal bunkers, but steam power replaced dependence on the wind, making journey times more predictable and quicker, and increased the manoeuvrability of ships, making it easier to sound inshore and hazardous waters, and to operate during bad weather. Moreover, maritime steam technology developed rapidly, with the screw propeller (placed at the stern) increasing mobility from the 1840s. Steamships were soon used extensively by the British, for example in the Crimean War with Russia of 1854–6. The global range of British commitments fed into the development of strategic communications for political, military and economic purposes, with the resulting development of technology. This was an important aspect of logistical capability.

The necessary extension of the network of British coaling stations made possible by the global nature of Britain's empire ensured that its steam-powered armoured warships could be used in deep waters across the world. In late 1861, as war with the Union apparently neared, Britain, the leading producer in the world, sent coal to New World bases, notably Bermuda, to support a larger naval presence there. In 1898, even an incomplete list of British naval bases included Wellington, Fiji, Sydney, Melbourne, Adelaide, Albany, Cape York (Australia), Labuan (North Borneo), Singapore, Hong Kong, Weihaiwei (China), Calcutta, Bombay, Trincomalee, Colombo, the Seychelles, Mauritius, Zanzibar, Mombasa, Aden, Cape Town, St Helena, Ascension, Lagos, Malta, Gibraltar, Alexandria, Halifax, Bermuda, Jamaica, Antigua, St Lucia, Trinidad, Port Stanley in the Falkland Islands and Esquimalt (British Columbia). An unwelcome reliance on British colliers encouraged the Americans to move to oil-firing steam engines in 1913. France had the second-largest empire in the world, and its overseas naval bases included Martinique, Guadeloupe, Oran, Bizerta, Dakar, Libreville, Diego Suarez, Obok, Saigon, Kwangchowan, New Caledonia and Tahiti. Germany from the 1880s developed bases in Africa, China and the Pacific.

An approach focused on the strengths of the imperial powers can risk denying a role to their opponents. This is misleading as there were significant defeats for imperial forces and, as a result, continued independence for Afghanistan and Ethiopia, victors respectively over Britain in 1842 and Italy in 1896. Resistance could also force the imperial forces not only to adapt militarily but also to seek a degree of consensus in the eventual outcome.

Nevertheless, force was the key element, as also with the American conquest of what became the Western United States. Thus, Donald MacAlister, who served with the 'field force' sent against the Aro Confederacy in South-East Nigeria in November 1901, wrote:

> We have to break through the jungle in single file. In order to prevent flank attacks flankers are sent out who cut paths through the jungle parallel (22 November). ... Our carriers and bushmen have cleared the bush all round and everywhere trees are being felled and the ruins of the huts pulled down. ... We had the Maxim [machine gun] pouring into the bush this morning (25 December).

Firepower was certainly a major factor in many imperial wars of expansion. This was the case, for example, with the success of Britain at the expense of the Zulus in southern Africa in 1879, especially with the crucial victory of Ulundi, and over the Mahdists of Sudan in 1895–9, particularly at Omdurman in 1898. Mass attacks on British defensive forces reliant on firepower failed in both cases and in others, which was a variation on the shift already apparent within the West in the face of firepower towards the obsolescence of such attacks. Victories were more impressive when won, as in these cases, at the expense of powers that were otherwise successful against local foes, a situation also seen with American defeats of the Comanche and the Sioux.

Japan, from the Meiji Restoration of 1868, was the leader among the non-Western powers that adapted to the new weaponry. This process was also seen with Egypt, Abyssinia/Ethiopia and Turkey and, less successfully, China and Persia. Nevertheless, the social, economic and political contexts and requirements did not always make such adaptation to the parameters of new technology easy. At the same time, the concept of conservatism can be overplayed, as adaptation reflected not just value systems but also understandings of effectiveness based on priorities. Moreover, the 'agency' based on this adaptability or domestication was one that was encouraged by outside powers seeking allies and recruits.

At any rate, the erosion of Western advantage was apparent at the same time as the latter was demonstrated. In 1904, a British force reached Lhasa, the capital of Tibet, the first time a Western force had done so, but in 1905, at Tsushima, the Russian fleet was totally defeated by the Japanese. A different imperialism to that of the West was now very much in evidence.

CHAPTER 30

China from Crisis to Consolidation, 1839–1949

In a war of revolutionary character, guerrilla operations are a
necessary part. This is particularly true in a war waged for the
emancipation of a people who inhabit a vast nation ... the
development of the type of guerrilla warfare characterised
by the quality of mass is both necessary and natural. ...
We consider guerrilla operations as but one aspect of our total
or mass war. ... All the people of both sexes from the ages of
sixteen to forty-five must be organised into anti-Japanese
self-defensive units.

                                        Mao Zedong, Communist leader, 1937

A standard global military history tends to push China to the side-
lines, emphasising instead the West. Thus, more space is usually
given to the Thirty Years War (1618–48) or the English Civil Wars
(1642–51) than to the contemporaneous Manchu (Qing) conquest
of China, but the latter was larger in scale and more significant.
In addition, the warfare China faced from the Opium War with

Britain in 1839–42 to the end, in 1949, of the last Chinese civil war, was crucial, not only for its history but also more broadly that of East Asia and, indirectly, that of the world as a whole.

Moreover, the experience of that period, and its subsequent presentation in Chinese public history, help underline the current Chinese determination to prevent any recurrence through weakness. Indeed, the process by which a lesson is 'learned' through military history very much comes to the fore in this case, providing the Chinese with a narrative for their past and the Communist Party with a justification for its position.

The current Chinese emphasis is a nationalist one, on the need to be vigilant in defending the homeland from foreign threats. Indeed, much destruction was inflicted between 1839 and 1945 by Britain, France and, most especially, repeatedly and recently, Japan, especially in 1894–5 and 1931–45.

Nevertheless, it was not overseas powers that conquered China. Indeed, the last time there was a complete foreign conquest was the Manchu (Qing) takeover in the mid-seventeenth century. Moreover, that was only achieved with the help of serious division within China, and the Ming defections that caused, which greatly helped enable the Manchu to make a swifter conquest than that of the Mongols in the thirteenth century. In the event, prominent defectors, in turn, launched the Rebellion of the Three Feudatories against the Manchu in the late 1670s.

Domestic revolution repeatedly was the source of the greatest challenges in the period 1839–1949, in the end totally overthrowing the existing system in 1911–12 and 1946–9. The Taiping Revolution of 1850–64 was a sustained crisis on a great scale, with much of southern China brought under the control of the Heavenly Kingdom established by the Taipings, whose large conscript armies were willing to take heavy casualties. In contrast, the Qing armies were backed by regional militia and foreign mercenaries. This was total war in which each side inflicted devastation on the supporters of the other, slaughtering many hundreds of thousands. The revolution was eventually defeated. In contrast, the next significant uprising, the anti-foreigner and anti-Christian Boxer Rising was able to win partial government support, only to be suppressed by foreign forces in 1900–1.

The twentieth century saw the Qing government finally overthrown in 1911–12, with Wuhan the original site of revolution and southern China the centre of opposition which was spread in part by telegram. A brief civil war saw Yuan Shikai, the key general in the regime, defeat the revolutionaries in the Battle of Yangxia in late 1911, before making a deal with them and becoming the first president of the new republic. He later declared himself emperor in 1915, only in 1916 to face a series of rebellions in the south in the National Protection War, and to die of natural causes.

His career is both one of many might-have-beens and a reminder that the role of the military strongman became stronger as dynastic monarchies failed, a process also seen in Persia in the 1900s, and Hungary and Turkey in the 1920s. Military strongmen also came to the fore in Mexico in the 1910s. This situation helped ensure that control over the military was important across a range of political systems, including those dominated by army figures. Partly as a result, surveillance of the military became more important, and some states developed national guards in part as a parallel army that was designed to counterbalance the regular one.

In China, there was a collapse of central control, and provincial warlords dominated the country from 1916 to 1928. Their continual jockeying for position was a form of war as government and government as war. More seriously, it was inherently unstable and destructive, *The Times* referring on 6 September 1924 to 'the merciless kidnapping by soldiers of thousands of peaceable Chinese for transport and trench-digging in the districts about Shanghai ... a state of terror'. The instability of the warlord era was a legacy of pre-World War One change in China, a process also seen in Mexico, but this was accentuated by the subsequent failure to create a successful government. Much of the warfare of the 1920s, which was frequently very large scale, can be seen in terms of the anarchic self-interest of the warlords, and their kaleidoscope alliances as they manoeuvred for advantage and to offset movements.

The use of railways was important in the movement of troops and support.

In the event, the Guomindang, the nationalist movement established by Sun Yat-sen, was able, under Jiang Jieshi (Chiang Kai-shek), to act as a form of successful warlordism with national pretensions, overcoming most of the warlords in the Northern Expedition in 1926-8, the largest military campaign of the decade, and one in which Shanghai and Beijing were taken. However, Manchuria under its warlord remained in effect independent and, as such, a target for Japanese expansionism from 1931. In 1931-2, the Japanese overran Manchuria, which became a major source of resources for their economy and military. This success encouraged interest in further expansionism.

Jiang Jieshi created a new national government that was challenged by recalcitrant warlords, notably in 1930. More seriously, it was opposed by the Communists, former allies, with whom there was a civil war from 1927. Initially, the Communists sought to seize cities, but they failed there and, instead, came, through necessity, to focus on rural areas. This civil war was large-scale in the early 1930s, with the Communists in response to the large-scale Guomindang assault on their bases in 1934 launching the so-called 'Long March' to more remote fastnesses. In 1937, the Communist leader, Mao Zedong, published *On Guerrilla Warfare*, a pamphlet calling for a popular revolutionary struggle.

In the event, that year the full-scale war launched by the Japanese began a lengthy struggle that neither side could win. Inflicting heavy defeats, the Japanese captured Beijing, Shanghai and Nanjing (with much slaughter of civilians) in 1937, and Guangzhou and Wuhan in 1938. However, the Chinese mounted a determined defence and there was hard fighting, notably in capturing Shanghai. Moreover, the British chiefs of staff noted in December 1939 that 'Japanese authority in China is limited to certain main centres and to lines of communication, and Chinese guerrilla forces continue to take considerable toll of Japanese garrison posts'. Although the Japanese made further gains in 1942 and, in particular, 1944-5, they were unable to knock China out of the war.

The Japanese were to remain in control of much of China until the end of World War Two, indeed mounting a successful offensive in central China in 1942 and capturing even more of it in 1944–5, not least overrunning the south in order to create an overland route between Vietnam and north China and thus lessen the possible damage from American naval attack on maritime routes. Furthermore, by their advances, the Japanese sought to thwart American plans to base in China bombers with which Japan could be attacked. Japanese success obliged the Americans to rely on capturing Pacific island bases from which Japan could be bombed, which they did in the Mariana Islands in 1944.

The end of World War Two was soon followed in China by a resumption in conflict by the Communists. Assisted by the Soviet Union, whereas the Americans provided much more limited assistance to the Guomindang, the Communists outfought their opponents in the largest-scale war in the world since 1945. They benefited from numbers, Soviet equipment and good commanders, winning crucial battles in 1948–9. The Guomindang were affected by divisions but fought with more determination than some commentators allowed and their defeat was not some inevitable consequence of social conditions.

In 1949, the Guomindang position collapsed, the leaders taking refuge in Taiwan. The following year, the Communists seized Hainan and Tibet. However, plans to occupy Taiwan were thwarted by an American commitment to its defence that owed a lot to the intensification of the Cold War when China intervened in 1950 in the Korean War. War had delivered a decisive verdict in China, but Western military commitment combined with South Korean determination then prevented this extending to an additional Chinese victory. Mao Zedong's optimism about revolutionary enthusiasm defeating regular forces proved misplaced. After the Korean War ended in 1953, the Chinese did not fight again until a brief and successful war with India in 1962 and, thereafter, until they attacked Vietnam in 1979. Indeed, although border clashes with Vietnam continued until 1991, China was involved in less foreign conflict than either the Soviet Union or the United States.

CHAPTER 31

World War One

The world stands on the threshold of the 'aeronautical era.' During this epoch the destinies of all people will be controlled through the air. . . . Mountains, deserts, oceans, rivers, and forests, offer no obstacles. In a trice, aircraft have set aside all ideas of frontiers. The whole country now becomes the frontier and, in case of war, one place is just as exposed to attack as another place.

Brigadier General Billy Mitchell, the vigorous protagonist of American air power, very much saw a new potential, beginning his *Winged Defense: The Development and Possibilities of Modern Air Power* (1925).

There was a heavy bombardment on the battalion on our left, against whom they advanced in waves presenting excellent targets for cross-fire.

Lieutenant-Colonel Percy Worrall, British army, about a German attack near the Lys Canal in the Spring Offensives, 14 April 1918

The nature of pre-war Austrian and German planning scarcely accorded with the unconvincing argument that Europe somehow slid or sleepwalked into war, an approach that risks turning perpetrators into victims and, to a degree, satisfying misleading national myths of victimhood. Instead, the willingness of key figures to turn to war accelerated a breakdown of deterrence and combined with a strategic confusion at the heart of decision making, especially about risk-taking. Alongside this came the extent to which the dynamic of the crisis meant that constructive ambiguity about commitments between allies, notably Germany and Austria, was no longer possible.

While planning for a war is not simple proof of intent of causing one, pressure from the military was highly significant, and in a context in which many of the decision makers, often living in a militaristic bubble, had lost the sense of the fragility of peace and order. Moreover, there was a widespread confusion of strategic and operational factors, and notably so by short-war advocates who assumed that a successful campaign would lead to the end of the war.

In particular, the significance to Britain's entry into the war of the German violation of Belgian neutrality, a strategy-led decision taken essentially by the Germans for the operational reasons of the ease of campaigning against France, was fundamental to the nature of the war. It is untrue to say that Germany lacked a strategic framework within which to consider operational issues, but this framework was inadequately thought out, and seriously so. This British entry alone was not responsible for the failure of Germany's short-war strategy, as Britain would have been very exposed had France been driven, as in 1940, to capitulate; but it was very important to it. So also with the German inability thereafter to settle on reasonable goals that could end the war on the basis of a compromise peace.

Within Germany, there was a lack of the cross-governmental organisations necessary to provide the broader strategic formulation that settling on reasonable goals required. Wilhelm II failed to pull together military and civilian advice, while, under all of its leaders, the army's general staff treated naval power and diplomacy as superfluous and was contemptuous of civilian advice. Co-ordination with all of Germany's allies was deficient. The same flaws were to be seen in the next world war and, again, were linked to a structural problem in learning lessons. Moreover, although tactically adept, and often also so in operational terms, German commanders lacked the knowledge and training appropriate to engage with the range of necessary strategic tasks.

That they proved better in operational terms than their Austrian and Russian counterparts did not make up for the last flaw. The Austrian inability to cope was shown in 1914, against Russia and even Serbia. Poorly equipped, mobilised and commanded, the Austrian forces were deployed with inadequate concern for the seriousness of the strategic situation facing Austria and showed a more general failure to learn from experience. The decision for offensives against both Russia and Serbia was exacerbated by a reliance on frontal tactics. Moreover, Austrian command went on proving inadequate. In 1914, even the German army failed to coordinate the moves on their left flank in France with their overall actions and demonstrated serious operational incoherence on the right flank. And their army had problems with equipment, logistics and discipline.

German strategic planning, strongly influenced by their rapid victories in the 1864–71 wars of German unification, aimed at achieving a rapid collapse of the enemy by a massive sudden blow, but took no account of what would happen if this failed. In 1914, in part over-impressed by the size of the Russian army, the Germans saw the greatest threat as coming from Russia, and underrated the long-term challenge from Britain. In 1945, fears of Russia, in the shape of the Soviet Union, were to be vindicated, but, in 1914, the mishandled Russian offensive lacked the capacity for rapid development, in part due to logistical drawbacks arising from transport difficulties, notably poor roads.

These were also to be factors when the Germans in turn attacked on the Eastern Front, the centre of their offensive concerns in 1915, but so also was the determination of the Russian defensive. It is useful to look for parallels in World War Two. Thus, Russian defence increasingly has been argued to be a key factor in thwarting the German attacks in 1941, 1942 and 1943. Moreover, that element requires more attention for the earlier war as it helps explain why the Germans did not succeed on the Eastern Front until 1917–18. In contrast, Serbia was conquered in 1915, while Romania, which was in a more vulnerable situation than Russia, was largely defeated in 1916 by attacking forces that combined speed and manoeuvre, unbalancing the Romanians who failed to respond to the dynamism of the attack. An earlier success against Russia, comparable to that, on a very different geographical scale, against France in 1940, would have put the Western Allies in a very difficult situation, which indeed helps explain the pressure in Britain and France for attacks to draw off German resources from the war with Russia. In practice, though attempted each year, coordinated Allied offensives proved difficult, although, in late 1918, simultaneous pressure by the Western Allies on the four Central Powers helped greatly in the sense of crisis that was significant to their giving up the conflict.

In contrast to the siege-like confrontation on the Western Front, the experience of fighting was different in the East, with greater mobility and less artillery support. That contrast posed specific tactical and operational issues, and these help undermine the tendency to think in terms of a common experience of the conflict. So also with the scholarly analysis of trench warfare on the Western Front, which presents an account very different from that of an essentially unitary system, although the latter remains the popular view. Thus, as part of a rapid German learning process, in place of a simple linear defence came first one of several lines of trenches, and then a zonal one, with the German *Siegfriedstellung* (to the British the Hindenburg Line) offering mutually supporting concrete bunkers surrounded by obstacle belts, and thus providing a defence in depth.

On the Western Front, defensive systems developed in an interaction with those of the attack. The evolution of artillery tactics of creeping barrage and deep bombardment had made linear defensive lines more vulnerable during late 1916, and this led to the new defensive system. The German frontline became a series of lightly manned outposts, and the British were moving in this direction in 1918. Combatants, moreover, had to get used to new experiences of conflict, with new sensations.

The British situation was somewhat different, but there were serious problems with the strategic planning, not least the degree to which the government lost control of the military strategy with there being a lack of higher defence mechanisms in which strategic options could be seriously debated. Related to this, the relationships between ways and means were unprobed, as were the consequences of the military commitments to France and Belgium. In numbers, Britain lacked the army to match its commitments and, once the numbers were gained, notably in 1916, the army did not have the necessary training or sufficient appropriate equipment until 1917. British strategy was to a degree 'captured' by France in the sense of the political and military requirements of alliance with France.

World War One was always understood as a world war, and one with global consequences. Yet, the war was far more focused on Europe than its sequel, both as far as conflict on land was concerned and also with regard to the war at sea and, even more, in the air. Conflict between aircraft began in World War One, although air power remained largely tactical, not strategic.

In the case of the war on land, at sea and in the air, there has been a greater understanding by scholars of the extent to which interactive learning processes occurred, not least in the development both of trench systems and of attack techniques, including the more effective use of artillery. This use benefited from the greater provision of information, one that stemmed in large part from aerial photography. This was an aspect of the application of knowledge that was so important to the course of the conflict, and one that ensured that the war ended with very different fighting techniques to that of its start, so that, by late 1917, gunners could calibrate their guns for every shot and, in doing so, take account of air temperature, barrel wear and propellant power. This process did not so much need new technology, but new devices were invented to help, ensuring that what had not been feasible in 1914 was now practical, and readily so. Wind speed and air temperature were given to artillery several times daily on the Western Front. Information was integrated and rapidly transmitted in a process that responded to the greater complexity of war and the more sophisticated understanding of capability, ensuring more accurate and appropriate bombardment, not least in coordination with the infantry. And so also with a range of weapons and practices, for example the production and use of maps.

The weakness of the Germans at the strategic and operational levels, demonstrated in the offensives on the Western Front in 1914 and 1916, were seen again in 1918. Pressure was poorly applied and rested on misjudged assumptions about the vulnerability of the Allies' political will to events at the front and concerning the fighting determination of the Allies. In part, the German lack of strategic realism, notably about political implications, and of the ability to create 'the bridge' between tactics and operations on the one hand, and the 'political wish-list' on the other, rested on the understanding that Germany's comparative advantage lay at the tactical level, and not the strategic, with tactical success unable to create a winning strategy.

Eventually, on all the surviving fronts in 1918 (the Eastern Front had ended with Russia's collapse and surrender), the Allies, despite the strain of continued casualties, brought to fruition earlier developments in their armies. They had gathered the resources and developed the mechanisms necessary to sustain their advance and offensive in the face of continued opposition. In this way, the Allies acquired the operational dynamic that gave effect to their strategy, and were able to deliver decisive military blows. These reflected Allied improvements in fighting as well as in resource utilisation, but also serious deficiencies in German fighting methods and notably so at the operational level. In contrast, helped by a new unity of command, the Allies proved more effective operationally and thereby helped make 1918 the tipping point. There was also a more systematic approach to conflict, one seen moreover in the next world war. Seeking to raise the effectiveness of the army as a whole, rather than to focus on élite units, British improvements and adaptability outweighed those of the Germans, and this brought great benefits in the more fluid closing stage of the war. The Americans, who entered the war on the Allied side in 1917, had a sharper learning curve and this helped ensure heavy casualties for them in 1918, although they still played an important part in Allied operations.

The decisive blows were not measured so much in territory occupied, but rather in the pressure of defeat that affected all the Central Powers. In particular, aside from its own serious failure, the German military leadership had also been greatly influenced by Bulgaria's decision to seek an armistice, which threatened, through putting pressure on Austria and Turkey, the unravelling of the alliance, and by the Austrian collapse, which opened the way for an Italian advance into Bavaria. This proved a classic instance of the placing of operational success in terms of the centrality of strategy, and of the related evaluation of the value of particular territories.

The German defeats in 1918 had not dictated the end of the war, and indeed the Allies were planning on its continuation into 1919. Nevertheless, the Central Powers had failed, and their individual strategies had all become redundant, both militarily and politically. Strategic capability, on land, at sea and in economic terms, had been shown by the ability of the more politically adept Allies to attract more states to their side from 1915, and in the skill in integrating and deploying greater resources than their opponents.

CHAPTER 32

The Interwar Years

ASSESSING THE THREAT

In hindsight, the period 1919–38 appears dominated by thinking through the lessons of the traumatic experience of World War One and in preparing for the next world war. Much discussion today of this period focuses on the development of new weapons systems, notably aircraft, tanks, aircraft carriers and submarines, and on the ideas involved, notably those of commentators such as J.F.C. Fuller and Basil Liddell Hart for tanks and Giulio Douhet for aircraft. A key theme in military speculation was certainly that of the potential of aircraft to provide a totally different source of military decisiveness.

In practice, however, there was not in these years the degree of change that some had anticipated or that fascinates later writers, in part because the conflicts of this period, notably the civil wars in Russia, China and Spain, were very different to World War One. Indeed, Major-General Sir Percy Rawcliffe, in his report on the Franco-British Mission in 1920 to Poland, then at war with Russia, observed:

The tide of battle has surged backwards and forwards more in response to psychological and emotional factors than to the results of hard blows on either side, and the possibilities of manoeuvre have once more reached a pitch of development that has not been seen in Europe since the days of Napoleon. Coming so quickly on the heels of the long stagnation, which was the feature of the war on the Western Front, the antithesis is all the more striking.

The last point underlines the extent to which technology did not dictate a particular outcome. He continued by arguing that the lower density of troops compared to the Western Front was crucial, as it ensured that defenders and attackers lacked cohesion, depth and reserves.

Much of the subsequent discussion on the military in this period focuses on the question of whether the correct responses were made to the possibilities of new technology, notably in the shape of aircraft and tanks. This question looks towards the issue of the German and Japanese offensives in 1939–42 and, notably, the problem of the ability to adapt to the possibilities of blitzkrieg, the German application of mechanisation in order to ensure rapid advances. This approach is valuable. However, it should be regarded as linked to, and in practice subordinate to, the very tasking of the military. This was notably a consequence of the perception of who were the likely opponents. In the 1920s, and into the early 1930s, there was no apparent need to assume that such a large-scale conflict would occur. Therefore, technology and politics need to be reconciled in our consideration, with strategy presented as the active response to the geopolitical challenges that were faced, and strategic planning therefore a key context for procurement, training and deployment.

An indicative, and far from exhaustive, list of specific concerns and tasks is useful in highlighting the issue. Britain was the leading world empire and its military tasks in 1919–21 included occupation responsibilities, notably in Germany but also in Turkey, wide-ranging participation in the Russian Civil War, conflict with Afghanistan, instability in the Punjab, rebellion in Ireland, Iraq and Egypt, war in British Somaliland and challenges to interests in Iran.

1922–30 again saw a range of issues, including concern about the possibility of war with Turkey over, first, Constantinople and the Dardanelles and, subsequently, its border with Iraq, as well as instability in the Arabian peninsula, and attacks on interests in China. In 1931–8, Japanese, Italian and German expansionism were all serious problems, but there were also rebellions or disturbances in the empire, notably on the North-West Frontier of India and in Palestine (the Arab Rising), but also in Jamaica, Malta and Myanmar.

This incomplete list leaves out the possibility that tensions or disputes with other major powers, notably France and the United States, might lead to conflict. With hindsight, and notably in light of the developing challenges in the 1930s, these scenarios might appear implausible, but they led not only to speculation but also to planning, notably to American plans for war with Britain, including the invasion of Canada.

The variety of these challenges helps explain why it was so difficult to determine strategy, and therefore the relevant geography of a likely conflict. Military historians considering this period are apt to underplay the challenge of rebellion and to focus on symmetrical conflict between the conventional forces of independent states, but that was not a certainty as far as planners were concerned. Instead, they had to consider the hypotheticals of future conflict in such circumstances against the more pressing immediate issues of security within the empire. These latter issues were enhanced because of the extent to which the army was responsible for what in effect was civil policing.

Moreover, the reliance of the imperial system on native troops, notably in South Asia, underlined the need to emphasise the security of relevant areas. The same was not the case for the navy, and this point underlines the very different strategic dimensions of the particular branches of the military.

The concerns of imperial defence when faced by 'native' opposition helped explain the reluctance of some generals to engage with what they saw as the hypotheticals of developing tank forces for conflict in Europe. An appreciation of the operational possibilities of the tank was seen within the army by practical modernisers, but they had to be more aware of financial restrictions than the publicists criticising from outside, notably Basil Liddell Hart.

Imperial defence, moreover, encouraged an emphasis on air power as the best means to deter or fight Germany. This was a reflection of confidence about the damage that could be done by bombing and of the most worrying aspect of German power, the potential strength of the Luftwaffe, its air force. German air attack could not be deterred by France's border-ward defences, notably the Maginot Line. Hitler came to power in 1933 and pledged to overthrow the 1919 Versailles settlement. Given the later situation, this might appear clearly to have been the foremost threat to the international order and British interests; but Germany only turned to war in 1939, whereas Japan did so in 1931 and Italy in 1935. Each of these challenged British interests and Britain's ideas of international order and relations, and threatened to lead to further problems. Indeed, Japan launched a full-scale invasion of China in 1937 while Italy encouraged Arab opposition to British control.

Strategic uncertainty therefore surrounded the prioritisation of the challenge posed by these three powers, and the resulting geography of prioritisation. This uncertainty was enhanced by a lack of clarity as to how these powers would respond to negotiations and/ or pressure, by uncertainty over alliances, and by the presence of other threats, notably the Soviet Union. Thus, rearmament was affected not only by limitations in industrial capacity and capability, and by financial problems, but also by a lack of certainty over tasking and appropriate force structure. Clarity over allies and enemies was necessary in order to produce effective strategic plans.

If Japan was the leading challenge to Britain, then the principal response would be naval, specifically the development of a powerful naval base in Singapore such that it could be used to defend the British empire in South-East Asia, Australasia and India from Japanese attack, while also serving for force-projection to East Asian waters. This naval policy had many aspects and variants, including a network of bases to support the movement of warships and aircraft, co-operation with Australia, New Zealand and Canada against Japan, and alliance with the United States.

Italy posed a similar, but different, set of priorities. The much expanded Italian navy represented a major threat to the British in the Mediterranean and, with that, to the British route to the Indian Ocean via the Suez Canal. At the same time, war over the Abyssinia Crisis in 1935–6 would also have involved both army and air force, as, indeed, war with Italy was to do from 1940. The army would need to defend Egypt, Sudan, British Somaliland and Kenya from invasion from the neighbouring Italian colonies of Libya, Eritrea and Italian Somaliland, while the air force would help protect the colonies, including Malta, and would also be used to bomb Italy.

Germany also posed a naval challenge, but the German navy appeared weaker as a strategic challenge than those of Japan and Italy because, until the conquest of Denmark, Norway and France in 1940, Germany lacked significant naval room for manoeuvre or access to the North Atlantic. Nevertheless, despite its strength as the world's foremost naval power, Britain did not have a navy capable of fighting Germany, Italy and Japan simultaneously. That was the product of the stop on capital ship construction under the Washington Naval Treaty of 1921–2, as well as the lack of sufficient British industrial capability and fiscal strength; to which was added the increased strength of these three powers. However, to expect the arithmetic of naval power to provide for conflict at once with all three states was to anticipate a margin of superiority that was unreasonable given the state of the country and the fact that the potential enemies were well apart geographically, but also one that diplomacy sought to avoid the need for.

Allowing for the significance and consequences of serious rivalries between the views of the key ministries, the Treasury, Foreign Office and Admiralty, British naval strategy planned that, if necessary, operations against threats arising simultaneously would be conducted sequentially in separate theatres. This strategy assumed that operational flexibility could help lessen the constraints posed by tough fiscal limits. In addition, war, it was hoped with reason, was likely to bring Britain the support of allies, notably France against Germany and Italy, and the United States against Japan, which, indeed, was to be the case.

The German Luftwaffe was a much greater threat to Britain itself than the Italian, Japanese and, indeed, Soviet air forces. As a result, the strategic need for air defence was dependent on the prospect of war with Germany. To that end, whereas aircraft could be moved, radar stations were fixed facilities. Thus, the defence of Britain, as opposed to that of particular imperial interests, however crucial, involved very different means as well as ends.

The challenge from Germany was also linked to views about the European order and Britain's relationship to it. Italy might be a threat to Albania (1939), and try to be one to Greece (1940) but, alone, was not likely to prevail against France and, indeed, did not seek to do so. Instead, it was Germany that posed the major threat to other states in Western Europe, and Germany and the Soviet Union in Eastern Europe. The question of whether Britain should send troops to the Continent to counter such a threat was a difficult one, not least because there was no peacetime conscription, while the Indian army was not to be deployed in Western Europe. With Belgium, the Netherlands, Denmark and Norway resolved to remain neutral, the sole room for manoeuvre would be France and the strategic option of the build-up of a large army in Britain to send to France was not an encouraging one in light of the range of British commitments and the experience of World War One.

Thus, speculations about the next war related practically not only to the issue of what weapons systems could achieve, in absolute and relative terms, but what they would be expected to achieve in light of specific tasks. The hypotheticals interacted in an extraordinarily dynamic situation. With the benefit of hindsight, it is possible to point to serious flaws in the decisions taken by British policymakers, but it is also worth underlining the difficulties of assessing links between challenges and commitments, as well as the problems of prioritisation. This is instructive because it prepared the way for the position today, and the multiple uncertainties for Western (and other) powers. Much of the value of history rests in its capacity to help us understand issues in the modern world. In this case, the latter also assists greatly in an appreciation of the issues of the past.

CHAPTER 33

World War Two

> Bombing on a vast scale is the weapon upon which we
> principally depend for the destruction of German economic
> life and morale ... we believe that by these methods applied
> on a vast scale the whole structure on which the German
> forces are based can be destroyed. As a result these forces will
> suffer such a decline in fighting power and mobility that
> direct [British] action will once more become possible.
>
> British strategic review, 16 August 1941

A war supposedly settled by Allied superiority in resources, World
War Two provides the opportunity to discuss that factor in military
history. A world war on an unprecedented scale, this struggle
was the basis for the post-war order/disorder, but set a model
of warfare that has not yet been repeated, whether in specifics,
notably the use of the atom bomb, areas in conflict, or the size of
the armed forces. Indeed, from the perspective of the 2020s, it is the
atypicality of the world war that is most striking and, linked to that,

the extent to which it established a misleading pattern for the consideration of war.

Thus, in the decades after the war it was insurrectionary struggle that was to the fore, whereas, although the resistance to German and Japanese occupations had played a role, notably in China, this had not been crucial during World War Two. It had been fought by large militaries manned by conscripts but, by the 2020s, the pattern was very much one of smaller militaries manned by professional volunteers. In addition, the mobilisation of all of the resources of society seen in World War Two was not the case subsequently for major powers engaged in conflict and those wars, such as the commitments in Vietnam and Afghanistan for the United States and the Soviet Union respectively, were clearly wars of choice and not of necessity.

The war is close enough for us to have from it very many individual voices, both military and civilian, and there is also extensive film footage and photographic and sound records. This closeness of memorialisation and very tactile quality has its advantages. Thus, a member of the British force that intervened in Greece in 1944 in a struggle between resistance organisations, one of the large number of struggles that fitted under the umbrella title of the world war, recorded the difference between this and the more conventional operations of the war:

> The enemy was just the same as any other Greeks as far as we knew, they didn't have any uniform as such. ... It was a situation that was quite completely different to the way we had been used to fighting. ... As an average infantryman, one of the first questions that you ask is 'Which way is the front?' so that you know if the worst comes to the worst which way you can go to get out of the bloody place. In this sort of situation, which is a typical urban 'battlefront', it's all around you.

At the same time, general impressions, however fortified by film footage from the period, can be highly misleading, as with the disproportionate focus on the German blitzkrieg attacks of 1939–41, attacks that failed to overcome the Soviet Union in 1941.

Explanations of Allied victory in the war have tended to adopt the explanation of the defeated, namely that they were out-resourced, and notably so both due to the strength and reach of the world's leading economy, the United States, and because this was the first oil war, with oil crucial to weapons systems on land, sea and in the air, and with the Allies dominating oil reserves.

These factors were certainly apparent, and massive resources were required to sustain war against both Germany and Japan. The size of the invasion fleet that attacked Normandy on 6 June 1944, D-Day, was made more impressive by the Allied deployment that summer of other invasion fleets in the Mediterranean and the Pacific. So also with air power. The formidable Anglo-American Combined Bomber Offensive on Germany inflicted very serious damage on its war economy and obliged the Luftwaffe to focus on home defence, rather than supporting the army. At the same time, the Americans mounted a major air offensive on Japan from 1944.

Yet, resources alone cannot explain the outcome of war. In particular, the counterpart to an emphasis on Allied resources is usually accompanied by a stress on Axis fighting qualities and notably so of Germany. This is a mistaken perspective for a number of reasons.

First, the idea of an aggregate national fighting quality is mistaken. Units in all armies vary in their characteristics; and that variation is sharpened by the extent to which opponents and tasks vary greatly, and notably so for Britain and the United States.

Second, the Germans are generally praised for the success of their blitzkrieg (lightning war) methods in 1939–41, in particular the defeat of France in 1940 that had eluded them in World War One. However, blitzkrieg was never an official German term but rather a description of adding an armoured and air power lead component to very traditional German approaches to war. In prac-tice, the ad hoc nature of blitzkrieg helps put supposed German operational brilliance in 1939–41 in its proper context, as does the extent to which it arose from sequential war-making and one-front campaigning. Moreover, much of the German army in 1939 was heavily reliant on railways and draught animals.

The potential of weaponry and logistics based on the internal combustion engine, notably in powering tanks, was less fully grasped than talk of blitzkrieg might suggest, not least because, despite the popular view that the German army was largely mechanised, much of the German army was unmechanised, heavily dependent on horse-drawn supplies, and walked into battle. *Panzergrenadiers* (mechanised infantry) were only a minority of the German infantry. The absence of adequate mechanisation, at nearly all levels, reduced the effectiveness and range of German advances; although, even had there been more vehicles, there were the issues both of their maintenance and, more seriously, the availability of oil. In light of the latter factor, the question of 'fitness for purpose' occurs anew. In addition, the successful German invasions of Poland (1939), France (1941), Yugoslavia (1941) and Greece (1941) owed much in practice to the poor response of opponents, notably the location and use of reserves.

Third, there are different levels of war, most usually the tactical, operational and strategic, and it is possible to do better at one than another. Thus, there is a widespread perception that in this conflict the German military was better at the tactical than the strategic level. This, indeed, was particularly so with reference to the German attack on the Soviet Union in 1941. German assessments drew on the flaws revealed in the Soviet invasion of eastern Poland in 1939 and, even more, in the initial stages of the Soviet attack on Finland in 1939–40, the 'Winter War', as well as on assumptions based on the effect of Stalin's extensive purges of the military leadership from 1937 to 1941, purges themselves fed by the German provision of forged information. These assessments failed adequately to note the success of the Red Army in the last (successful) stage of the 'Winter War', as well as subsequent improvements, while, anyway, for the Soviet Union as for other powers, there was a major contrast between weaknesses on the offensive and capabilities in defence. Furthermore, Russian military defeat and total political collapse in World War One in 1917 encouraged the Germans to feel that victory could again be had. Letters indicate that many German troops were confident that the war would be speedily over. Nevertheless, despite their misjudgement of the Red Army, appreciable casualties were antici-pated by the Germans, who deployed as many troops as they could.

The Germans, however, did not understand the Soviet ability to compensate for casualties and lost equipment, and notably the potential of the Soviet economy, especially in tank production. They also planned to overrun production facilities fast, thus making them unimportant. Most German generals were confident that they had developed a military system able to defeat the Soviet Union, and did not appreciate Soviet geography, including the impact of the weather on the roads.

There is also the question of the German and Japanese ways of war, and whether national cultures of war-making, with their emphasis on short wars characterised by offensive operations designed to lead to total victory, encouraged the resort to war and, indeed, helped cause German and Japanese failure. The political cultures of individual states were bound up with these distinctive goals and types of war-making.

Fourth, Allied fighting quality improved with time, and against both Germany and Japan. Having been taken by surprise and outfought by the Japanese in the winter of 1941–2, the Americans, Australians and British all learned to fight effectively in the envi-ronments in question. The Americans did so to devastating effect in the Pacific War, which had begun with a Japanese air attack on the American naval anchorage at Pearl Harbor on Hawaii, and continued with very far-flung Japanese gains within six months, including the modern states of Malaysia, the Philippines, Indonesia and Myanmar. After the cumulative total defeat of the Japanese fleet, notably at Midway (1942) and Leyte Gulf (1944), the war ended with the Americans preparing an invasion of Japan itself. Air power had proved particularly effective against warships, the Americans using carriers to overcome some of the challenges of the Pacific War, a naval war fought across unprecedented distances.

The Soviets, who had lost large numbers of men in 1941, were able to impose major defeats on the Germans from late 1942 and to destroy the major portion of the German army. In particular, the Soviets implemented pre-war ideas of 'deep battle' in order to be able to provide a sustained operational capability that came to fruition in 1944–5, against first Germany and then Japan. These tactical and operational improvements then exploited the many failures of Axis strategy, notably the lack of effective coordination and the absence of viable war goals. The relative availability of resources for both sides should be set in this context.

The failure of the powers that launched each world war to translate their initial victories into lasting political or military success helped to give an attritional character to each struggle, and at the strategic level of the conflict as a whole, as well as in the nature of the fighting on individual fronts. In World War Two, Allied attacks simultaneously on Germany from a number of directions proved more successful than in the previous world war, and the cumulative pressure was intense. This owed most to the total failure of Hitler's strategy bound up in the attack on his one-time Soviet ally. Having sought to impose sequential warfare and prioritisation on other powers, Hitler had simultaneous warfare and total commitment imposed on Germany, with a multi-front war. He talked the language of total commitment, but could not win the resulting war. German fighting quality could not match that of opponents who also benefited from superiority in resources.

This was to be matched for Japan in 1945 with Soviet entry into the war that August, helping lead to Japan's surrender. However, that surrender owed more to the American use of atomic bombs on Hiroshima and Nagasaki, a potent demonstration of hitherto unprecedented lethality. That ensured that the Americans did not need to mount the large-scale invasion they had been planning.

The war subsequently set the parameters for much popular understanding of the nature of conflict, and notably so in America, for which it was the cradle of its subsequent global primacy. The war also encouraged the post-war maintenance both of conscription and of military–industrial systems. However, by its very nature, the war proved highly atypical, notably because the Cold War did not become a full-scale conflict.

CHAPTER 34

The Cold War

> Today your government and its military advisors appear to
> have accepted the concept that the way to defeat Communism
> in Vietnam is by bombing when clearly the precepts garnered
> from World War Two should have told them that ideas cannot
> be dislodged by bombs.
>
> Major-General John 'Boney' Fuller, British thinker,
> to an American correspondent, 1965

Rockets, their tips ominously pointing skywards, ready to deliver
nuclear or thermonuclear cataclysm, presided over the imagination
of contemporaries during the Cold War, the confrontation between
the United States and the Soviet Union that dominated international relations for the forty-five years following World War Two.
Leaders, such as the Chinese dictator from 1949 to 1976, Mao
Zedong, speculated about losses in hundreds of millions dead in
the event of war with the United States. Fiction frequently returned
to the possibility of such a war.

Yet, Hiroshima and Nagasaki in 1945 were the only cities to be pulverised by such bombs, and the far more powerful devices available from the 1950s, notably hydrogen bombs, were not used in attack. That was not for want of crises in which war came close, notably in 1962 (the Cuban Missile Crisis) and 1983. However, the Soviet ability to end the American monopoly of such weapons helped make deterrence more serious (and dangerous) from 1949. There was a tension between a possible stalemate borne of Mutually Assured Destruction (MAD) and innovations in weapons delivery and planned usage.

Thus, subsequent attacks were designed to deter rivals from a first strike or surprise assault. To that end, having initially been carried by aircraft and then on land-based rockets, nuclear warheads were also mounted on rockets fired from submarines, which were mobile and therefore hard to detect. So also with the intermediate or limited range weaponry, notably lorry-mounted nuclear rockets and cruise missiles, that were increasingly deployed in the 1980s. These increased the uncertainty bound up in any resort to attack.

The two sides prepared and planned for conflict with each other, with planning a key element of the Cold War. This planning was made far more dangerous because both were armed first with atomic bombs and then with the more lethal hydrogen ones, as well as with relevant delivery systems. Indeed, in July 1955, when American, Soviet and British leaders met in Geneva for the first time since 1945, Dwight Eisenhower, American president from 1953 to 1961, emphasised that any nuclear war would, due to the windborne spread of radioactivity, end life in the northern hemisphere, and thus, in an unprecedented globalisation, ensure that whichever power launched a nuclear attack would also be destroyed by it. This was a totally different prospectus to what he had faced when in command of the invasion of German-held Normandy in 1944.

The MAD threatened by massive nuclear stockpiles, and by the increased vulnerability following the development and deployment of intercontinental missiles, eventually brought a measure of stability, in part by giving substance to the use of the concept of deterrence. However, it was only in hindsight that this was to be seen as a success. At the time, there was a great risk that deterrence would not work and, instead, that the very danger that the other side would strike first would encourage a move to war. The Berlin Crisis of 1961 and, even more, the Cuban Missile Crisis of 1962 highlighted this risk, while the deployment, in the 1970s, of rockets with multiple independently targeted re-entry vehicles increased the danger. In the early 1980s, against a background of increased mistrust and the deployment of new missile systems, Cold War tensions rose to a peak, notably in 1983 when the Soviet early-warning system reported an American attack only for the reports to be correctly treated as false alarms.

The concentration of nuclear weaponry in a divided Europe also encouraged the major nuclear powers, the United States and the Soviet Union, to pursue their ambitions elsewhere, in what for them, although not for many of those who suffered the consequences, was a form of limited war. This process was facilitated by the collapse of the Western European imperial systems from the late 1940s to the mid-1970s.

Growing tension between, and within, states had represented a failure of the hopes that it would be possible to use the United Nations to ensure a new peaceful world order. In 1943, the United States, the Soviet Union, Britain and (Nationalist, Guomindang) China, had agreed the Moscow Declaration on General Security, including the establishment of 'a general international organisation, based on the principle of sovereign equality'. The resulting United Nations was established in 1945, but it proved the setting, not the solution, for growing East–West tensions and, although it could assemble forces, certainly did not lead to the world army that had been envisaged by some. Both sides were fired by ideology and both aspired to a new world order conforming to their beliefs, as in the American determination to create both a new world order and an Atlantic community, each described in terms of *the* (not *a*) 'Free World'.

Discussing the Cold War enables us to assess the role of ideology in causing and sustaining conflict. In the respective worldviews, the world should, by default, progress towards their system and therefore any attempts to resist was an act of aggression. From 1945, despite serious military limitations on both sides, each side increasingly felt threatened, and seriously so, by the other, both militarily and ideologically. This sense of threat helped define and strengthen the sides.

Fear, indeed, was a driving element in the causes and escalations of the successive stages of the Cold War, while also being a unifier of state and society, or, at least, a would-be unifier from the perspective of governments and commentators that sought accordingly to impose discipline and maintain ideological control. This fear was to be seen across societies, including in popular culture, from films to youth organisations. Internal surveillance was presented as an aspect of conflict, as in Communist Albania, where thousands of individual pillboxes were constructed as part of a defence system. In many countries, the security services were boosted as part of an active front in the ongoing conflict.

Aside from missiles, the Cold War indeed saw a multiple competition, notably in supporting protégés, in arms races and rivalry, across the Third World, in espionage, and in cultural and intellectual opposition. While some of the rivalry interacted with decolonisation struggles in the Third World, many other factors were involved. There were also more clear-cut Cold War conflicts, with Communist regimes trying to conquer non-Communist counterparts. Failure for the Communists in the Korean War was followed eventually in 1975 by total success in Vietnam, Laos and Cambodia.

The combination of realist and idealist factors that determined the policies of states and, notably, empires, was apparent with the protagonists in the Cold War. American intervention, puppet regimes and economic direction in Central and South America and the Caribbean were similar, up to a point, to Soviet activity in Eastern Europe. Albeit in a different ideological context, the concept of powers' regions, or 'spheres of influence' in nineteenth-century language, has recurred as a major one in the 2000s and, even more, 2010s, indeed has been central more recently to the Chinese and Russian practice of international relations and bellicosity. This situation both poses a major challenge to the current norms of the world order, and should also encourage a reconsideration of earlier examples, as during the Cold War. Then it proved difficult to prevent interference in what were perceived as 'spheres' of influence, notably with Soviet support for Cuba and Nicaragua, and American for the Afghan resistance.

The end of the Japanese empire in 1945 created another area of confrontation between the West and the East in the shape of East Asia, first with the Chinese Civil War (1946–9) and then in the Korean War (1950–53) in which the Soviets were able to rely on their newly victorious Chinese Communist allies. Success in the Chinese Civil War had encouraged Mao to believe that technological advantages, especially in air power, which the Americans dominated, could be countered, not least by determination. This was a 'realist' belief in the prospect of victory, albeit one heavily conditioned by ideological suppositions. However, as had also been done by the Japanese in World War Two, American resilience, resources and fighting quality were underestimated by the Chinese. To a degree, the Korean War became the sole war between any of the world's leading military powers since 1945, and, arguably, in 1950, China was not yet such a power.

In turn, the American belief that air power could isolate the battlefield, and dominate larger ground forces there, led to misplaced confidence, as was seen in particular in the Vietnam War. These points throw suggestive light on the extent to which the theory, doctrine and infrastructure of nuclear deterrence might later have not worked had there been conflict between the major powers. The serious miscalculations shown in Korea in 1950, by the Americans, and also earlier by Communist planners who did not anticipate an American intervention in South Korea, did not provide encouraging instances of the effectiveness of deterrence. As with other conflicts, the Korean War showed how what was intended as a distinct and very limited conflict became a larger-scale and, for a while, indeterminate one.

Like so much of the military history bound up in the apparent legitimacy of present-day regimes, the Korean War continues to attract the propaganda coverage it had from the first, notably in

North Korea, where its aggression is ignored. China refers to the struggle as 'The War to Resist America and Aid Korea', and continues to present it as self-defence against American invasion threats. The heavy costs of the struggle are also underplayed. In contrast, the American coverage is more balanced, not least on command flaws.

If American intervention in Vietnam greatly delayed the Communist success there and drove up its cost, it had serious consequences also for America's public finances, military confidence and international reputation. This led the Americans to become more wary about committing regular forces.

In the late 1970s and 1980s, Cold War conflict focused on sub-Saharan Africa and, to a lesser extent, Central America. There was success for the Soviet bloc in the former, notably in Angola, and, less directly, Zimbabwe, but not in the latter. Nor were the Soviets able to overcome American-supplied resistance after they invaded Afghanistan in 1979.

There was also a significant Cold War dimension to the Arab–Israeli struggle, especially the October War of 1973, with a stand-off between the American and Soviet Mediterranean fleets and the arming of both sides. In this and other respects, there was a linkage between particular areas of tension. Thus, the American position in the Mediterranean was weakened by the Vietnam commitment, thereby providing the Soviets with opportunities. In turn, the end of the American commitment to the Vietnam War and the American-mediated Israel–Egypt peace settlement in 1978 helped offset Soviet activity in the Middle East, and weakened the Soviet client state, Syria. Conflicts in the Middle East proved a means of demonstrating the proficiency of armaments, although the repeated failure of Arab forces had more complex causes, ranging from Israeli fighting quality to deficiencies in the highly politicised Arab command structures.

The range and scale of the conflicts were such that the term Cold War is not especially helpful, as it can suggest a wary deterrence rather than the reality of many killed. Ultimately, the most significant outcomes were the success of the Communists in the Chinese Civil War, establishing a system that has lasted to the present, unlike the total failure of Soviet and Eastern European Communism of 1989–91. As a consequence, the key period of the Cold War was that in the immediate aftermath of World War Two, and the Chinese Communists won despite the Americans then having a monopoly of nuclear weaponry. In 1989, China used its army to curb dissent, whereas the Soviet Union did not do so in 1989–91.

CHAPTER 35

Wars of Decolonisation

The period 1943–91 saw the biggest transfer of territorial control in world history. Wars of decolonisation as a topic usually focus on anti-imperial struggles and, classically, the fall of the Western European empires, with particular stress on the French failures in Vietnam (1946–54) and Algeria (1956–62), and the conflicts in which the Dutch, British and Portuguese struggled to preserve their imperial position, but with the Western European empires swept away by 1976.

These conflicts counterpointed the theory and practice of wars of national liberation with those of counter-insurgency warfare. Prefiguring later American problems in Vietnam and Iraq, the French discovered in Vietnam (1946–54) and then Algeria (1956–62) that a superiority in conventional weaponry could not deliver a military verdict, and that the politics of the situation proved intractable. And that was exacerbated by the extent to which the Communist great powers helped the opponents of the European colonial powers. The latter made a formidable effort in the case of

France, Portugal and Britain. The French mounted a major effort in Algeria, and were able to suppress their opponents in sweep and destroy operations, but not to end opposition. Including locally recruited Africans, who rose from 30 per cent of the total in 1966 to 42 per cent by 1973, the Portuguese army increased from 79,000 men in 1961 to 217,000 in 1974, a greater percentage under arms than any army bar Israel. In Portuguese Africa, 149,000 men were deployed.

Altering the perspective, however, offers a different vista. Here the wars of decolonisation begin in World War Two with the complete collapse of the German and Japanese empires, beginning in late 1942 and gathering pace in 1944, in turn. They end in 1989–91, with the collapse of the Soviet system, first in Eastern Europe and then in the Soviet Union itself. Consideration at this range emphasises the variety of the process being discussed. Moreover, it invites comparative assessments. This includes both what is more classically covered and also the military dimension which was most to the fore with the collapse of the Italian, German and Japanese empires, and least with the Soviet system.

Western decolonisation was an in-between stage. Factors that come to the fore include the very variable extent to which large-scale conflict played a role in decolonisation and even if looking only at the Western European empires. Thus, France abandoned its sub-Saharan empire with scant difficulty, and Britain did the same in West and East Africa, and the West Indies.

The great potential significance of external support, indeed intervention, emerges repeatedly, and for both insurgencies and counter-insurgency forces. This support could take military form, notably in the provision of arms and advisors, especially by the leading Cold War rivals, but also sometimes that of troops.

However, political backing could be as, or more, important, as with international recognition, diplomatic pressure and the disengagement of allies. Most of Portugal's allies were unwilling to provide support in its struggle to preserve its empire, while the Americans actively discouraged the Dutch in what became (and remains) Indonesia, and did not support the French over Algeria. In all those cases, independence was conceded while all the key cities were still under the control of the imperial power.

Anti-imperialism became (and remains) more complex when it was applied to states that were non-Western and did not consider themselves imperial, for example India in Kashmir and Punjab, Egypt in Yemen, China in Tibet, Ethiopia in Eritrea, Tigray and the Ogaden, Nigeria in Biafra, Congo in Katanga, Oman in Dhofar, Indonesia in Northern Sumatra, East Timor and Western New Guinea, Pakistan in East Pakistan and Baluchistan, Myanmar in tribal territories, Turkey, Iraq, Iran and Syria, all in Kurdish areas, Sudan in Southern Sudan and Serbia within Yugoslavia. In each case, the political causes, course and consequences of the conflict were different. However, in every case, force was very much involved in the struggles both to maintain and to overthrow control. Indeed, non-violent resistance was more common as a concept than a reality, although it did play an important role in the overthrow of the Soviet empire and its client regimes in 1989–91.

There was total failure for the rebels in Kashmir, Tibet, Biafra and Katanga, but eventual success in some of the other cases, such as East Timor and Eritrea. A common feature of all these struggles was the weakness or breakdown of ideas of state incorporation in the face of nationalisms, and even so if the latter were defined as separatism or terrorism.

And so also for struggles on a smaller scale, as, unsuccessfully, with Basque resistance to Spanish rule, or that of Catholic Irish nationalists to the status of Northern Ireland within the United Kingdom. On the other hand, these movements had a disproportionate political impact, which represented success of a sort.

It is all too easy to assume that insurgencies are bound to succeed, and that they were an aspect of modern warfare with a long pedigree, for example back to the American Revolution of 1775–83. Nevertheless, in practice, there was no clear proficiency for counter-imperial opposition. Thus, by the end of the 1950s, the concept of success through revolutionary warfare that had appeared so clear after the results of the Chinese Civil War (in practice far from a war of insurgency) and the anti-French Vietnam conflict of

1946–54 appeared, instead, far more problematic. This was as a result of major British counter-insurgency successes in Malaya and Kenya, the first against a Communist insurrection and the second against a more tribally based opposition. In practice, the situation had been varied throughout, not least with the total failure, in the late 1940s and early 1950s, of insurgencies in Greece, the Philippines and the Baltic Republics, the first two Communist and the last anti-Communist.

Moreover, many insurgencies were often not won or lost but, instead, ended in stalemate. However, the reality and understanding of what that entailed were far from fixed, with the assessment and degree of compromise very much part of the politics of the situation. Readers are invited to assess what they would be prepared to accept in such a scenario. Throughout, a key element is the degree to which the government is willing to resist insurrection or, more particularly, to go on resisting, and, linked to that, the position of the military. Thus, in 1974, in both Portugal and Ethiopia, discontented army officers overthrew their governments, which, albeit very differently, affected the willingness to sustain anti-imperial rebellions: in Portugal this was followed by the abandonment of Portugal's African empire in Angola, Guinea-Bissau and Mozambique, the largest surviving European empire at that stage.

In contrast, the new Ethiopian regime made a major effort to sustain control over Eritrea and also, successfully, fought Somalia to regain control of the Ogaden district. Military regimes, such as those of Ethiopia and Myanmar, or the Nigerian government during the Biafran War of 1967–70, tended to be especially active in resisting separatist struggles (decolonisation in another perspective). The Nigerian forces benefited from overwhelming numerical superiority and air and sea control, although the role of ethnic and factional considerations weakened the army's fighting competence. Starvation via blockade was used to help destroy Biafran separatism. And yet, not only with military regimes. In opposing Basque and Catholic Irish nationalists, the governments of Spain and Britain benefited from the willingness of their military/security systems to sustain a long struggle. In the British case, it was probably important that the army was volunteer and not conscript.

Other military or militarised regimes engaged in risky wars, as with the Argentine invasion of the Falkland Islands in 1982, and also the Iraqi attack on Iran in 1980 that launched a major conflict lasting until 1988 and that was intended to 'free' Khuzestan, an area with a majority Arab population. The first was successful militarily in the short term in that the Falklands fell to surprise attack by the far larger invasion force. However, the Argentineans were unable to move to the political table of compromise because a robust response by the British government led to a war in which the Argentineans were defeated. At the same time, by keeping this a limited struggle, fought near and on the Falklands, the British were able to prevail: there was no attempt to invade Argentina. In contrast, Iraq and Iran failed to limit their goals and means. This also helped lead to an intractable struggle with very heavy casualties to both, not least because of the deliberate targeting of civilian populations in order to drive up the cost of the war and to sap resolve.

Some civilian governments were also very active in maintaining control, for example those of Israel in the Gaza Strip and on the West Bank of the Jordan, and of India in Kashmir. These struggles could also be linked to war with neighbouring states, notably those of India with Pakistan, and of Israel with Egypt, Syria and Jordan. Indeed, territories gained in such conflicts could then become the base for what were wars of decolonisation. As each of those cases indicated, a determination to remain in control could thwart insurgent forces. Thus, although Israel ended its occupation of the Gaza Strip, the successive intifadas on the West Bank of the Jordan that began in 1987 failed to end Israeli rule, while Indian forces have retained control of their part of Kashmir seized in 1947–8.

In the Soviet empire in 1989–91, the politicians were not prepared to sustain a fight to maintain imperial control, although in part this was a consequence of the failure in 1991 of a short-lived attempt by authoritarian Communist loyalists to overthrow the liberalising government of the Soviet Union.

This political element was more significant than the inherent strengths or weaknesses of insurgencies and/or revolutionary warfare. This point underlines the extent to which the issues bound up in capability have to be assessed and presented in a comparative context, and with there being no single measure. It is all too easy to explain success and failure, and to build narrative patterns and analytic frameworks accordingly, but that does not make such explanations adequate or accurate.

CHAPTER 36

Conflict Since the Cold War

The period 1990–2021 demonstrates the problems of assessing the character of modern warfare, and therefore, by extension, what earlier should be considered modern, modernisation, progressive and, accordingly, worthy of attention. The headline conflicts are those involving the United States, notably the two Gulf Wars of 1991 and 2003 with Iraq, and the lengthy commitment in Afghanistan. Total American success in both Gulf Wars in defeating Iraq's conventional military encouraged a technologically based optimism about a leap forward in military capability, with terms such as paradigm shift, AirLand Battle, Revolution in Military Affairs, and Transformation, all employed with zeal, and notably so by American commentators for whom the rhetoric of total power appeared vindicated by the apparent experience of complete victory.

However, a reprise of the tactical and technological myopia seen during the Vietnam War became clear, both with the problems facing the American occupation in Iraq from 2003 and also in Afghanistan from 2001. It rapidly became apparent that it would not be possible to dictate the situation as a result of the technological, organisational and doctrinal changes that had been highlighted as aspects of the supposed leaps forward in capability. As so often, output did not equate with outcome, and protection, rather than offensive action, became a key theme which, to a degree, gave the initiative to the insurgent.

As a result, the limitations of the intervening power attracted attention. However, there were broader issues about the nature of strategy in the contexts of uncertain domestic support for a sustained foreign presence, with, in particular, pressure to bring back troops from dangerous foreign postings. This, for example, became an issue also for the French in Mali, where troops were sent against al-Qaeda-linked groups in 2013; by 2021, there was pressure to bring to an end an apparently intractable commitment.

There had also been a serious failure to appreciate the nature of Afghan and Iraqi society, and notably the strengths of sectarianism and tribalism. The overlapping character of force and organisation were differently seen in both societies. As in the former Yugoslavia, the Caucasus, the Sahel and more generally, sectarian and ethnic links were important in both societies. For example, Izzat Ibrahim al-Douri, the deputy to Saddam Hussein of Iraq, who had commanded a special unit to kill opponents of the Ba'ath party, became, in 1968, an interior minister with in effect the same role. He was important to the 1979 coup that took Saddam to power and, as deputy commander of the armed forces, was given the honorary rank of Lieutenant-General, often wearing uniform, and keenly supporting the wars Saddam launched against Iran and Kuwait. Yet, as Sheikh of the Naqshbandi Sufi Islamic religious order, Al-Douri also had a separate source of authority, and it played a major role in the insurgency against the American-backed government that succeeded Saddam after he was overthrown in 2003, and in the rise of the Islamic State movement. Such careers were a norm in a world in which distinctions between force and the military and/or the military and politics were far from clear-cut.

So also with sectarianism and tribalism in Yugoslavia, a federal state, in the early 1990s. Divisions between the republics were matched by tensions within, and, in 1991, conflict began as the Serbian-dominated Yugoslav army sought to suppress Slovene and Croatian moves towards independence. Having failed to maintain Yugoslavia, the Serbs sought to force through a Greater Serbia, with episodic conflict until 1999, notably in Bosnia in 1992–5 and, to a lesser extent, Kosovo in 1996–9. A large number of those killed were civilians, and maybe 4.4 million people fled their homes. Crimes against humanity were all too common, and by all combatants. Alongside Croatian and Bosnian forces, American-led interventions, principally in the form of air attack, were important in stopping Serbia and bringing peace.

A different problem of perception and analysis occurred from the very focus on conflicts in which the United States intervened, at the expense of the much wider-ranging pattern of conflict, notably in Africa, but also in other parts of the world, including the Caucasus, Burma, Nepal and Sri Lanka. This range indicated the varied factors that played a role in conflict and success. For example, in Sri Lanka, the Tamil insurrection was crushed in 2009, with heavy civilian casualties and no discrimination between non-combatants and armed rebels. Exacerbated by chemical weapons, such brutality also appeared to 'work' for the Syrian government in the 2010s, first in preventing its overthrow and then in defeating its opponents.

Yet, other factors were also significant, including, in Sri Lanka, the Indian government dropping its support for the insurgents who had also lost backing from the civilian population. In Syria, the West was unwilling to develop its tentative support for the opposition, that became serious from 2012, to the Assad regime, which could draw on Russian military backing, notably arm support. Similarly, the Algerian government was able to secure French support against Islamist insurrection in the 1990s.

Alongside the warfare of insurrections and foreign interventions, which, combined, led to the fall of the Gaddafi regime in Libya in 2011, came confrontation between the major powers.

Thus, beginning with the Russian seizure of Crimea from Ukraine in 2014, there was increased talk of a new Cold War. Tension markedly rose between China and Russia on one side, and America on the other; and that despite the unprecedented economic interdependence of America and China.

In addition to these tensions have come the rivalries of assertive regional powers, and notably so in the Middle East, with Turkey under President Erdoğan in the late 2010s and the early 2020s seeking to play a major role in the Caucasus, Syria, Iraq, the eastern Mediterranean, Libya and Somalia, employing historical claims and religious propaganda to that end, and using both its expanded armed forces and weaponry, including drones. Moreover, Turkey has proved willing to sustain the commitment despite the heavy financial costs and economic problems it has faced. So also, albeit to very varying extents, with Egypt, Iran, Israel, Saudi Arabia, Qatar and the United Arab Emirates, the first four all continuing earlier patterns of regional assertiveness.

As a result, many local conflicts have become the seat of regional tensions, as with the long-standing conflicts in Iraq, Lebanon, Libya, Syria and Yemen. In Libya, the United Arab Emirates allied with Egypt, and Turkey took opposite sides in the civil war, while, in 2015, Saudi Arabia and the United Arab Emirates sent troops into Yemen to fight the Houthis, a Shia rebel group backed by Iran. Drones were deployed in all these conflicts.

There is also an interventionism in the shape of coups, as in 2013, when the military seized power in Egypt from an elected Islamist government; the military looking to the United States and the government to Turkey. Tens of thousands of political prisoners were seized and many killed. In turn, foreign states sought to help suppress what was presented as subversion, as in 2020 with Russia in Belarus and Cuba in Venezuela. Such a presence used force, but the 'troops' employed were mostly security agents; and the nature of the intervention was not in the form of tanks rolling across frontiers but, rather, the forceful suppression of demonstrators. There was no comparable foreign intervention in the lawlessness that played a role alongside American politics in 2020–21.

The overlap of domestic violence and international intervention was also seen in the Sahel belt of sub-Saharan Africa. Thus, the failure to suppress Islamist rebellion in northern Mali helped, in 2012 and 2020, to cause coups, which were normative in a state that had earlier seen coups in 1968 and 1991. In turn, France intervened in its former colony from 2013, as it has elsewhere in its ex-African empire, notably in the Central African Republic. France has been joined by allies, including the United States and Britain, and in 2020 the Americans accordingly built a large drone airbase near Agadez in Niger. The jihad has spread widely, notably into Burkina Faso and Niger, and beyond that to overlap with other violent Islamist movements like that in northern Nigeria. Jihadists in Mali use improvised explosive devices, rockets, motorbikes and pick-up trucks, and, when attacked, move to another area. In turn, the French have deployed five thousand troops and use aircraft, helicopters and drones in their attacks.

As with Yugoslavia in the 1990s, in both the Middle East and sub-Saharan Africa, religion is important in conflict, as also in the Caucasus, with Christian Armenia opposed to Muslim Azerbaijan. In the Middle East, violence in part stems from the collapse of the Turkish empire, but also from the degree to which the current political order does not match with traditional interpretations of the Koran. Far from becoming less common, religious-linked conflict has become more so in the 2010s and early 2020s, including in South-East Asia and in Mozambique, where an Islamic insurgency began in 2017 and has become more active.

In all these cases, vicious and deliberate brutality towards civilians was part of both insurgency and counter-insurgency actions, if not policies. To that extent, war was total, and the casualties in part a matter of those deliberately driven to become refugees, and thus warnings and burdens. Clearing land of the current occupiers was a traditional goal and means but was now carried out with different weaponry.

All of these conflicts were very deadly and disruptive. And so also for other wars such as the 1998–2000 border war between Eritrea and Ethiopia that cost about 100,000 lives. For that in

Congo in 1996–2003, the epicentre of an African Great War, the figure was probably about 3–5.5 million deaths, although mainly due to wartime disease and starvation, rather than the slaughter that was probably responsible for 400,000 deaths. As in the past, it is necessary to look at far more than the West in order to get a firmer grasp of war and its future.

CHAPTER 37

War Today
CONFRONTATIONS WITHIN STATES

It is commonplace to focus on the great powers when discussing war today, and we will look at that in the next section. But to do so avoids the necessary focus on what are now, and may in the future be, the prime causes, sites and means of conflict. Ideology and material factors combine to ensure a high degree of pressure on societies affected by the major, indeed, transformative, population, environmental and social changes of recent years. The most likely precipitant of animosity will be the consequences of the unprecedented population increase taking place across much of the world. This increase will create 'pinch points' in terms of resources, notably land, water, food, fuel and government jobs, these interacting with ethnic, religious, social and religious factors and justifications, as in 2020, for example, with ethnic rivalries helping to cause conflict in Ethiopia and Ivory Coast. In the former, the federal forces fighting the Tigrayans were joined by Amhara militiamen.

Ethnic pressure exists irrespective of the contentious questions of the extent, speed, causes and consequences of climate change, although that has clearly been important in the past, and not only with the coming and passing of the Ice Ages, but also with those of the 'Little Ice Age', from roughly 1300 to about 1850.

Whatever the timescale of climate change, and it clearly accelerated and became cumulative, in the early twenty-first century an even more immediate pressure across much of the world stems from the massive rise in the global population. This rise has not been countered by increases in deaths due to disease nor, so far, by Malthusian factors focused on famine. In a rapidly accelerating pattern, the world's population reached one billion in about 1804, two in 1927, three in 1960, four in 1974, five in 1987, six in 1999, seven in 2012 and 7.8 in 2020, and is currently regarded as likely to rise to 9.8 by 2050 and probably 10.9 by 2100. This rise is particularly marked in Africa and India, but not in Europe or Japan, where indeed there are falls. Africa's population is predicted to rise from one billion in 2019 to nearly 2.4 by 2050, with more than half of its population under twenty-five by then. By 2050, Nigeria is likely to be the third most populous state in the world, replacing the United States behind India and China.

This situation has major implications, for states both directly and indirectly affected, not least when combined with resource flows, or with gender imbalances leading to a relative shortage of young women. Earlier optimism that rising prosperity will lead to a decline in fertility, with the world population peaking at 9.5 billion in 2050, has been discarded. This further throws light on pressures over resources. In particular, there is a huge potential for conflict over water, both within and between many states. Water is already a grave problem in a large number of countries including, most acutely, Yemen, where, but for other reasons, the government was overthrown in an insurgency in 2015. Worried about limits on the water coming downriver, Egypt has threatened to destroy the dam Ethiopia is building on the Blue Nile.

These and other pressures can be made more pressing by the nature of the context, notably a perception of challenge from others within particular communities. In addition, an international dimension is readily present, not least due to large-scale migration.

This is a long-standing pattern, seen for example in the large-scale slaughter of Haitians in the neighbouring Dominican Republic in 1937.

The 'pinch points' over resources and grievances will probably be particularly acute in cities. Despite their greater exposure to infectious diseases, the percentage of the world's rising population who live in cities will continue to increase. Although individual predictions vary, the trend is clear. The United Nations suggests that, while more than half of the world's population of seven billion lived in cities in 2012, by 2030 the number will be more than five billion. There are also projections that three-quarters of the global population by 2050 will be living in cities, with most of the increase occurring in Asia, notably India, and Africa. Indeed, in 2015, about 56 per cent of the thousand largest urban areas were in Asia, as well as the eight most populous urban agglomerations.

Cities therefore serve to highlight the issue of managing unprecedented growth, not least because of concerns about the social and political consequences of unsuccessful expansion. It is scarcely surprising that dystopias are now very much seen in terms of urban chaos and an unmanaged cityscape – a theme that links imaginative works, such as the vision of Gotham City (New York) in the *Batman* films (1989–2019), and of the city in *Blade Runner* (1982), to more grounded studies. Indeed, it is in urban locations that change affects human drama with the most intensity and pungency, and receives the most attention.

The net effect will be a geography of insurgency in which urban areas are usually its key locations and sites of conflict, as in the Kurdish part of Turkey in the winter of 2015–16. Thus, in Pakistan, it will be Karachi, not the mountainous fringe in Waziristan, that is the central area of risk; in Brazil, São Paulo and not Amazonia; in India, the big cities, not the Naxalites in Odisha; and in China, the same, and not ethnic areas, notably Xinjiang and Tibet. Although rural insurgency is a problem in many states, including Myanmar and India, the focus may well be on urban activism, as for China in Hong Kong in 2020, and warfare, and on the related problems of surveillance and counter-insurgency. Moreover, rural areas tend to be the source of military personnel, as in Latin America; and cities, conversely, are of ideological agitators.

Across much of the world, lawlessness may already or will overlap with internal conflict. This is apparent even more where precautions are made. The United States provides an instance: police forces have become militarised, with all sorts of body armour, armoured vests, helmets, army rifles, armoured vehicles and special optical equipment (including night-fighting sights). Police trade shows display this equipment lavishly, and federal subventions exist to help purchase it. The deployment of police in the disorder in 2020–21 at times had a militarised character.

Among the dynamic elements in the future on the global scale will probably be the relationship between insurgencies and criminal networks, each of whom benefit greatly from the other. Such networks pose a major threat to order in a number of states, including Mexico and Colombia, and can contribute to their being to a degree failed states; although that term is more properly employed for those where the entire central government has collapsed. Criminal networks can also have links to states, while, correspondingly, the authority of the latter can be a protection racket enforced by violence and challenged by the same means. That element can interact with economic and political inequalities between, and within, communities, with the violence both top-down and bottom-up.

There is also continuity from the conflicts of the Cold War, not only in terms of divisive issues, but also with reference to weaponry and warriors. Second-hand weapons have a long life, especially firearms, but also higher-specification weaponry.

Tension and violence do not necessarily lead to insurgent activity, let alone a full-blown insurgency. Many states with a high population growth rate, for example Senegal and Zambia, do not suffer from civil war nor from proactive factors of control designed to prevent the possibility of insurgency, in other words the deterrent aspects of counter-insurgency.

Nevertheless, it is likely that violence between groups within a state will frequently involve a defiance of the authority of the latter, and thus constitute an insurgency. This is particularly so as most states seek to monopolise violence.

In opposition to this attempt, the cheapness and ready availability of lethal weapons is a key element, and is likely to become more so with ease of manufacture, not least from plastic using 3D printers. Such weapons may have inferior specifications, but the conflicts in Afghanistan and Iraq in recent decades have indicated that 'improvised' weaponry can be deadly and can be readily developed to counter the defences of the protection and counter-weaponry of regular forces. In particular, 'improvised explosive devices' in the shape of roadside bombs have had a major impact on convoys, leading to the strengthening of vehicles. The same has also been seen elsewhere, as in Mali.

The relationship seen from 1990 to 2007 – of about 220,000 people killed in inter-state wars, compared to over 3.6 million dying as a result of conflict within states – is likely to continue. It certainly has in the period 2008 to 2015. In considering this, and other issues, there are problems with definitions and measurements. For example, how far should the violence in Iraq from 2004 be classified as an aspect of the 2003 war? How many people in Congo or Sudan would have died of disease and malnutrition, whether or not there had been war? Nevertheless, the trend in casualties between different types of war is apparently clear. Moreover, these material pressures interact with ideological tensions between belief-based groups, with religious and ethnic animosities particularly apparent.

The extent to which these confrontations within states then overlap with tensions and violence between states can be part of the equation in helping such conflict to spread or at least threaten neighbours, as with Yemen in recent years.

In terms of the means of conflict, anti-societal violence is a key element, one, moreover, frequently discussed in terms of 'ethnic cleansing'. This captures the extent to which the issue is presented as the very presence of people, a situation encapsulated in Hitler's genocidal 'war' against Jews, rather than simply the military operations of regular forces. Thus, war becomes a struggle between groups in a 'total' framework and 'format', and where the combatants are as much those wielding knives and flaming brands, and killing babies, as being or fighting regular forces. Linked to this, sexual violence, in the form of rape and the seizure of women, was very much linked to a drive to dominate, humiliate and cause pain. Conflict in the former Yugoslavia, in Rwanda, Congo, the Caucasus, the Sahel and Sudan all took this form in the 1990s and thereafter. 'Front lines' came to be a matter of the defended villages of particular ethnic groups, which was a long-standing pattern in some areas, for example the former Yugoslavia.

Regular forces can appear weak, if not hapless, in this context, in part by seeking a type of combat, with a readily definable enemy, to make sense of their weaponry, training and doctrine that is inappropriate. Aircraft do not stop demonstrating crowds, as was shown in Cairo during 'the Arab Spring' in 2011, when the government was overthrown. In contrast, benefiting from a degree of popular support, the Egyptian army was able to seize power there in 2013. An attempt by militaries to regain relevance was particularly associated in the 2000s with the development of ideas and training for urban conflict, and of 'doctrine' and weaponry accordingly. At the same time, those engaged in such struggles tended, as in Libya and Syria, to rely on local militias that were as much to do with anti-societal brutality as any 'doctrine' of urban warfare. The response varies greatly by society and state. There is no sign that this will stop.

CHAPTER 38

The Confrontations of Major Powers

Alongside conflicts between states comes the discussion of warfare in terms of the advanced weaponry being deployed by major powers. Thus, just as the Cold War after 1945 rapidly led to a move into nuclear confrontation and the speedy development, first, of hydrogen bombs and, then, of intercontinental rockets, there has been a rapid move in the revived Cold War since 2014 into the spheres of cyberwarfare, hypersonic weaponry and space warfare. Indeed, space weaponry could destroy satellites which are vital to communications and surveillance, and have been a major adjunct of American power, as used for example in the 2003 Gulf War with Iraq. In 2020, the NATO secretary-general Jens Stoltenberg noted: 'Fast, effective and secure satellite communications are essential for our troops. The space environment has fundamentally changed in the last decade. Some nations, including Russia and China, are developing anti-satellite systems that could blind, disable or shoot down satellites.' China has the Dong Neng interceptor and the

SC-19 missile, and Russia the PL-19 Nudol system. This capability threatens the American 'C2' command and control.

Expenditure on advanced weaponry had been cut after the Cold War, as the Western powers, including the United States, sought to take a 'peace dividend', while Russia was seriously affected by fiscal crisis. This expenditure, however, rose in the 2000s, not least due to the American 'War on Terror', and then even more in the 2010s. The most strongly growing major power, China, has proved particularly active so that, by the end of 2020, it had 360 commissioned warships (US Navy 297), as well as over 1,250 ground-launched ballistic missiles and cruise missiles with ranges between 500 and 5,500 kilometres. Politically as well as economically, China is able to make a major military commitment.

In the United States, expenditure, which in large part, as during the Vietnam War, is debt-fuelled, rose again under President Trump (2017–21). Russia under Vladimir Putin, who has dominated its politics since 2000, also associated its identity with an active military profile and presence, the latter seen in particular in Syria. The major growth in Russian expenditure has seen a marked increase in capability in conventional forces, notably tanks and aircraft, but more Russian investment has focused on a range of missile types that together provide lethal coverage of Europe and nearby waters.

In 2019, the top ranking states in military expenditure, in $billion, were:

USA	732
China	261
India	71.1
Russia	65.1
Saudi Arabia	61.9
France	50.1
Germany	49.3
Britain	48
Japan	47.6
South Korea	43.9

In comparison, in 2000, the United States spent $295 billion, Russia 59, China 41, and the then 17 European NATO powers 162.5. Inflation between 2000 and 2019 was modest.

These figures are not strictly comparable by country and date, not only because of the possibility of under-reporting, which is a frequent issue with China, but also because of the very different rates of pay and social support for the military. Nevertheless, the key elements are readily apparent. The major spenders are Western (USA, France, Germany, Britain) and the leading Asian economies (China, India, Japan and South Korea), with Russia, the rival of the United States in the Cold War, no longer in the top three of spenders, while the wealthiest of the oil states, Saudi Arabia, comes fifth, with two other oil states, the USA and Russia, prominent. The fall in the price of oil has hit other major spenders in the past, notably Iran and Iraq and, to a lesser extent, Angola and Libya. The low price of money in the 2010s and early 2020s, with interest rates historically slight, by making borrowing easier, has helped increase and sustain military expenditure.

Per capita expenditure can also be very different, the list usually including Israel, Singapore and Kuwait, alongside the aggregate heavyweights of the United States and Saudi Arabia. In terms of the percentage of resources in a society devoted to war, North Korea would be high up, because the state, both authoritarian and paranoid, squeezes living standards to that end. This enabled North Korea in January 2021 to claim to have under development not only a multi-warhead missile, underwater-launched nuclear missiles and solid-fuel long-range missiles, but also spy satellites, all intended to threaten the United States.

Alongside the cutting-edge weaponry at the strategic level is that at the tactical level, notably with drones. Initially, these were for aerial reconnaissance, but they rapidly expanded in function, lethality, size and milieux, including those designed for submarine weaponry. As such, there is interest in hybrid or overlap weaponry, as in that of drones and torpedoes, or drones and mines. The emphasis on drones meant that the human dimension is that of distant controllers who do not have to confront the facts and danger of conflict.

Moreover, being able to dispense with combatants ensures that the nature of military vehicles has changed. Thus, in place of aircraft carriers, which are themselves highly vulnerable to attack, notably by swarm weaponry, come warships that can fire drones and cruise missiles from shorter and smaller firing platforms as they are not subject to the G forces that affect pilots and thus lessen the desired speed of take-off. Drones also offer a supply dimension, being, for example, developed by the United States to take supplies to nuclear submarines, thus prolonging their time on station. The use of drones links to greater interest in robotic warriors and weapons, and in artificial intelligence (AI). Research is active in all of these spheres. For example, the American V60 Q-UGV is a robot that can cross terrain and sense, scan and communicate a wide range of environmental factors. AI is designed to link sense, scan and fire technologies and systems at a speed and sophistication humans are unable to match. China and Russia have the comparable software, and each power has also to consider the technology that others can develop in order to thwart such processes.

Directional pulse weapons are another area of development. In 2020, China claimed to have used microwave weapons focusing high-frequency electro-magnetic pulses to make Indian positions in a contested area of the Himalayas too painful to retain, leading the troops to retreat.

The confrontations between powers revolve not only between the capabilities in weapons systems but also around the particular areas in contention, such as the East and South China Seas, the trade-offs of differing weapons systems, for example the potential viability of 'access-denial' weapons, and the extension of range through proxy conflicts and forces. The first was increasingly the case with exercises as in 2020, the biannual American-Japanese military exercises, which included amphibious landings intended to signal resolve to recapture the Senkaku Islands in the East China Sea were China to seize them. 'Access-denial' weapons are principally ground-based missiles directed in particular against carriers, although these may be replaced by autonomous swarms of drones that are not dependent on distant control systems. The spread of innovation matches that prior to World War One, but with weapons envisaged that can 'shrink' the world and even more dramatically lessen the chances of those who did not get in the first blow.

The strength of deterrence in such a context is unclear, not least that of asymmetrical capability, as with Taiwan's purchase of American mobile land-based precision missiles designed to operate against a Chinese invasion. Other second- or third-rank powers are similarly having to consider how best to protect themselves from major states, and thereby deter attacks by increasing the cost attacking them poses. Thus, Sweden has reversed its post-Cold War arms run-down in order to confront what is seen as a more menacing Russia.

The resort to force is frequently at issue. In November 2020, shortly before a standard anti-ballistic missile, SM-311A, was successfully fired from an American warship to shoot down a dummy intercontinental ballistic missile, thus providing a layered defence network for the United States, including against North Korea, President Trump was allegedly talked out of bombing Iran's main nuclear site, its uranium enrichment facility at Natanz, when his senior officials warned him that it could begin a regional conflict. The possibility of an Israeli attack on the site has been much mentioned.

War planning has become far more intense since the mid-2010s, and notably for conflict between China and the United States. The planning has to consider both symmetrical (similar weapons systems, methods and goals) and asymmetrical, rivalries and clashes; and, as with the Cold War, the potential interaction between the symmetrical and the asymmetrical is unclear and therefore part of the planning matrix. In November 2020, General Sir Nick Carter, head of the British military, publicly warned about the risk of a World War Three:

> we need to be conscious of these risks. . . . The real risk we have
> with quite a lot of regional conflicts that are going on at the

moment is you could see escalation lead to miscalculation. More people perhaps get involved, more weaponry gets involved, and before you can contain it, it leads to the sides ending up in a full-blown war ... the threat is evolving the whole time, the threat is modernising in certain quarters, and of course we need to modernise as well. ... Park some capabilities perhaps from the industrial age. ... Look forward to some of the capabilities you need for an information age.

Opponents will act to lessen the value of such capabilities, which underlines the inherently dynamic nature of the situation, one that has become more volatile as the world has 'shrunk' markedly over the last century in space–time terms. There is no sign that the populations of major powers wish for war, but that is not a key element in the preparedness for conflict that is insistent at the level of weapons-development and procurement.

CHAPTER 39

Theorists of Military History

How best should military history be presented, discussed and explained? What is war? One of the standard issues with the subject is the way in which the same old thinkers get mentioned when it is discussed, and frequently with a repetition of past arguments and established problems. Sun Tzu, Clausewitz, Jomini and Fuller dominate consideration of war on land, and Mahan and Corbett that at sea. Moreover, the standard approach to the subject, both academic and popular, focuses on great commanders, on major wars and on supposedly decisive battles. Thus, Clausewitz and Jomini had their reputations made as commentators on warfare in the light of French Revolutionary and Napoleonic conflicts, Fuller and Liddell Hart as commentators on World War One and the way to avoid such another costly impasse, and Mahan and Corbett on Britain as the great naval power in the period 1689–1815, and notably its conflict with France.

Others have of course been added to the list, including Frunze and Mao Zedong on revolutionary warfare in the twentieth century, and Callwell and (very differently) Galula for counter-insurgency operations; while the inclusion of Sun Tzu and Mao Zedong represent a major effort to engage with the rising significance of China as a military power. There has not been a comparable focus on India, which is now the world's leading population. Separately, air power brought in its exponents and analysists (the two overlapping to a damaging effect), notably Douhet and Mitchell.

There are, however, a number of issues with much of the standard commentary, and in terms of content, range and tone. First, there is a preference for assessing the theories of military thinkers, rather than the thoughts, still less actions, of military actors. The overwhelming majority of the latter do not leave such theoretical accounts, and certainly not in any systematic fashion, but the problem with considering military thinkers is that that tells you about . . . military thinkers. They do not necessarily get at all close to those who made the decisions, nor their reasons for doing so, and tend to tell you about their own views, fitting others into these preconceptions and exaggerating their impact. Thus, Basil Liddell Hart was happy to pose as a neglected prophet in his own country, Britain, who, however, was influential for the German development of blitzkrieg and for Israeli operations in the Six-Day War of 1967. This greatly exaggerated his significance.

Second, there is a marked emphasis in much of the theory on conflict between states rather than within them. Indeed, civil wars tend to be addressed only when both sides have formal military structures, as in the English (1642–8) and American (1861–5) civil wars, or quasi-formal structures.

Third, the discussion is usually of battle, and not skirmish or 'small war' (or blockade at sea), despite the frequency and significance of the latter. This significance has risen considerably since World War Two, and the 'decisive battle' approach is not very helpful in this context. It is more useful when the number of units is small, as with warships or modern aircraft, and therefore their destruction becomes more significant.

Fourth, much of the world is 'primitivised' in the standard account, with the general simplification and primitivisation of many of the combatants, especially steppe peoples and African polities. There is a tendency to present them as less sophisticated (and diverse) than 'settled' states, especially if the latter are reliant on large-scale agriculture and industry, and/or Western (European and North American) or East Asian. This creates an insistent geography of significance, with an assumption that best practice is synonymous with 'developed societies', which also tend to have militaries and military commentary formalised in a 'modern' fashion. Thus, the 'undeveloped' societies only appear to gain relevance if they copy aspects of the best practice, in other words Westernise, or the equivalent.

Stated like that, the standard position is clearly problematic. Effective militaries, such as the Huns in the fifth century, the Mongols in the thirteenth, the armies of Timur the Lame in the fourteenth and the Manchu in the seventeenth, all of which were non-European cavalry forces, are apt to be underplayed, or treated as likely to fail in the long term, although most types of military can be seen to fail in the long term. In part, this approach is due to an emphasis, instead, on Western infantry forces. This process is taken further if the stress is on a military–industrial nexus, or 'complex' as the seedbed of the advanced weaponry of modern warfare, with terms such as industrial, advanced and modern all having clear connotations.

By their rural and non-industrial nature, steppe societies do not produce such systems. As a result, they can appear inherently redundant. This is so even if the redundancy was frequently not given effect until the nineteenth century. Indeed, this redundancy was both a cause and a consequence of the age of imperialism of that period, which, in reality, was just another such age, as there is no one age of imperialism. In the treatment of steppe societies, there is, indeed, a teleology (we know where we are going and it is both inevitable and good) at play, as so often in military history. This teleology is supposedly defined by a movement towards inherently more effective technological proficiencies and organisational methods.

However, this teleology, which draws heavily on the variations of modernisation theory, and frequently uses the language of military revolutions as a description and explanation of change, does not appear so secure from the perspective of the 2020s. By then, Mexican crime cartels as a whole have more armed men than many European armies.

Culture is a key concept for military history, for an emphasis on the way in which war can be seen and experienced differently in particular cultural settings offers an opportunity to move beyond supposedly universal propositions in understanding the nature of conflict. Moreover, this approach is necessary if fighting in, or against, these settings, in order to appreciate the impact of force and the understanding there of success. These points emerged very clearly with the American commitments in Iraq and Afghanistan, and the difficulties they faced.

Most modern Western commentators in particular have little or nothing to say about religious values, and their role in helping create and sustain specific attitudes to victory and defeat, suffering and loss, and thus to the acceptability of casualties. Yet, as conflict in recent decades in the Islamic world has repeatedly shown, tactical, operational and strategic equations of success, and thus practicality, can all be affected by this factor, a point that has been seen repeatedly in the early accounts of warfare. Indeed, the relative neglect of religion is a problem with one of the most interesting theories about military history, that advanced in the eighteenth century by writers such as Edward Gibbon, William Robertson and Adam Smith. They were convinced that history was a matter of development through socio-economic stages, notably from hunter-gatherers, to pastoral societies, agrarian counterparts and then urban-based systems, with political and military systems varying accordingly. This thesis, which can be extended to include modern societies, allows for differences in physical and human environments around the world, but not for their counterparts in terms of ideological variations.

Whether with Prussian military theorist Clausewitz, or with Gibbon, who was writing a half-century earlier, we are dealing with ideas over the *longue durée*, an attempt to capture the essence of war. However, most theorisation in practice is very short term. It is an analysis of recent conflicts in order to attempt to understand the capabilities of possible opponents. For example, the Germans analysed the poor Soviet performance in the Winter War with Finland in 1940, which encouraged them to plan the attack on the Soviet Union in 1941, although, as yet another instance of the tendency of theory and analysis to confirm bias, they underplayed the key point, after serious early defeats, of eventual Soviet victory in the Winter War.

Such military analysis was prone to support convenience and was apt to confirm institutional, national and social bias. Thus, looking to the problems of the moment and the threat of forthcoming conflict, the American Air Corps analysts, assessing the failure of the German Luftwaffe in the air offensive on Britain in 1940, attributed it to a lack of strategic bombers, rather than the overall deficiencies of the Luftwaffe and the role of Britain's integrated air defence system. This encouraged investment in strategic bombers. In July 1941, Air War Plans Division No. 1 offered a comprehensive plan for defeating Germany by means of air power, which was an instance of the likely right opponent helping to push forward both the doctrine and the crucial support.

There is a widespread tendency to treat flaws in analysis and institutional bias as factors in the past, but there is no reason to believe that there are not similar problems at present, notably for weapons procurement and the 'doctrine' that reflects ideas. Moreover, the vexed and disputatious nature of strategic reviews highlights the role of choice in tasking, prioritisation, procurement and doctrine, and, correspondingly, the extent to which these and other factors have a legacy that affects not only subsequent choices but also the frameworks within which they are posed, debated and implemented. 'Planning for the last war' is a simplistic way of phrasing this point, as it is far more insistent as a process, and one that arises from, and addresses, the need to consider experience. That consideration is ultimately the theorisation of war.

Military theory is very separately advanced through popular culture, with a repeated emphasis on individual heroism, collective bravery and the group cohesion that helps cement resolve. This was a powerful factor in the earliest recorded literature, and remains important in modern literature, electronic games and other media. The theory here is of the triumph of will, although there can be a providentialism and fatalism that ensures a heroic failure, as with the Spartans at Persian hands at Thermopylae in 480 BCE, or the Texans at Mexican hands at the Alamo in 1836. Failure itself then becomes a form of triumphant will.

This form of commentary attracts the most attention, and not least because of the popularity, strengthened from the 1970s, of 'face of battle' accounts, with their emphasis on the stories of individual combatants, and the related use of oral history. This approach downplays background elements of great significance, such as strategy, logistics and communications, and focuses, instead, on the tactical dimension and also on willpower. The two are linked in such factors as unit cohesion.

Modern cultures are particularly apt to respond to visual stimuli and 'lessons'. Those can focus on tales of heroism, as well as the particular capabilities of weaponry, which frequently provide the visual images. Thus, the specific medium of the history provides a message, and one that, in this case, is a long way from the use of written text, which is more readily able to suggest ambiguity and qualifications. Visual media, moreover, are more accessible for usage across much of the world. These media are where the theories of military history, generally implicit theories, are being expressed, and they offer the modern equivalents to the oral epics that were so important in the past. Again, that suggests links, or at least resonances, across the ages.

Conclusions

> While in the barn I was much affected by seeing and hearing
> a lad of about eleven or twelve years of age, who was wounded
> in one of his knees. The little fellow's cries, from the pain of
> his wound, his crying after his dead mother, and saying that
> he should die, was so affecting that it was not soon forgotten
> by me. He was a midshipman belonging to one of the
> gunboats.
>
> Shadrach Byfield, a badly wounded British soldier of the
> aftermath of the British-Native American victory over the
> Americans at Frenchtown (today Monroe, Michigan), 1813

The cruelty of war is not only visited on the living. At the height of the fighting over Fort St Elmo on Malta in 1565, the bodies of three dead Knights of St John were decapitated and disembowelled by the Ottomans before being nailed to wooden crosses that were floated across Valletta harbour in order to discourage the sending of further reinforcements. When the fort fell, only five badly wounded knights were captured. They also were nailed on crosses that were floated across the harbour.

Humans frequently frame their conflicts in a cosmic way that includes religious frameworks and other ideological struggles. This developmental model of a certain form of providential identity did not determine the effectiveness or otherwise of certain social and political systems, either in their own terms or with reference to the competitive context in which they had to operate. Explicitly or implicitly, there is always a moral dimension to conflict, even with animals. Right from the beginning, there was a moral argument that humans are inherently more valuable than animals. Many of the ancient philosophers of the Western world, at least, often began developing their theories of morality and ethics by drawing the distinction between humans and animals. In the Judaeo-Christian tradition, the Genesis creation account clearly delineates humans as above animals in the hierarchy of creation.

Wars today can be far shorter than the time it takes to write a chapter, let alone a book, and yet there is no shortage of lengthy books on war that if dropped from any height might well be fatal to a pedestrian on the ground. A short book, however, risks both simplifying the nature of war in order to provide a clear account and using a causal narrative in order apparently to explain developments. All then usually falls into a pat analysis, with technological proficiency in weaponry generally the measure of proficiency and the sorcerer's apprentice of steadily more deadly, if not frenetic, conflict. Weaponry provides both a developmental narrative and analysis, and a way to rank, and link, past, present and future. It also answers to the strong interest in the material culture of war, the sense that conflict is about things and that these give strength to humans.

The approach here is deliberately different. The omissions reflect not only the need for an economy of space (and one of the academic readers demanded at least a doubling of the length, which was definitely not the brief), but also an implicit critique of the standard account. Where here is the familiar narrative and such staples as Gustav Adolf of Sweden (r. 1611–32), the Thirty

Years War (1618–48), the Battle of Sadowa (1866) and so on? And with similar exclusions for other contexts, for example the Mexican–American War of 1846–8 or the Russo-Japanese War of 1904–5. You, reader, are invited to consider this because, in discussing what we include and what we leave out, the element of assessment in choice and of choice in assessment comes to the fore. That follows on from the discussion offered in the previous chapter.

The sense here is that it is non-Western military history that requires more attention, not only as an important share of the historical space but also because consideration of it subverts the standard analytical approach. Thus, the classic turning points and interpretative ideas of the Western approach mean relatively little or nothing if the world's military history is viewed from Delhi or Beijing. Indeed, in the West as a whole, this process can be seen, with far too much of the discussion a matter of France, Germany, Italy, Britain and the United States, and not, for example, of Eastern Europe or Latin America. The latter in particular appears to drop out of the general perspective after the Latin American Wars of Independence of the 1810s–20s, or the end of the Chile–Peru–Bolivia War of the Pacific (1879–83), albeit with possibly a brief reference to the Bolivia–Paraguay–Chaco War of 1932–5 and to Cold War-era conflicts in Central America, notably in Nicaragua and El Salvador. Such an approach underplays the far wider significance of civil conflict in Latin America.

If we 'decentre' military history, we move away from a baton-passing exercise, of one key weapon, or leader, or state, or military system, being replaced by another, with supposedly decisive battles, marking these changes, such as the major Swedish victory over Imperial (Austrian) forces at Breitenfeld (1631) and the French one over the Spaniards at Rocroi (1643), as in conventional accounts. This is an approach, in practice, that is apt to be self-fulfilling in its convenience, rather than based on an understanding of the ambiguities of change or, indeed, questions of relative significance, and not only those at a global level.

The proposal, instead, here is at once to offer an analysis of the past, a perspective on the present and a prospectus for the future. In doing so, a key point is that there is no clear hierarchy of military capabilities, certainly within the species, as opposed to towards other species. Rather, there are varied challenges and responses set by very different taskings and environments, both physical and human, such that war is a medium of questions, and not a message of an answer.

The key divide is that of wars between states as opposed to conflict within them. It is only if both the latter, and also the non-West, are given sufficient attention that a sounder understanding of war can develop. This has to engage with war as a continuum of experience, and not as a single, 'true' or essential state. Thus, in 1970, in response to Québécois terrorism, the Canadian government invoked the War Measures Act, its sole use in peacetime, and sent troops onto the streets. Terrorism was more broadly presented as war, and by both sides. So, for example, with the al-Qaeda assault on America in 2001, the resulting American declaration of a 'War on Terror' and, in 2020, when Gérald Darmanin, the French interior minister, declared, after a terrorist attack on a church in Nice: 'We are in a war against an enemy that is both inside and outside.'

A strategy of decisive battle and destruction of the enemy's armed forces is valuable and appropriate when dealing with regimes held up by bayonets. In these cases, the destruction of the armed forces has direct political results as it undermines the security of the regime, even if resistance can continue. However, this strategy can be inappropriate when dealing with polities or movements based on a different source of power.

Far from this being a new feature of warfare, it is one that has long been seen, for example with wars of religions or other ideological and cultural struggles. Religious division is more persistent than was anticipated in the twentieth century when secular ideologies seemed to the fore. Indeed, since the Cold War ended, such division has been more pronounced. To a degree, notably with crises for the Soviet Union in Afghanistan and Poland in the 1980s, it was the persistence of religious identity and activism that was responsible for the outcome of the Cold War; although much else was also at stake. This serves as a reminder of the degree to which changing aspects of conflict, notably weaponry and tactics, are matched by others, such as causation, that see greater continuity.

It is not clear which element should take precedence, nor how best to establish causal links in terms of what is presented as development. Rather than there being a core 'character' to military history, different elements, instead, come to the fore. Thus, perception is important to the understanding of war. This necessarily directs attention to the issues bound up in perception, issues which include those of presentation.

Moreover, it is only if this is done that Western powers will adequately understand the non-Western environments in which they might seek to operate, which has been the pattern of recent centuries. This pattern might be reversed, but a similar point could probably then be made. In the meantime, the various strands of humanity are having to move on post-Cold War narratives, while also making sense of themselves in light of identities, resource and problem pinch points.

There is a need for a less Western-centric military history, and for the avoidance of the primitivisation of non-Western military capabilities. The allocation of space in this book is an attempt to rise to this challenge. There is no one answer, and this is necessarily, as with all history, an interim report, but the intention is clear. Force is a key element in history. War, even if the scale may be modest and the technology limited, is not just the cause and consequence of change, but also an activity and experience that is at once more protean and more extensive.

Selected Further Reading

Biddle, S., *Nonstate Warfare: The Military Methods of Guerillas, Warlords, and Militias* (2021)

Black, J., *Air Power: A Global History* (2016)

Bryce, T., *Warriors of Anatolia: A Concise History of the Hittites* (2019)

France, J., *Western Warfare in the Age of the Crusades, 1000–1300* (1998)

Friday, K., *Samurai, Warfare and the State in Early Medieval Japan* (2004)

Gommans, J., *Mughal Warfare: Indian Frontiers and Highroads to Empire, 1500–1700* (2002)

Graff, D., *Medieval Chinese Warfare, 300–900* (2002)

Haldon, J., *Warfare, State and Society in the Byzantine World 560–1204* (1999)

Hamblin, W.J., *Warfare in the Ancient Near East to 1600 BC: Holy Warriors at the Dawn of History* (2006)

Kennedy, H., *The Armies of the Caliphs* (2001)

Kilcullen, D., *Out of the Mountains: The Coming Age of the Urban Guerrilla* (2014)

Lorge, P., *War, Politics and Society in Early Modern China, 900–1795* (2005)

Macola, G., *The Gun in Central Africa: A History of Technology and Politics* (2016)

May, T., *The Mongol Conquests in World History* (2012)

Reid, R., *Warfare in African History* (2012)

Roy, K., *Military Thought of Asia: From the Bronze Age to the Information Age* (2020)

Starkey, A., *European and Native American Warfare, 1675–1815* (1998)

Thornton, J., *Warfare in Atlantic Africa, 1500–1800* (1999)

Vandervort, B., *Wars of Imperial Conquest in Africa, 1830–1914* (1998)

Waldron, A., *The Great Wall of China: From History to Myth* (1990)

Index